Joseph Lincoln's Essential Cape Cod Reader

Joseph C. Lincoln

Foreword by: Priscilla Dalrymple

Schiffer Publishing Ltd®

4880 Lower Valley Road, Atglen, PA 19310 USA

Acknowledgments

Many thanks to Priscilla Dalrymple of the Chatham Historical Society for agreeing to write a foreward for this collection and helping use keep true to the style and spirit of Joseph C. Lincoln.

Library of Congress Card Number: 2006920603

Edited by Nathaniel Wolfgang-Price
Designed by Mark David Bowyer
Type set in Americana XBd BT / Dutch 801 RM BT

ISBN: 0-7643-2453-5
Printed in China

Published by Schiffer Publishing Ltd.
4880 Lower Valley Road
Atglen, PA 19310
Phone: (610) 593-1777; Fax: (610) 593-2002
E-mail: Info@schifferbooks.com

In Europe, Schiffer books are distributed by
Bushwood Books
6 Marksbury Ave.
Kew Gardens
Surrey TW9 4JF England
Phone: 44 (0) 20 8392-8585; Fax: 44 (0) 20 8392-9876
E-mail: info@bushwoodbooks.co.uk
Free postage in the U.K., Europe; air mail at cost.

Table of Contents

Foreword

Joseph Crosby Lincoln endeared himself to the American public over a span of forty years by writing, with humor and insight, about the people he knew best--Cape Codders. But, one may well ask, did Lincoln's Cape Cod, and its roster of colorful characters, ever really exist? Proof positive comes from the hundreds of letters he received from readers claiming they knew the identity of one or more of the people he portrayed. Lincoln was adamant, though, that he never depicted specific individuals, and that all his characters were composites. If some of their expressions and eccentricities seem exaggerated, he explained that life on the Cape in the late 19th and early 20th century "was far less sophisticated and standardized than now, and individual peculiarities and characteristics had more opportunity to persist and develop."

Lincoln's basic appeal, of course, was that he told a good story, or "yarn" as he called it, that held your attention right up to the inevitably-happy ending, though along the way his characters struggle with very real problems. Serious themes run through some of his novels--water pollution and typhoid in *Dr. Nye of North Ostable*, for instance, and racial prefudice in *The Portygee*, but always, virtue is eventually rewarded and vice satisfactorily punished. This approach edged Lincoln out of the literary mainstream as the 20th century progressed, and left him in a regional backwater. Critics were hailing the depressing "realism" of a new crop of writers, and Lincoln, from their standpoint, was passe. He defended himself vigorously, saying "I insist that a reasonable cheerful attitude toward life is not optimism or sentimental falderal...that is the realest of realism, because it is the outlook of the average sane human being."

Lincoln's "sane human being" -- the Cape Cod version, in any case, had a large dose of common sense and an acute appreciation of the foibles and weaknesses of his fellow man. From this material he produced countless humorous situations which, above all, accounted for his immense popularity, and separated him from a raft of other writers dealing with similar subject matter.

Today Lincoln can be read for his detailed descriptions of an era long gone, and now of historical interest, or he can simply be enjoyed as a delightful escape from our problem-wracked world. In either case, the rewards will be great.

-Priscilla Dalrymple, Chatham Historical Society

The Chatham Historical Society

The Chatham Historical Society's Atwood House Museum, in Chatham, Massachusetts, includes the Joseph Lincoln Room, featuring displays relating to the author's life and works, as well as a complete collection of his first editions, the handwritten manuscript of "The Portygee," and several Harold Brett paintings done as illustrations for Lincoln's books.

Elsewhere in the museum, besides the 1752 house itself, are extensive collections of maritime paintings, ship models, nautical artifacts, antique tools, Sandwich glass, Elmer Corwell miniatures, Parian Ware, Rose Medallion china, and the famous Stallknecht murals. A recent addition is a gallery devoted to a history of commercial fishing in Chatham.

Introduction

Cape Cod holds a particular image in the minds of the American people. When spoken, it conjures up images of lonely houses perched over the gray Atlantic, tiny fishing villages, and weather beaten old sailors in oil skins and rubber boots with corncob pipes clenched between their teeth. Cape Cod has become a symbol of nostalgia for the simple life of the seaside villages portrayed in books and movies. A number of American writers wrote books and stories about or set on Cape Cod, but Joseph C. Lincoln (1870-1944) is perhaps the most well known of these writers and undoubtedly was the most successful. Throughout his literary career beginning with the publication of a collection of poems entitled *Cape Cod Ballads* in 1902 and ending with the novel *The Bradshaws of Harniss* published in 1943 (a year before his death) Lincoln wrote over forty novels and plays, two works of nonfiction, and many more short stories and poems. While some critics scoffed at the sentimentality, and the predictability of his novels, Lincoln never lost his humor and remained true to his goal of portraying the Cape Cod he remembered from his childhood. Despite his critics, Lincoln's novels were particularly popular, sold thousands of copies, and were reprinted numerous times.

The images depicted in Lincoln's novels were so vivid and accurate that he has been called a historian rather than a writer of fiction. Lincoln succeeded in recording the very nature, both good and bad of life on the Cape. The unfailing courage of the foremast hand who stands full-face into the gale lives side by side with the spiteful small-mindedness of the town gossip.

Joseph C. Lincoln was born in Brewster, Mass. on Cape Cod and even though he spent a good part of his life in other parts of the United States most of his literature never ventured a few miles beyond the lonely strip of land that is Cape Cod.

Thirty-one abridged works will touch on the "essentials" of Lincoln's writing and paint a beautiful picture of the place and the the people that Joseph C. Lincoln loved so much.

CAPE COD BALLADS

THE COD-FISHER

Where leap the long Atlantic swells
In foam-streaked stretch of hill and dale,
Where shrill the north-wind demon yells,
And flings the spindrift down the gale;
Where, beaten 'gainst the bending mast,
The frozen raindrop clings and cleaves,
With steadfast front for calm or blast
His battered schooner rocks and heaves.
To same the gain, to some the loss,
To each the chance, the risk, the fight:
For men must die that men may live—
Lord, may we steer our course aright
Yet well he knows—where'er it be,
On low Cape Cod or bluff Cape Ann—
With straining eyes that search the sea
A watching woman waits her man:
He knows it, and his love is deep,
But work is work, and bread is bread,
And though men drown and women weep
The hungry thousands must be fed.
To some the gain, to some the loss,
To each his chance, the game with Fate:
For men must die that men may live—
Dear Lord, be kind to those who wait.

THE SONG OF THE SEA

Oh, the song of the Sea—
The beautiful song of the Sea!
The mighty note from the ocean's throat,
The laugh of the wind in glee!
And swift as the ripples flee
With the surges down the shore,
It bears me back, o'er life's long track,
To home and its love once more.
I stand at the open door,
Dear mother, again with thee,
And hear afar on the booming bar
The beautiful song of the Sea.

THE WIND'S SONG

Oh, the wild November wind,
How it blew!
How the dead leaves rasped and rustled,
Soared and sank and buzzed and bustled
As they flew;
While above the empty square,
Seeming skeletons in air,
Battered branches, brown and bare,
Gauntly grinned;
And the frightened dust-clouds, flying.
Heard the calling and the crying
Of the wind,—
The wild November wind.
Oh, the wild November wind,
How it rang
Through the rigging of a vessel
Rocking where the great waves wrestle!
And it sang,
Light and low, that mother's song;
And the master, staunch and strong,
Heard the sweet strain drift along—
Softened, thinned,—
Heard the tightened cordage ringing
Till it seemed a loved voice singing
In the wind,—
The wild November wind.

THE LIFE-SAVER

(Dedicated to the Men in the United States Life-saving Service)

When the Lord breathes his wrath above the bosom of the waters,
When the rollers are a-poundin' on the shore,
When the mariner's a-thinkin' of his wife and sons and daughters,
And the little home he'll, maybe, see no more;
When the bars are white and yeasty and the shoals are all a-frothin',
When the wild no'theaster's cuttin' like a knife;
Through the seethin' roar and screech he's patrollin' on the beach,—
The Gov'ment's hired man fer savin' life.

He is rigger, rower, swimmer, sailor, doctor, undertaker,
And he's good at every one of 'em the same:
And he risks his life fer others in the quicksand and the breaker,
And a thousand wives and mothers bless his name.
He's an angel dressed in oilskins, he's a saint in a "sou'wester",
He's as plucky as they make, or ever can;
He's a hero born and bred, but it hasn't swelled his head,
And he's jest the U.S. Gov'ment's hired man.

"THE EVENIN' HYMN"

When the hot summer daylight is dyin',
And the mist through the valley has rolled,
And the soft velvet clouds ter the west'ard
Are purple with trimmings of gold,—
Then, down in the medder-grass, dusky,
The crickets chirp out from each nook,
And the frogs with their voices so husky
Jine in from the marsh and the brook.
And the noise of the frogs and the crickets
And the birds and the breeze are ter me
Lots better than high-toned supraners,
Although they don't get to "high C";
And the church, with its grand painted skylight,
Seems cramped and forbiddin' and grim
'Side of my old front porch in the twilight
When God's choir sings its "Evenin' Hymn."

THE MEADOW ROAD

Just a simple little picture of a sunny country road
Leading down beside the ocean's pebbly shore,
Where a pair of patient oxen slowly drag their heavy load,
And a barefoot urchin trudges on before:
Yet I'm dreaming o'er it, smiling, and my thoughts are far away
'Mid the glorious summer sunshine long ago,
And once more a happy, careless boy, in memory I stray
Down a little country road I used to know.
I hear the voice of "Father" as he drives the lumbering steers,
And the pigeons coo and flutter on the shed,
While all the simple, homelike sounds come whispering to my ears,
And my heart leaps gayly upward, like the foam upon the sea,
As I watch the breakers tumbling with a roar,
And the ships that dot the azure seem to wave a hail to me,
And to beckon to a wondrous, far-off shore.

* * * * *

Just a simple little picture, yet its charm is o'er me still,
And again my boyish spirit seems to glow,
And once more a barefoot urchin am I wandering at will
Down that little country road I used to know.

THE VILLAGE ORACLE

"I am Sir Oracle, and when I ope my lips let no dog bark!"

Old Dan'l Hanks he says this town
Is jest the best on earth;
He says there ain't one, up nor down,
That's got one half her worth;
Says I "D'jer ever travel, Dan?"
"You bet I ain't!" says he;
"I tell you what! the place I've got
Is good enough fer me!"
He says the other party's fools,
'Cause they don't vote his way;
He says the "feeble-minded schools"
Is where they ought ter stay;
Says I, "D'jer ever read it, Dan?"
"You bet I ain't!" says he;

"And when I do; well, I tell you,
I'll let you know, by gee!"
He says that all religion's wrong
'Cept jest what he believes;
He says them ministers belong
In jail, the same as thieves;
Says I, "D'jer ever hear 'em, Dan?"
"You bet I ain't!" says he;
"I'd never go ter hear 'em; no;
They make me sick ter see!"
Some fellers reckon, more or less,
Before they speak their mind,
And sometimes calkerlate or guess,—
But them ain't Dan'l's kind.
Says I, "How d' yer know you're right?"
"How do I know?" says he;
"Well, now, I vum! I know, by gum!
I'm right because I be!"

THROUGH THE FOG

The fog was so thick yer could cut it
'Thout reachin' a foot over-side,
The dory she'd nose up ter butt it,
And then git discouraged an' slide;
No noise but the thole-pins a-squeakin',
Or, maybe, the swash of a wave,
No feller ter cheer yer by speakin'—
'Twas lonesomer, lots, than the grave.
I set there an' thought of my trouble,
I thought how I'd worked fer the cash
That bust and went up like a bubble
The day that the bank went ter smash.
"And," says I, "All my life I've been fightin'
Through oceans of nothin' but fog;
And never no harbor a-sightin'—
Jest driftin' around like a log;
No matter how sharp I'm a-spyin',
I never see nothin' ahead:
I'm sick and disgusted with tryin'—
I jest wish ter God I was dead."
It wa'n't more'n a minute, I'm certain,
The words was jest out er my mouth,
When up went the fog, like a curtain,
And "puff" came the breeze from the south;
And 'bout a mile off, by rough guessin',
I see my own shanty on shore,
And Mary, my wife and my blessin',
God keep her, she stood in the door.
And I says ter myself, "I'm a darlin';
A chap with a woman like that,
To set here a-grumblin' and snarlin',
As sour as a sulky young brat—
I'd better jest keep my helm steady,
And not mind the fog that's adrift,
For when the Lord gits good and ready,
I reckon it's certain ter lift."

THE BALLADE OF THE DREAM-SHIP

My dream-ship's decks are of beaten gold,
And her fluttering banners are brave of hue,
And her shining sails are of satin fold,
And her tall sides gleam where the warm waves woo:
While the flung spray leaps in a diamond dew
From her bright bow, dipping its dance of glee;
For the skies are fair and the soft winds coo,
Where my dream-ship sails o'er the silver sea.
My dream-ship's journeys are long and bold,
And the ports she visits are far and few;
They lie by the rosy shores of old,
'Mid the dear lost scenes my boyhood knew;
Or, deep in the future's misty blue,
By the purple islands of Arcady,—
And Spain's fair turrets shine full in view,
Where my dream-ship sails o'er the silver sea.
My dream-ship's cargo is wealth untold,
Rare blooms that the old home gardens grew,
Sweet pictured faces, and loved songs trolled
By lips long laid 'neath the churchyard yew;
Or wondrous wishes not yet come true,
And fame and glory that is to be;—
Hope holds the wheel all the lone watch through,
Where my dream-ship sails o'er the silver sea.

MAY MEMORIES

To my office window, gray,
Come the sunbeams in their play,
Come the dancing, glancing sunbeams, airy fairies of the May;
Like a breath of summer-time,
Setting Memory's bells a-chime,
Till their jingle seems to mingle with the measure of my rhyme.
And above the tramp of feet,
And the clamor of the street,
I can hear the thrush's singing, ringing high and clear and sweet,—
Hear the murmur of the breeze
Through the bloom-starred apple trees,
And the ripples softly splashing and the dashing of the seas;
See the shadow and the shine
Where the glossy branches twine,
And the ocean's sleepy tuning mocks the crooning in the pine;
Hear the catbird whistle shrill
In the bushes by the rill,
Where the violets toss and twinkle as they sprinkle vale and hill;
Oh, the skies of blissful blue,
Oh, the woodland's verdant hue,—
Oh, the lazy days of boyhood, when the world was fair and new!
Still to me your tale is told
In the summer's sunbeam's gold,
And my truant fancy straying, goes a-Maying as of old.

BIRDS'-NESTING TIME

The spring sun flashes a rapier thrust
Through the dingy school-house pane,
A shining scimitar, free from rust,
That cuts the cloud of the drifting dust,
And scatters a golden rain;
And the boy at the battered desk within
Is dreaming a dream sublime,
For study's a wrong, and school a sin,
When the joys of woods and fields begin,
And it's just birds'-nesting time.
He knows of the spot by the old stone wall,
Where the sunlight dapples the glade,
And the sweet wild-cherry blooms softly fall,
And hid in the meadow-grass rank and tall,
The "Bob-white's" eggs are laid.
He knows, where the sea-breeze sobs and sings,
And the sand-hills meet the brine,
The clamorous crows, with their whirring wings,
Tell of their treasure that sways and swings
In the top of the tasselled pine.

* * * * *

And so he dreamed, with a happy face,
Till the noontide recess came,
And when't was over, ah, sad disgrace,
The teacher, seeing an empty place,
Marked "truant" against his name;
While he, forgetful of book or rule,
Sought only a tree to climb:
For where is the boy who remembers school
When the cowslip blows by the marshy
And it's just birds'-nesting time?

SUMMER NIGHTS AT GRANDPA'S

Summer nights at Grandpa's—ain't they soft and still!
Just the curtains rustlin' on the window-sill,
And the wind a-blowin', warm and wet and sweet—
Smellin' like the meadows or the fields of wheat;
Just the bullfrogs pipin' in amongst the grass,
Where the water's shinin' like a lookin'-glass;
Just a dog a-barkin' somewheres up along,
So far off his yelpin' 's like a kind of song.
Summer nights at Grandpa's—ain't it fun ter lay

In the early mornin' when it's gettin' day—
When the sun is risin' and it's fresh and cool,
And you 're feelin' happy coz there ain't no school?—
When you hear the crowin' as the rooster wakes,
And you think of breakfast and the buckwheat cakes;
Sleepin' in the city's too much fuss and noise;
Summer nights at Grandpa's are the things for boys.

GRANDFATHER'S "SUMMER SWEETS"

Grandfather's "summer sweets" are ripe.
  Out on the gnarled old tree,
Out where the robin redbreasts pipe,
  And buzzes the bumblebee;
Swinging high on the bending bough,
  Scenting the lazy breeze,
What is the gods' ambrosia now
  To apples of gold like these?
Ruddy the blush of their maiden cheeks
  After the sunbeam's kiss—
Every quivering leaflet speaks,
  Telling a tale of bliss;
Telling of dainties hung about,
  Each in a verdant wreath,
Shimmering satin all without,
  Honey and cream beneath.
Barefoot, trip through the meadow lane,
  Laughing at bruise and scratch;
Come, with your hands all rich with stain
  Fresh from the blackberry patch;
Come where the orchard spreads its store
  And the breath of the clover greets;
Quick! they are waiting you here once more,—
  Grandfather's "summer sweets."

MIDSUMMER

Sun like a furnace hung up overhead,
Burnin' and blazin' and blisterin' red;
Sky like an ocean, so blue and so deep,
One little cloud-ship becalmed and asleep;
Breezes all gone and the leaves hangin' still,
Shimmer of heat on the medder and hill,—
Labor and laziness callin' to me:
"Hoe or the fishin'-pole—which'll it be?"
There's the old cornfield out there in the sun,
Showin' so plain that there's work ter be done;
There's the mean weeds with their tops all a-sprout,
Seemin' ter stump me ter come clean 'em out;
But, there's the river, so clear and so cool,
There's the white lilies afloat on the pool,
Scentin' the shade 'neath the old maple tree—
"Hoe or the fishin'-pole—which'll it be?"
Dusty and dry droops the corn in the heat,
Down by the river a robin sings sweet,
Gray squirrels chatter as if they might say:
"Who's the chump talkin' of workin' to-day?"
Robin's song tells how the pickerel wait
Under the lily-pads, hungry for bait;
I ought ter make for that cornfield, I know:
But, "Where's the fishin'-pole? Hang the old hoe!"

THE WATCHERS

When the great, gray fog comes in, and the damp clouds cloak the shore,
And the tossing waves grow dim, and the white sails flash no more,
Then, over the shrouded sea, where the winding mist-wreaths creep,
The deep-voiced Watchers call, the Watchers who guard the Deep.

* * * * *

"Hear! hear! hear! Hark to the word I bring!
Toilers upon the sea, list to the Bell-buoy's ring!
List, as I clash and clang! list, as I toss and toll!
Under me yawns the grave, under me lies the shoal

Where the whirling eddies wait to grapple the drowning crew,
And the hungry quicksand hides the bones of the ship it slew.
Swift on the outward tack! quick, to the seaward bear!
Toilers upon the sea, here is the shoal! Beware!"
"Hear! hear! hear! Hark to me, one and all!
Toilers upon the sea, list to the Fog-horn's call!
List to my buzzing cry! list, as I growl and groan:
Here is the sullen shore where the white-toothed breakers moan;
Where the silky ripples run with the wolf-like wave behind,
To leap on the struggling wreck and worry and gnaw and grind,
To toss on the cruel crag the dead with his streaming hair!
Toilers upon the sea, here are the rocks! Beware!"
"Hear! hear! hear! Hark to my stormy shriek!
Toilers upon the sea, the Whistling-buoy would speak!
List to my sobbing shout! list, for my word is brief:
Death is beneath me here! death on the sunken reef
Where the jagged ledge is hid and the slimy seaweeds grow,
And the long kelp streamers wave in the dark green depths below,
Where, under the shell-clad hulk, the gaunt shark makes his lair,—
Toilers upon the sea, here is the reef! Beware!"

* * * * *

And then, o'er the silent sea, an answer from unseen lips,
Comes in through the great, gray fog, the word from the mist-bound ships,—
A chorus of bell and horn, faint and afar and clear,—
"Thanks, O Guard of the Deep! Watchers, we hear! we hear!"

A RAINY DAY

Kind er like a stormy day, take it all together,—
Don't believe I'd want it jest only pleasant weather;
If the sky was allers blue, guess I'd be complainin',
And a-pesterin' around, wishin' it was rainin'.
Like a stormy mornin' now, with the water dashin'
From the eaves and from the spouts, foamin' and a-splashin',
With the leaves and twigs around, shinin' wet and drippin',
Shakin' in the wind with drops every-which-way skippin'.
Like ter see the gusts of rain, where there's naught ter hinder,
Sail acrost the fields and come "spat" against the winder,
Streakin' down along the panes, floodin' sills and ledges,
Makin' little fountains, like, in the sash's edges.
But I like it best inside, with the fire a-gleamin',
And myself, with chores all done, settin' round and dreaming
With the kitten on my knee, and the kettle hummin',
And the rain-drops on the roof, "Home, Sweet Home" a-drummin'.

THE SURF ALONG THE SHORE

Ye children of the mountain, sing of your craggy peaks,
Your valleys forest laden, your cliffs where Echo speaks;
And ye, who by the prairies your childhood's joys have seen,
Sing of your waving grasses, your velvet miles of green:
But when my memory wanders down to the dear old home
I hear, amid my dreaming, the seething of the foam,
The wet wind through the pine trees, the sobbing crash and roar,
The mighty surge and thunder of the surf along the shore.
The dear old Cape! I love it! I love its hills of sand,
The sea-wind singing o'er it, the seaweed on its strand;
The bright blue ocean 'round it, the clear blue sky o'erhead;
The fishing boats, the dripping nets, the white sails filled and spread;—
For each heart has its picture, and each its own home song,
The sights and sounds which move it when Youth's fair memories throng;
And when, down dreamland pathways, a boy, I stroll once more,
I hear the mighty music of the surf along the shore.

AT EVENTIDE

The tired breezes are tucked to rest
In the cloud-beds far away;
The waves are pressed to the placid breast
Of the dreaming, gleaming bay;
The shore line swims in a hazy heat,
Asleep in the sea and sky,
And the muffled beat where the breakers meet
Is a soft, sweet lullaby.
The great sun sinks, and the gray fog heaps
His cloak on the silent sea;
The night-wind creeps where the ocean sleeps,
And the wavelets wake in glee;
Across the bay, like a silver star,
There twinkles the harbor-light,
And faint and far from the outer bar
The sea-birds call "Good-night."

Cape Cod Stories

The Count and the Manager
(Abridged)

The way we got into the hotel business in the first place come around like this: Me and Cap'n Jonadab went down to Wellmouth Port one day 'long in March to look at some property he'd had left him.

We got there after a spell and set down on the big piazza with our souls full of gratitude and our boots full of sand. Great, big, old-fashioned house with fourteen big bedrooms in it, big barn, sheds, and one thing or 'nother, and perched right on top of a hill with five or six acres of ground 'round it.

The next morning after ballasting up with the truck we'd bought at the store we went out on the piazza again, and looked at the breakers and the pine trees and the sand, and held our hats on with both hands.

"Jonadab," says I, "what'll you take for your heirloom?"

"Well," he says, "Barzilla, the way I feel now, I think I'd take a return ticket to Orham and be afraid of being took up for swindling at that."

Neither of us says nothing more for a spell, and, first thing you know, we heard a carriage rattling somewhere up the road.

"Judas!" says Jonadab, "there's somebody COMING!"

There WAS somebody coming—a feller in a buggy, and he hitched his horse to the front fence and come whistling up the walk.

He was a tall chap, with a smooth face, kind of sharp and knowing, and with a stiff hat set just a little on one side. His clothes was new and about a week ahead of up-to-date, his shoes shined till they lit up the lower half of his legs, and his pants was creased so's you could mow with 'em.

"Cap'n Wixon?" he says to me, sticking out a gloved flipper.

"Not guilty," says I. "There's the skipper. My name's Wingate."

"Glad to have the pleasure, Mr. Wingate," he says. "Cap'n Wixon, yours truly."

We shook hands, and he took each of us by the arm and piloted us back to the piazza, like a tug with a couple of coal barges.

"My name's Brown—Peter T. Brown. I read about your falling heir to this estate, Cap'n Wixon, in a New Bedford paper. Soon as I read the paper I came right down to look at the property. Having rubbered, back I go to Orham to see you. Your handsome and talented daughter says you are over here. That'll be about all—here I am. Now, then, listen to this."

He went under his hatches again, rousted out a sheet of paper, unfolded it and read something like this—I know it by heart:

"The great sea leaps and splashes before you as it leaped and splashed in the old boyhood days. Forgotten are the cares of business, the scramble for money, the ruthless hunt for fame. Here are perfect rest and perfect peace.

"Now what place would you say I was describing?" says the feller.

"Heaven," says Jonadab, looking up, reverent like.

You never see a body more disgusted than Brown. "Get out!" he snaps. "Do I look like the advance agent of Glory? Listen to this one."

He unfurls another sheet of paper, and goes off on a tack about like this:

"You who sit in your luxurious apartments, attended by your liveried servants, eating the costly dishes that bring you dyspepsia and kindred evils, what would you give to go back once more to the simple, cleanly living of the old house in the country? The old home, where the huckleberry pies that mother fashioned were swimming in fragrant juice, where there were no voices but those of the wind and sea; no—"

"Don't!" busts out Jonadab. "Don't! I can't stand it!" He was mopping his eyes with his red bandanner. I was consider'ble shook up myself. As for Peter T. Brown, he fairly crowed.

"It gets you!" he says. "I knew it would. And it'll get a heap of others, too. Well, we can't send 'em back to the old home, but we can trot the old home to them, or a mighty good imitation of it. Here it is; right here!"

And he waves his hand up toward Aunt Sophrony's cast-off palace.

Cap'n Jonadab set up straight and sputtered like a firecracker. A man hates to be fooled.

"Old home!" he snorts. "Old county jail, you mean!"

And then that Brown feller took his feet down off the rail, hitched his chair right in front of Jonadab and me and commenced to talk.

And HOW he did talk! Fore he got through he talked a thousand dollars out of Cap'n Jonadab, and it takes a pretty hefty lecture to squeeze a quarter out of HIM. To make a long yarn short, this was his plan:

He proposed to turn Aunt Sophrony's wind plantation into a hotel for summer boarders.

"But 'twill cost so like the dickens to furnish it," I says.

"Furnish it!" says he. "Why, that's just it! It won't cost nothing to furnish it—nothing to speak of. All I want from you folks is a little money—I'll chuck in two hundred and fifty myself—and you two can be proprietors and treasurers if you want to. But active manager and publicity man—that's yours cheerily, Peter Theodosius Brown!"

Well, he talked all the forenoon and all the way to Orham on the train and most of that night. And when he heaved anchor, Jonadab had agreed to put up a thousand and I was in for five hundred and Peter contributed two hundred and fifty and experience and nerve.

And the "Old Home House" was off the ways. And by the first of May 'twas open and ready for business, too.

You never see such a driver as that feller Brown was. He had a new wide piazza built all 'round the main buildings, painted everything up fine, hired the three best women cooks in Wellmouth—and there's some good cooks on Cape Cod, too—and a half dozen chamber girls and waiters.

And the advertisements! They was sent everywheres. By the middle of April most of our money was gone, but every room in the house was let and we had applications coming by the pailful.

There was one old chap that we'll call Dillaway—Ebenezer Dillaway. He runs the Dillaway Combination Stores that are all over the country. He come to the Old Home House with his daughter, and he took to the place right away. Said 'twas for all the world like where he used to live when he was a boy. He liked the grub and he liked the cornhusks and he liked Brown.

His daughter liked Brown, too, and 'twas easy enough to see that Brown liked her. She was a mighty pretty girl, the kind Peter called a "queen," and the active manager took to her like a cat to a fish.

Me and Jonadab see how things was going, and we'd look at one another and wink and shake our heads when the pair'd go by together.

But all that was afore the count come aboard. We got our first letter from the count about the third of June. The writing was all over the plate like a biled dinner, and the English looked like it had been shook up in a bag, but it was signed with a nine fathom, toggle-jinted name that would give a pollparrot the lockjaw, and had the word "Count" on the bow of it.

You never see a feller happier than Peter T. Brown.

"Can he have rooms?" says Peter. "He says he's a count and he'll be advertised as a count from this place to where rolls the Oregon."

And he was, too. The papers was full of how Count What's-his-Name was hanging out at the Old Home House, and we got more letters from rich old women and pork-pickling money bags than you could shake a stick at.

The count himself hove in sight on June fifteenth. His talk was like his writing, only worse, but from the time his big trunk with the foreign labels was carried upstairs, he was skipper and all hands of the Old Home House.

And the funny part of it was that old man Dillaway was as much gone on him as the rest. Anyway, from the minute the count come over the side it was "Good-by, Peter." The foreigner was first oar with the old man and general consort for the daughter. It worried Peter—you could see that. He'd set in the barn with Jonadab and me, thinking, thinking, and all at once he'd bust out:

"Bless that Dago's heart! I haven't chummed in with the degenerate aristocracy much in my time, but somewhere or other I've seen that chap before."

For the first two weeks the count paid his board like a major; then he let it slide. Jonadab and me was a little worried, but he was advertising us like fun, so we judged he was a good investment. But Peter got bluer and bluer.

One night we was in the setting room—me and Jonadab and the count and Ebenezer.

The count was spinning a pigeon English yarn of how he'd fought a duel with rapiers. When he'd finished, old Dillaway pounded his knee and sung out: "That's bus'ness! That's the way to fix 'em! No lawsuits, no argument, no delays. Just take 'em out and punch holes in 'em. Did you hear that, Brown?"

"Yes, I heard it," says Peter, kind of absent-minded like. "Fighting with razors, wan't it?"

Now there wan't nothing to that—'twas just some of Brown's sarcastic spite getting the best of him—but I give you my word that the count turned yellow under his brown skin, kind of like mud rising from the bottom of a pond.

"What-a you say?" he says, bending for'ards.

"Mr. Brown was mistaken, that's all," says Dillaway; "he meant rapiers."

"But why-a razors—why-a razors?" says the count.

Now I was watching Brown's face, and all at once I see it light up like you'd turned a searchlight on it. Then he grinned and begged pardon and talked a blue streak for the rest of the evening.

Next day he was the happiest thing in sight, and when Miss Dillaway and the count went Lover's Nesting he didn't seem to care a bit. All of a sudden he told Jonadab and me that he was going up to Boston that evening on bus'ness and wouldn't be back for a day or so. He wouldn't tell what the bus'ness was, either, but just whistled and laughed and sung, "Good-by, Susannah; don't you grieve for me," till train time.

He was back again three nights afterward, and he come right out to the barn without going nigh the house. He had another feller with him, a kind of shabby dressed Italian man with curly hair. "Fellers," he says to me and Jonadab, "this is my friend, Mr. Macaroni; he's going to engineer the barber shop for a while."

Well, we'd just let our other barber go, so we didn't think anything of this, but when he said that his friend Spaghetti was going to stay in the barn for a day or so, and that we needn't mention that he was there, we thought that was funny.

But Peter done a lot of funny things the next day. One of 'em was to set a feller painting a side of the house by the count's window, that didn't need painting at all. And when the feller quit for the night, Brown told him to leave the ladder where 'twas.

That evening the same crowd was together in the setting room. Peter was as lively as a cricket, talking, talking, all the time. By and by he says: "Oh, say, I want you to see the new barber. He can shave anything from a note to a porkypine. Come in here, Chianti!" he says, opening the door and calling out.

And in come the new Italian man, smiling and bowing and looking "meek and lowly, sick and sore," as the song says.

Well, we laughed at Brown's talk and asked the Italian all kinds of fool questions and nobody noticed that the count wan't saying nothing. Pretty soon he gets up and says he guesses he'll go to his room, 'cause he feels sort of sick.

And I tell you he looked sick. He was yellower than he was the other night, and he walked like he hadn't got his sea legs on. "Now that's too bad!" says Brown. "Spaghetti, you needn't wait any longer." So the other Italian went out, too.

And then Peter T. Brown turned loose and talked the way he done when me and Jonadab first met him. He told of this bargain that he'd made and that sharp trade he had turned, while we set there and listened and laughed like a parsel of fools. And every time that Ebenezer'd get up to go to bed, Peter'd trot out a new yarn and he'd have to stop to listen to that.

It was just about quarter past one and we was laughing our heads off at one of Brown's jokes, when out under the back window there was a jingle and a thump and a kind of groaning and wiggling noise.

"What on earth is that?" says Dillaway.

"I shouldn't be surprised," says Peter, "if that was his royal highness, the count."

He took up the lamp and we all hurried outdoors and 'round the corner. And there, sure enough, was the count, sprawling on the ground with his leather satchel alongside of him, and his foot fast in a big steel trap that was hitched by a chain to the lower round of the ladder. He rared up on his hands when he see us and started to say something about an outrage.

"Oh, that's all right, your majesty," says Brown. "Hi, Chianti, come here a minute!"

When the new barber showed up the count never made another move, just wilted like a morning-glory after sunrise. But you never see a worse upset man than Ebenezer Dillaway.

"But what does this mean?" says he, kind of wild like. "Why don't you take that thing off his foot?"

"Oh," says Peter, "he's been elongating my pedal extremity for the last month or so; I don't see why I should kick if he pulls his own for a while. You see," he says, "it's this way: "Ever since his grace condescended to lend the glory of his countenance to this humble roof," he says, "it's stuck in my mind that I'd seen the said countenance somewhere before. The other night when our conversation was trifling with the razor subject and the Grand Lama here"—that's the name he called the count—"was throwing in details about his carving his friends, it flashed across me where I'd seen it. About a couple of years ago I was selling the guileless rural druggists contiguous to Scranton, Pennsylvania, the tasty and happy combination called 'Dr. Bulger's Electric Liver Cure,'. I made my headquarters at Scranton, and, while there, my hair was shortened and my chin smoothed in a neat but gaudy barber shop, presided over by my friend Spaghetti here, and my equally valued friend the count."

"So," says Peter, smiling and cool as ever, "when it all came back to me, as the song says, I journeyed to Scranton accompanied by a photograph of his lordship. I was lucky enough to find Macaroni in the same old shop. It seems his majesty had hit up the lottery a short time previous for a few hundred and had given up barbering. It may be," says Brown, "that he thought he might marry some rich girl. There's some fool fathers, judging by the papers, that are willing to sell their daughters for the proper kind of tag on a package like him."

Old man Dillaway kind of made a face, as if he'd ate something that tasted bad, but he didn't speak.

"And so," says Peter, "Spaghetti and I came to the Old Home together, he to shave for twelve per, and I to set traps, etcetera. I left the ladder by his grace's window, thinking he might find it handy after he'd seen his friend of other days, particularly as the back door was locked.

"And now," goes on Brown, short and sharp, "let's talk business. Count," he says, "you are set back on the books about sixty odd for old home comforts. We'll cut off half of that and charge it to advertising. But the other thirty you'll have to work out. I'll give you twelve dollars a week to chip in with Macaroni here and barber the boarders."

But Dillaway looked anxious. "Look here, Brown," he says, "I wouldn't do that. I'll pay his board bill and his traveling expenses if he clears out this minute. It seems tough to set him shaving after he's been such a big gun around here."

I could see right off that the arrangement suited Brown first rate and was exactly what he'd been working for, but he pretended not to care much for it.

"Oh! I don't know," he says. "I'd rather be a sterling barber than a plated count. But anything to oblige you, Mr. Dillaway." So the next day there was a nobleman missing at the Old Home House, and all we had to remember him by was a trunk full of bricks. And Peter T. Brown and the "queen" was roosting in the Lover's Nest; and the new Italian was busy in the barber shop. And before the season was over the engagement was announced. Old Dillaway took it pretty well, considering. The old man said he'd been hoping for a son-in-law sharp enough to run the "Consolidated Stores" after he was gone, and it looked, he said, as if he'd found him.

The South Shore Weather Bureau
(Abridged)

"But," says Cap'n Jonadab and me together, "but,"we says, "will it work? Will anybody pay for it?"

"Work?" says Peter T. "Well, maybe 'twouldn't work if the ordinary brand of canned lobster was running it, but with ME to jerk the lever and sound the loud timbrel—why, say! it's like stealing money from a blind cripple that's hard of hearing."

"Yes, I know," says Cap'n Jonadab. "But this ain't like starting the Old Home House. This is peddling weather prophecies when there's the Gov'ment Weather Bureau running opposition—not to mention the Old Farmer's Almanac, and I don't know how many more," he says.

Brown took his patent leathers down off the rail of the piazza, give the ashes of his cigar a flip and he says: "Confound it, man!" he says. "You can throw more cold water than a fire-engine. Old Farmer's Almanac! This isn't any 'About this time look out for snow' business. And it ain't any Washington cold slaw like 'Weather for New England and Rocky Mountains, Tuesday to Friday; cold to warm; well done on the edges with a rare streak in the middle, preceded or followed by rain, snow, or clearing.' No siree! this is TO-DAY'S weather for Cape Cod, served right off the griddle on a hot plate, and cooked by the chef at that. You don't realize what a regular dime-museum wonder that feller is," he says.

Well, I suppose we didn't. You see, Jonadab and me, like the rest of the folks around Wellmouth, had come to take Beriah Crocker and his weather notions as the regular thing, like baked beans on a Saturday night.

'Twas in the early part of May follering the year that the "Old Home House" was opened. Passages was booked all through the summer and it looked as if our second season would be better'n our first. Then the Dillaway girl she thought 'twould be nice to have what she called a "spring house-party" for her particular friends 'fore the regular season opened. So Peter he thought 'twould be nice, too, and for a week it was "all hands on deck!"getting ready for the "house-party."

Two days afore the thing was to go off the ways Brown gets a letter from Belle, and in it says she's invited a whole lot of folks from Chicago and New York and Boston and the land knows where, and that they've never been to the Cape and she wants to show 'em what a "quaint" place it is. "Can't you get," says she, "two or three delightful, queer, old 'longshore characters' to be at work 'round the hotel? It'll give such a touch of local color," she says. So out comes Peter with the letter.

"Barzilla," he says to me, "I want some characters. know anybody that's a character?"

"Well," says I, "there's Nate Slocum over to Orham. He's about the toughest character I can think of, offhand, this way."

"Oh, thunder!" says Brown. "I don't want a crook. What I'm after is an odd stick; a feller with pigeons in his loft. Not a lunatic, but jest a queer genius—little queerer than you and the Cap'n here."

After a while we got his drift, and I happened to think of Beriah and his chum, Eben Cobb. Beriah's pet idee was foretelling what the weather was going to be. And he could do it, too, better'n anybody I ever see. He'd smell a storm further'n a cat can smell fish, and he hardly ever made a mistake.

Peter said Beriah and Eben was just the sort of "cards" he was looking for and drove right over to see 'em. He hooked 'em, too.

So the special train from Boston brought the "house-party" down, and our two-seated buggy brought Beriah and Eben over. The city folks thought they was "just too dear and odd for anything," and made 'em bigger fools than ever, which wa'n't necessary.

The second day of the "party" was to be a sailing trip clear down to the life-saving station on Setuckit Beach. It certainly looked as if 'twas going to storm, and the Gov'ment predictions said it was, but Beriah said "No," and stuck out that 'twould clear up by and by. So they sailed away, and, sure enough, it cleared up fine. And the next day the Gov'ment fellers said "clear" and Beriah said "rain," and she poured a flood. And, after three or four of such experiences, Beriah was all hunky with the "house-party."

So, when the party was over, 'round comes Peter, busting with a new notion. What he cal'lated to do was to start a weather prophesying bureau all on his own hook, with Beriah for prophet, and him for manager and general advertiser, and Jonadab and me to help put up the money to get her going. His idee was to send Beriah's predictions by telegraph to agents in every Cape town each morning, and the agents was to hand 'em to susscribers. First week a free trial; after that, so much per prophecy.

And it worked—oh, land, yes! it worked. Brown rigged up a little shanty on the bluff in front of the "Old Home," and filled it full of barometers and thermometers and chronometers and charts, and put Beriah and Eben inside to look wise and make b'lieve do something. And Beriah was right 'most every time.

We had to have Eben, though he wasn't wuth a green hand's wages as a prophet. But him and Beriah stuck by each other like two flies in the glue-pot, and you couldn't hire one without t'other.

In July, Mrs. Freeman—she had charge of the upper decks in the "Old Home" and was rated head chambermaid—up and quit, and being as we couldn't get another capable Cape Codder just then, Peter fetched down a woman from New York; one that a friend of old Dillaway's recommended. She was able seaman so far's the work was concerned, but she'd been good-looking once and couldn't forget it, and she was one of them clippers that ain't happy unless they've got a man in tow.

Her name was Kelly, Emma Kelly, and she was a widow. Men—except the boarders, of course—was scarce around Wellmouth Port. First the Kelly lady begun to flag Cap'n Jonadab and me, but we sheered off and took to the offing. So Emma had to look for other victims, and the prophet-shop looked to her like the most likely feeding-ground.

And, would you b'lieve it, them two old critters, Beriah and Eben, gobbled the bait like sculpins. If she'd been a woman like the kind they was used to—the Cape kind, I mean—I don't s'pose they'd have paid any attention to her; but she was diff'rent from anything they'd ever run up against, and the first thing you know, she had 'em both poke-hooked. She'd drop in at the weather-factory 'long in the afternoon and pretend to be terrible interested in the goings on there. "I don't see how you two gentlemen CAN tell whether it's going to rain or not. Do tell me, Mr. Crocker, will it be good weather to-morrer? I wanted to take a little walk up to the village about four o'clock if it was."

And then Beriah'd swell out like a puffing pig and put on airs and look out of the winder, and crow: "Yes'm, I jedge that we'll have a southerly breeze in the morning with some fog, but nothing to last, nothing to last. The afternoon, I cal'late, 'll be fair. I—I—that is to say, I was figgering on goin' to the village myself to-morrer."

Then Emma would pump up a blush, and smile, and purr that she was SO glad, 'cause then she'd have comp'ny. And Eben would glower at Beriah and Beriah'd grin sort of superior-like, and the mutual barometer, so's to speak, would fall about a foot during the next hour. The brotherly business between the two prophets was coming to an end fast, and all on account of Mrs. Kelly.

She played 'em even for almost a month; didn't show no preference one way or the other. Cap'n Jonadab and me was uneasy, for we was afraid the Weather Bureau would suffer 'fore the thing was done with; but Peter was away, and we didn't like to interfere till he come home. And then, all at once, Emma seemed to make up her mind, and 'twas all Eben from that time on. The fact is, the widder had learned, somehow or 'nother, that he had the most money of the two. Beriah didn't give up; he stuck to it like a good one, but he was falling behind and he knew it. As for Eben, he couldn't help showing a little joyful pity, so's to speak, for his partner, and the atmosphere in that rain lab'ratory got so frigid that I didn't know but we'd have to put up a stove.

The last of August come and the "Old Home House" was going to close up on the day after Labor Day. Peter was down again, and so was Ebenezer and Belle, and there was to be high jinks to celebrate the season's wind-up.

Of course, the weather must be good or it's no joy job taking females to Setuckit in a catboat. The night before the big day, Peter came out to the Weather Bureau and Jonadab and me dropped in likewise. Beriah was there all alone; Eben was out walking with Emma.

"Well, Jeremiah," says Brown, "what's the outlook for to-morrer?"

"Wall," says Beriah, goin' to the door, "I don't know, Mr. Brown. It don't look just right; I swan it don't! I can tell you better in the morning. I hope 'twill be fair, too, 'cause I was cal'lating to get a day off and borrer your horse and buggy and go over to the Ostable camp-meeting."

Now, I knew of course, that he meant he was going to take the widder with him, but Peter spoke up and says he: "Sorry, Beriah, but you're too late. Eben asked me for the horse and buggy this morning. Eben's going to take the fair Emma for a ride," he says. "Beriah, I'm afraid our beloved Cobb is, in the innocence of his youth, being roped in by the sophisticated damsel in the shoo-fly hat," says he.

Me and Jonadab hadn't had time to tell Peter how matters stood betwixt the prophets, or most likely he wouldn't have said that. It hit Beriah like a snowslide off a barn roof.

Next morning I met Eben prancing around in his Sunday clothes and with a necktie on that would make a rainbow look like a mourning badge.

"Hello!" says I. "You seem to be pretty chipper. You ain't going to start for that fifteen-mile ride through the woods to Ostable, be you? Looks to me as if 'twas going to rain."

"The predictions for this day," says he, "is cloudy in the forenoon, but clearing later on. Wind, sou'east, changing to south and sou'west."

"Did Beriah send that out?" says I, looking doubtful, for if ever it looked like dirty weather, I thought it did right then.

"ME and Beriah sent it out," he says, jealous-like. But I knew 'twas Beriah's forecast or he wouldn't have been so sure of it.

Pretty soon out comes Peter, looking dubious at the sky. "If it was anybody else but Beriah," he says, "I'd say this mornings prophecy ought to be sent to Puck. Where is the seventh son of the seventh son—the only original American seer?"

He wasn't in the weather-shanty, and we finally found him on one of the seats 'way up on the edge of the bluff.

"Hey, Elijah!" says Brown. "Does this go?" And he held out the telegraph-blank with the morning's prediction on it.

Beriah looked around just for a second. "The forecast for to-day," says he, "is cloudy in the forenoon, but clearing later on. Wind sou'east, changing to south and sou'west."

"Right you are!" says Peter, joyful. "We start for Setuckit, then."

So, after breakfast, the catboats loaded up, the girls giggling and screaming, and the men boarders dressed in what they hoped was sea-togs. They sailed away 'round the lighthouse and headed up the shore, and the wind was sou'east sure and sartin, but the "clearing" part wasn't in sight yet.

Beriah didn't watch 'em go. But by and by, when Eben drove the buggy out of the barn and Emma come skipping down the piazza steps, I see him peeking out of the little winder.

The Kelly critter had all sail sot and colors flying. "Oh!" she squeals, when she sees the buggy. "Oh! Mr. Cobb. Ain't you afraid to go in that open carriage? It looks to me like rain."

But Eben waved his flipper, scornful. "My forecast this morning," says he, "is cloudy now, but clearing by and by. You trust to me, Mis' Kelly."

"Of COURSE I trust you, Mr. Cobb," she says, "Of course I trust you, but I should hate to spile my gown, that's all."

They drove out of the yard, fine as fiddlers, and I watched 'em go. When I turned around, there was Beriah watching 'em too, and he was smiling for the first time that morning.

At ha'f-past ten it begun to sprinkle; at eleven 'twas raining hard; at noon 'twas a pouring, roaring, sou'easter, and looked good for the next twelve hours at least.

"Good Lord! Beriah," says Cap'n Jonadab, running into the Weather Bureau, "you've missed stays THIS time, for sure. Has your prophecy-works got indigestion?" he says.

But Beriah wasn't there. By two o'clock 'twas so bad that I put on my ileskins and went over to Wellmouth and telephoned to the Setuckit Beach life-saving station to find out if the clambakers had got there right side up.

They'd got there; fact is, they was in the station then, and the language Peter hove through that telephone was enough to melt the wires.

'Twas nearly eight when they drove into the yard and come slopping up the steps. The women-folks made for their rooms, but the men hopped around the parlor, shedding puddles with every hop, and hollering for us to trot out the head of the Weather Bureau.

"Bring him to me," orders Peter, stopping to pick his pants loose from his legs; "I yearn to caress him."

But Beriah didn't come to be caressed. 'Twas quarter past nine when we heard wheels in the yard.

"By mighty!" yells Cap'n Jonadab; "it's the camp-meeting pilgrims."

He jumped to open the door, but it opened afore he got there and Beriah come in.

Somebody outside says: "Whoa, consarn you!" Then there was a thump and a sloshy stamping on the steps, and in comes Eben and the widder.

I had one of them long-haired, foreign cats once that a British skipper gave me. 'Twas a yeller and black one and it fell overboard. When we fished it out it looked just like the Kelly woman done then.

Emma looked once round the room, and her eyes, fairly snapped. Then she went up the stairs three steps at a time.

Eben didn't say a word. He just stood there and leaked. Leaked and smiled. We didn't know what to make of it.

'Twas Beriah that spoke first. "He! he! he!" he chuckled. "Wasn't it kind of wet coming through the woods, Mr. Cobb? What does Mrs. Kelly think of the day her beau picked out to go to camp-meeting in?"

Then Eben came out of his trance. "Beriah," says he, "shake!" But Beriah didn't shake.

"I've got a s'prise for you, shipmate," goes on Eben. "Who did you say that lady was?"

Beriah didn't answer. I begun to think that some of the wet had soaked through the assistant prophet's skull and had give him water on the brain.

"You called her Mis' Kelly, didn't you?" gurgled Eben. "Wall, that ain't her name. Her and me stopped at the Baptist parsonage over to East Harniss when we was on the way home and got married. She's Mis' Cobb now," he says.

Well, the queerest part of it was that 'twas the bad weather was really what brought things to a head so sudden. Eben hadn't spunked up anywhere nigh enough courage to propose, but they stopped at Ostable so long, waiting for the rain to let up, that 'twas after dark when they was half way home. Then Emma—oh, she was a slick one!—said that her reputation would be ruined, out that way with a man that wa'n't her husband. If they was married now, she said—and even a dummy could take THAT hint.

I found Beriah at the weather-shanty about an hour afterwards with his head on his arms. "Mr. Wingate," he says, "I'm a fool, but for the land's sake don't think I'm SUCH a fool as not to know that this here storm was bound to strike to-day. I lied," he says; "I lied about the weather for the first time in my life; lied right up and down so as to get her mad with him."

But you ought to have read the letters Peter got next day from subscribers that had trusted to the prophecy and had gone on picnics and such like. The South Shore Weather Bureau went out of business right then.

The Mare and the Motor
(Abridged)

Them Todds had got on my nerves. 'Twas Peter's ad that brought 'em down. You see, 'twas 'long toward the end of the season at the Old Home, and Brown had been advertising in the New York and Boston papers to "bag the leftovers," as he called it. Besides the reg'lar hogwash about the "breath of old ocean" and the "simple, cleanly living of the bygone days we dream about," there was some new froth concerning hunting and fishing.

"Humph!" grunts Cap'n Jonadab. "Anybody but a born fool'll know there ain't any shooting down here this time of year."

Peter looked at him sorrowful. "Pop," says he, "did you ever hear that Solomon answered a summer hotel ad? This ain't a Chautauqua, this is the Old Home House, and its motto is: 'There's a new victim born every minute, and there's twenty-four hours in a day.' You set back and count the clock ticks."

Well, that's 'bout all we had to do. We got boarders enough from that ridiculous advertisement to fill every spare room we had, including Jonadab's and mine.

The Todds was part of the haul. He was a little, dried-up man, single, and a minister. He had a notion that he was a mighty hunter afore the Lord, like Nimrod in the Bible, and he'd come to the Old Home to bag a few gross of geese and ducks.

His sister was an old maid, and slim. She wore eye-glasses and a veil to "preserve her complexion," and her idee seemed to be that native Cape Codders lived in trees and ate cocoanuts. Whenever she piped "James" her brother had to drop everything and report on deck.

Them Todds was what Peter T. called "the limit, and a chip or two over." The other would-be gunners and fishermen were satisfied to slam shot after sandpeeps, or hook a stray sculpin or a hake. But t'wa'n't so with brother James Todd and sister Clarissa. "Ducks" it was in the advertising, and nothing BUT ducks they wanted. Finally we lost patience, and Peter T., he said they'd got to be quieted somehow, or he'd do some shooting on his own hook; said too much Toddy was going to his head. Then I suggested taking 'em down the beach somewheres on the chance of seeing a stray coot or loon or something—ANYTHING that could be shot at.

So the next morning we started, me and the Reverend James and Clarissa in the *Greased Lightning*, Peter's new motor launch.

Well, by and by Lonesome Huckleberries' shanty hove in sight, and I was glad to see it, although I had to answer a million questions about Lonesome and his history. His real name's long enough to touch bottom in the ship channel at high tide, so folks got to calling him "Huckleberries" because he peddles them kind of fruit in summer. Then he mopes around so with nary a smile on his face, that it seemed right to tack on the "Lonesome." So "Lonesome Huckleberries" he's been for ten years. He lives in the patchwork shanty on the beach down there, he is deaf and dumb, drives a liver-colored, balky mare that no one but himself and his daughter Becky can handle, and he has a love for bad rum and a temper that's landed him in the Wellmouth lock-up more than once or twice. He's one of the best gunners alongshore and at this time he owned a flock of live decoys that he'd refused as high as fifteen dollars apiece for. I told all this and a lot more.

When we struck the beach, Clarissa, she took her paint box and umbrella and mosquito 'intment, and the rest of her cargo, and went off by herself to "sketch."

James and me went perusing up and down that beach in the blazing sun looking for something to shoot. We frogged it up and down all the forenoon, but didn't git a shot at nothing but one stray "squawk" that had come over from the Cedar Swamp. I told James 'twas a canvasback, and he blazed away at it, but missed it by three fathom, as might have been expected. Finally, my game leg—rheumatiz, you understand—begun to give out.

So I flops down in the shade of a sand bank to rest, and the reverend goes poking off by himself. I cal'late I must have fell asleep, for when I looked at my watch it was close to one o'clock, and time for us to be getting back to port. I got up and stretched and took an observation, but further'n Clarissa's umbrella on the skyline, I didn't see anything stirring. Brother James wa'n't visible, but I jedged he was within hailing distance.

I started over toward the Greased Lightning. I'd gone only a little ways, and was down in a gully between two big hummocks, when "Bang! bang!" goes both barrels of a shotgun, and that Todd critter busts out hollering like all possessed.

"Hooray!" he squeals. "I've got 'em!"

Thinks I, "What in the nation does the lunatic cal'late he's shot?"

There was James, hopping up and down in the beach grass, squaling and waving his gun with one wing and there in front of him, was two ducks as dead as Nebuchadnezzar—two of Lonesome Huckleberries' best decoy ducks—ducks he'd tamed and trained, and thought more of than anything else in this world—except rum, maybe—and the rest of the flock was digging up the beach for home as if they'd been telegraped for, and squawking "Fire!" and "Murder!"

"I've got 'em!" hollers Todd. "I shot 'em all myself!"

"You everlasting—" I begun, but I didn't get any further. There was a rattling noise behind me, and I turned, to see Lonesome Huckleberries himself, setting on the seat of his old truck wagon and glaring over the hammer head of that balky mare of his straight at brother Todd and the dead decoys.

For a minute there was a kind of tableau, like them they have at church fairs—all four of us, including the mare, keeping still, like we was frozen. But 'twas only for a minute. Lonesome couldn't swear—being a dummy—but if ever a man got profane with his eyes, he did right then. Next thing I knew he tossed both hands into the air, clawed two handfuls out of the atmosphere, reached down into the cart, grabbed a pitch-fork and piled out of that wagon and after Todd.

"Run, you loon!" I hollers, desperate.

James didn't wait for any advice. He dropped his gun and put down the shore like a wild man, with Lonesome after him.

I was scart. I knew what Lonesome's temper was, 'specially when it had been iled with some Wellmouth Port no-license liquor. It looked bad to me. But I'd forgot sister Clarissa. 'Fore I'd limped fur I heard her calling to me.

"Mr. Wingate," says she, "get in here at once."

There she was, setting on the seat of Lonesome's wagon, holdin' the reins and as cool as a white frost in October.

"Get in at once," says she. I jedged 'twas good advice, and took it. When we rounded the sand hill we see the race in the distance. Lonesome had gained a p'int or two, and Todd wa'n't more'n four pitchforks in the lead.

"Make for the launch!" I whooped, between my hands.

The parson heard me and come about and broke for the shore. Todd splashed in to his waist and climbed aboard. James, he sees it's a close call, and he shins back to the engine, reaching it exactly at the time when the gent with the pitchfork laid hands on the rail. Then the parson throws over the switch and gives the starting wheel a full turn.

Well, you know the *Greased Lightning*? She don't linger to say farewell. Lonesome, being balanced with his knees on the rail, pitches headfust into the cockpit. Todd, jumping out of his way, falls overboard backward.

I yelled more orders than second mate on a coaster. Todd bubbled and bellered. Lonesome hung on to the rail of the cockpit and let his hair stand up to grow. Nobody was cool but Clarissa, and she was an iceberg.

"James," she calls, "get out of that water this minute and come here!"

James minded. He paddled ashore and hopped, dripping like a dishcloth, alongside the truck wagon.

"Now," says the lady, passing the reins over to me, "drive us home, Mr. Wingate, before that intoxicated lunatic can catch us."

It seemed about the only thing to do. I had some sort of a foggy notion that I'd drive along, pick up the guns and then get the Todds over to the hotel, afterward coming back to get the launch and pay damages to Huckleberries.

But the mare had made other arrangements. When I slapped her with the end of the reins she took the bit in her teeth and commenced to gallop.

Clarissa put in the time soothing James, who had a serious case of the scart-to-deaths, and calling me an "utter barbarian" for driving so fast. As for me, I wa'n't paying much attention to her—'twas the Cut-Through that was disturbing MY mind.

When you drive down to Lonesome P'int you have to ford the "Cut-Through." It's a strip of water between the bay and the ocean, and 'tain't very wide nor deep at low tide. But the tide was coming in now, and, more'n that, the mare wa'n't headed for the ford.

We struck that Cut-Through about a hundred yards east of the ford, and in two shakes we was hub deep in salt water. We crossed the first channel and come out on a flat where 'twasn't more'n two foot deep then. And then the most outrageous thing happened.

If you'll b'lieve it, that pesky mare balked and wouldn't stir another step.

"Drive on!" says Clarissa, pretty average vinegary. "You want to drown us!" says Miss Todd, continuing her chatty remarks. "I give you warning; if we reach the hotel, my brother and I will commence suit for damages."

"Commence suit!" I says. "I don't care WHAT you commence, if you'll commence to keep quiet now!" And then I give her a few p'ints as to what her brother had done, heaving in some personal flatteries every once in a while for good measure.

I'd about got to thirdly when James give a screech and p'inted. And, if there wa'n't Lonesome in the launch, headed right for us, and coming a-b'iling!

You never in your life heard such a row as there was in that wagon. Clarissa and me yelling to Lonesome to keep off—forgitting that he was stone deef and dumb—and James vowing that he was going to be slaughtered in cold blood. And the *Greased Lightning* p'inted just so she'd split that cart amidships, and coming—well, you know how she can go. She never budged until she was within ten foot of the flat, and then she sheered off and went past in a wide curve, with Lonesome steering with one hand and shaking his pitchfork at Todd with t'other.

He run up the Cut-Through a little ways, and then come about, and back he comes again, never slacking speed a mite, and running close to the shoal as he could shave. And past he goes, to wheel 'round and commence all over again.

Thinks I, "Why don't he ease up and lay us aboard? He's got all the weapons there is. Is he scart?"

And then it come to me—the reason why. HE DIDN'T KNOW HOW TO STOP HER. Here was us, stranded with a horse we couldn't make go, being chased by a feller who was run away with in a boat he couldn't stop!

Just as I'd about give up hope, I heard somebody calling from the beach behind us. I turned, and there was Becky Huckleberries,

Lonesome's daughter.

"Hi!" says she.

"Hi!" says I.

She held up the decoys.

"Who kill-a dem ducks?" says she.

I p'inted to the reverend. "He did," says I. "And he's willing to pay for 'em," I says.

"Pay thirty-five dolla?" says she.

"You bet!" says I.

But I'd forgot Clarissa. "Never!" says she. "We will never submit to such extortion. We'll drown first!"

Becky heard her. She didn't look disapp'inted nor nothing. "ALL right," says she; "GOO'-by."

The Todds stood it for a jiffy. Then James give in. "I'll pay it!" he hollers.

Even then Becky didn't smile. She just come about again and walked back to the shore.

“Hi, Rosa!” says Becky. And I give you my word that that mare started up, turned the wagon around nice as could be, and begun to swim ashore. When we got where the critter’s legs touched bottom, Becky remarks: “Whoa!”

“Here!” I yells, “what did you do that for?”

“Pay thirty-five dolla NOW,” says she.

Todd got his wallet from under hatches and counted out the thirty-five, keeping one eye on Lonesome, who was swooping up and down in the launch looking as if he wanted to cut in. I tied the bills to my jack-knife, to give ‘em weight, and tossed the whole thing ashore. Becky, she counted the cash and stowed it away in her apron pocket.

“ALL right,” says she.

Becky asked me how to stop the launch, and I told her. She made a lot of finger signs to Lonesome, and inside of five minutes the *Greased Lightning* was anchored in front of us. Old man Huckleberries was still hankering to interview Todd with the pitchfork, but Becky settled that all right.

Then Miss Huckleberries turned to us and smiled.

“ALL right,” says she; “GOO’-by.”

Them Todds took the train for the city next morning. James was kind of glum, but Clarissa talked for two. Her opinion of the Cape and Capers, ‘specially me, was decided. The final blast was just as she was climbing the car steps.

“Of all the barbarians,” says she; “utter, uncouth, murdering barbarians in—”

She stopped, thinking for a word, I s’pose. I didn’t feel that I could improve on Becky Huckleberries conversation much, so I says: “ALL right! GOO’-by!”

The Mark on the Door
(Abridged)

One nice moonlight evening me and Cap’n Jonadab and Peter T., having, for a wonder, a little time to ourselves and free from boarders, was setting on the starboard end of the piazza, smoking, when who should heave in sight but Cap’n Eri Hedge and Obed Nickerson. They’d come over from Orham that day on some fish business and had drove down to Wellmouth Port on purpose to put up at the Old Home for the night and shake hands with me and Jonadab.

We settled back for a good talk. After a spell somebody mentioned the Todds and I spun my yarn about the balky mare and the *Greased Lightning*. It tickled ‘em most to death, especially Obed.

“Ho, ho!” says he. “That’s funny, ain’t it. Them power boats are great things, ain’t they. I had an experience in one—or, rather, in two—a spell ago when I was living over to West Bayport. My doings was with gasoline though, not electricity. ’Twas something of an experience. Maybe you’d like to hear it.

“The yarn begins one morning when I went down to the shore after clams. I’d noticed the signs then. They was stuck up right acrost the path: ‘No trespassing on these premises,’ and ‘All persons are forbidden crossing this property, under penalty of the law.’ But land! I’d used that short-cut ever sence I’d been in Bayport—which was more’n a year—and old man Davidson and me was good friends, so I cal’lated the signs was intended for boys, and hove ahead without paying much attention to ‘em. ‘Course I knew that the old man—and, what was more important, the old lady—had gone abroad and that the son was expected down, but that didn't come to me at thetime, neither.

"I was heading for home about eight, with two big dreeners full of clams, and had just climbed the bluff and swung over the fence into the path, when somebody remarks: 'Here, you!' I jumped and turned round, and there, beating across the field in my direction, was an exhibit which, it turned out later, was ticketed with the name of Alpheus Vandergraff Parker Davidson— 'Allie' for short.

"All I could look at was teeth. There they was, a lovely set of 'em, in the mouth of the ugliest specimen of a bow-legged bulldog that ever tried to hang itself at the end of a chain. Allie was holding t'other end of the chain with both hands, and they were full, at that.

"'Here, you!' says Allie again. 'What are you crossing this field for?'

"'So's to get to t'other side of it, I guess,' says I.

"'Look here!' he says. 'I know who you are. Just because the gov'ner has been soft enough to let you countrymen walk all over him, it don't foller that I'm going to be. I'm boss here for this summer. I put those signs up,' he says, 'to keep just such fellers as you are off my property. They mean that you ain't to cross the field. Understand?'

"I understood. 'All right,' I says, picking up my dreeners and starting for the farther fence; 'I won't cross it again.'

"'You won't cross it now,' says he. 'Go back where you come from.'

"That was a grain too much. I told him a few things. He didn't wait for the benediction. 'Take him, Prince!' he says, dropping the chain.

"Prince was willing. He fetched a kind of combination hurrah and growl and let out for me full-tilt.

I simply couldn't reach the farther fence, so I made a quick jibe and put for the one behind me. And I couldn't make that, either. There was a little pine-tree in the lot, and I give one jump and landed in the middle of it. I went up the rest of the way like I'd forgot something, and then I clung onto the top of that tree and panted and swung round in circles, while the dog hopped up and down on his hind legs and fairly sobbed with disapp'intment.

"Allie was rolling on the grass.

"'Well, Reuben,' says he, lookin' up at me on the roost, 'you're a good deal handsomer up there than you are on the ground. I guess I'll let you stay there for a while as a lesson to you. Watch him, Prince.' And off he walks.

"'You everlasting clothes-pole,' I yells after him, 'if it wa'n't for that dog of yours I'd—'

"He turns around kind of lazy and says he: 'Oh, you've got no kick coming,' he says. 'I allow you to—er—ornament my tree, and 'tain't every hayseed I'd let do that.'

"And away he goes; and for an hour that had no less'n sixty thousand minutes in it I clung to that tree like a green apple, with Prince setting open-mouthed underneath waiting for me to get ripe and drop.

"Just as I was figgering that I was growing fast to the limb, I heard somebody calling my name. I unglued my eyes from the dog and looked up, and there, looking over the fence that I'd tried so hard to reach, was Barbara Saunders, Cap'n Eben Saunders' girl, who lived in the house next door to mine.

"'Why, Mr. Nickerson!' she calls. 'What are you doing up in that tree?'

"That was kind of a puzzler to answer offhand, and I don't know what I'd have said if friend Allie hadn't hove in sight just then and saved me the trouble.

"'Beg pardon, I'm sure,' says Allie. 'May I ask if that—er—deep-sea gentleman in my tree is a friend of yours?'

"Barbara kind of laughed and dropped her eyes, and said why, yes, I was.

"'By Jove! he's luckier than I thought,' says Allie, never taking his eyes from her face. 'And what do they call him, please, when they want him to answer?'

"'It's Mr. Nickerson,' says Barbara. 'He lives in that house there. The one this side of ours.'

"'Oh, a neighbor! That's different. Awfully sorry, I'm sure. Prince, come here. Er—Nickerson, for the lady's sake we'll call it off. You may—er—vacate the perch.'

"I waited till he'd got a clove-hitch onto Prince. He had to give him one or two welts over the head 'fore he could do it; the dog acted like he'd been cheated.

"'You see,' says Allie, talking to Barbara; 'the gov'nor told me he'd been plagued with trespassers, so I thought I'd give 'em a lesson. But neighbors, when they're scarce as ours are, ought to be friends. Don't you think so, Miss—? Er—Nickerson,' says he, 'introduce me to our other neighbor.'

"So I had to do it, though I didn't want to.

"'But Miss Saunders hasn't answered my question yet,' says Allie. 'Don't YOU think neighbors ought to be friends, Miss Saunders?'

"Barbara blushed and laughed and said she guessed they had. Then she walked away. I started to follow, but Allie stopped me.

"'Look here, Nickerson,' says he. 'I let you off this time, but don't try it again; do you hear?'

"'I hear,' says I. 'You and that hyena of yours have had all the fun this morning. Some day, maybe, the boot'll be on t'other leg.'

"Barbara was waiting for me. We walked on together without speaking for a minute. Then I says, to myself like: 'So that's old man Davidson's son, is it? Well, he's the prize peach in the crate, he is!'

"Barbara was thinking, too. 'He's very nice looking, isn't he?' says she. 'Twas what you'd expect a girl to say, but I hated to hear her say it. I went home and marked a big chalk-mark on the inside of my shanty door, signifying that I had a debt so pay some time or other.

"So that's how I got acquainted with Allie V. P. Davidson. And, what's full as important, that's how he got acquainted with Barbara Saunders.

"Shutting an innocent canary-bird up in the same room with a healthy cat is a more or less risky proposition for the bird. Same way, if you take a pretty country girl who's been to sea with her dad most of the time and tied to the apron-strings of a deef old aunt in a house three miles from nowhere and then fetch along, as next-door neighbor, a good-looking young shark like Allie, with a hogshead of money and a blame sight too much experience, and that's a risky proposition for the girl.

"Allie played his cards well; he'd set into a good many similar games afore, I judge. He begun by doing little favors for Phoebe Ann—she was the deef aunt I mentioned—and 'twa'n't long afore he was as solid with the old lady as a kedge-anchor. He had a way of dropping into the Saunders house for a drink of water or a slab of 'that delicious apple-pie,' and with every drop he got better acquainted with Barbara.

"I didn't see a great deal of what was going on, being too busy with my fishweirs and clamming to notice. Allie and me wa'n't exactly David and Jonathan, owing, I judge, to our informal introduction to each other.

"But, busy as I was, I see enough to make me worried.

"One Monday evening about the middle of the month I went over to Phoebe Ann's to borrow some matches. Barbara wasn't in—gone out to lock up the hens, or some such fool excuse. But Phoebe was busting full of joy. Cap'n Eben had arrived in New York a good deal sooner'n was expected and would be home on Thursday morning.

"I thought 'twas splendid for more reasons than one, and I went out feeling good. But as I come round the corner of the house there was somebody by the back gate, and I heard a girl's voice sayin': 'Oh, no, no! I can't! I can't!'

"If I hadn't trod on a stick maybe I'd have heard more, but the racket broke up the party. Barbara come hurrying past me into the house, and by the light from the back door, I see her face. 'Twas white as a clam-shell, and she looked frightened to death.

"Thinks I: 'That's funny! It's a providence Eben's coming home so soon.'

"And the next day I saw her again, and she was just as white and wouldn't look me in the eye. Wednesday, though, I felt better, for the servants on the Davidson place told me that Allie had gone to Boston on the morning train to be gone for good.

"Early that afternoon, as I was coming from my shanty to the bluff on my way to the shore after dinner, I noticed a steam-yacht at anchor two mile or so off the bar. Then I see a dingey with three men aboard rowing in, and I walked down the beach to meet 'em.

"There was a feller in a uniform cap steering the dingey, and, b'lieve it or not, I'll be everlastingly keelhauled if he didn't turn out to be Ben Henry, who was second mate with me on the old Seafoam.

"'Well, Ben,' says I, after we had shook hands, 'well, Ben,' I says, 'my shanty ain't exactly the United States Hotel for gilt paint and bill of fare, but I HAVE got eight or ten gallons of home-made cherry rum and some terbacker and an extry pipe. You fall into my wake.'

"'I'd like to, Obed,' he says; 'I'd like to almighty well, but I've got to go up to the store, if there is such a thing in this metropolus, and buy some stuff that I forgot to get in Newport. You see, we got orders to sail in a tearing hurry, and—'

"'Send one of them fo'mast hands to the store,' says I. 'You got to come with me.'

"He hemmed and hawed a while, but he was dry, and I shook the cherry-rum jug at him, figuratively speaking, so finally he give in.

"'You buy so and so,' says he to his men, passing 'em a ten-dollar bill. 'And mind, you don't know nothing. If anybody asks, remember that yacht's the *Mermaid*—M-U-R-M-A-D-E,' he says, 'and she belongs to Mr. Jones, of Mobile, Georgia.'

"So the men went away, and me and Ben headed for my shanty, where we moored abreast of each other at the table. After a spell I asked him about the man that owned the yacht.

"'Who? Oh—er—Brown?' he says. 'Why, he's—'

"'Brown?' says I. 'Thought you said 'twas Jones?'

"Well, that kind of upset him, and he took some cherry-rum to grease his memory. Then I asked more questions and he tried to answer 'em, and got worse tangled than ever.

"'Look here, Ben,' says I. 'You can't fetch port on that tack. The truth's ten mile astern of you. Who does own that yacht, anyway?'

"He looked at me mighty solemn—cherry-rum solemn. 'Obed,' he says, 'you're a good feller. The man that owns that yacht's named Davidson, and he's got a summer place right in this town.'

"'Davidson!' says I. 'DAVIDSON? Not young Allie Davidson?'

"'That's him,' says he.

"'But young Davidson's gone to Boston,' I says. 'Went this morning.'

"'That be hanged!' says Ben. 'All I know is that I got a dispatch from him at Newport on Monday afternoon, telling me to have the yacht abreast this town at twelve o'clock to-night, 'cause he was coming off to her then in his launch with a friend'.

"I didn't say much, being too busy thinking, but Ben went on telling about other cruises with 'friends.' Henry got speaking of one time down along the Maine coast.

"'But,' says I, referring to what he was telling, 'if she was such a nice girl and come from such nice folks, how—'

"'How do I know?' says he. 'Promises to marry and such kind of lies, I s'pose. And the plain fact is that he's really engaged to marry a swell girl in Newport.'

"He told me her name and a lot more about her. I tried to remember the most of it, but my head was whirling—and not from cherry rum, either. All I could think was: 'Obed, it's up to you! You've got to do something.'

"I was mighty glad when the sailors hailed from the shore and Ben had to go. I watched the dingey row off—the tide was out, so there was barely water for her to get clear—and then I went back home to think.

"Two and two made four, anyway I could add it up, but 'twas all suspicion and no real proof, that was the dickens of it. I couldn't speak to Phoebe Ann; she wouldn't b'lieve me if I did. I couldn't telegraph Cap'n Eben at Provincetown to come home that night; I'd have to tell him the whole thing and I knew his temper, so, for Barbara's sake, 'twouldn't do. I couldn't be at the shore to stop the launch leaving.

"No, 'twas up to me, and I thought and thought till after supper-time. And then I had a plan—a risky chance, but a chance, just the same. I went up to the store and bought four feet of medium-size rubber hose and some rubber tape. 'Twas almost dark when I got back in sight of my shanty, and instead of going to it I jumped that board fence that me and Prince had negotiated for, hustled along the path past the notice boards, and went down the bluff on t'other side of Davidson's p'int. And there in the deep hole by the end of the little pier, out of sight of the house on shore, was Allie's launch.

"I give one look around. Nobody was in sight. Then I ran down the pier and jumped aboard. Almost the first thing I put my hand on was what I was looking for—the bilge-pump.

"I fitted one end of my hose to the lower end of that pump and wrapped rubber tape around the j'int till she sucked when I tried her over the side. Then I turned on the cocks in the gasoline pipes fore and aft, and noticed that the carbureter feed cup was chock full. Then I was ready for business.

"I went for'ard, climbing over the little low cabin that was just big enough for a man to crawl into, till I reached the brass cap in the deck over the gasoline-tank. Then I unscrewed the cap, run my hose down into the tank, and commenced to pump good fourteen-cents-a-gallon gasoline overboard to beat the cars. Then I screwed the cap on again and went home, taking Allie's bilge-pump with me, for I couldn't stop to unship the hose. The tide was coming in fast.

"At nine o'clock that night I was in my skiff, rowing off to where my power-boat laid in deep water back of the bar. When I reached her I made the skiff fast astern, lit a lantern and set still in the pitch-dark, smoking and waiting.

"'Twas a long, wearisome wait. All I could think of was that gasoline. Was there enough in the pipes and the feed cup on that launch to carry her out to where I was? Or was there too much, and would she make the yacht, after all?

"It got to be eleven o'clock. I'd listened till my ear-drums felt slack, like they needed reefing. And then at last I heard her coming—CHUFF-chuff! CHUFF-chuff! CHUFF-chuff!

"And HOW she did come! She walked up abreast of me, went past me, a hundred yards or so off. Thinks I: 'It's all up. He's going to make it.'

"And then, all at once, the 'chuff-chuff-ing' stopped. Started up and stopped again. I gave a hurrah, in my mind, pulled the skiff up alongside and jumped into her, taking the lantern with me, under my coat. Then I set the light between my feet, picked up the oars and started rowing.

"I rowed quiet as I could, but he heard me 'fore I got to him. I heard a scrambling noise off ahead, and then a shaky voice hollers: 'Hello! who's that?'

"'It's me,' says I, rowing harder'n ever. 'Who are you? What's the row?'

"There was more scrambling and a slam, like a door shutting. In another two minutes I was alongside the launch and held up my lantern. Allie was there, fussing with his engine. And he was all alone.

"Alone he was, I say, fur's a body could see, but he was mighty shaky and frightened. Also, 'side of him, on the cushions, was a girl's jacket, and I thought I'd seen that jacket afore.

"'Hello!' says I. 'Is that you, Mr. Davidson? Thought you'd gone to Boston?'

"'Changed my mind,' he says. 'Got any gasoline?'

"'What you doing off here this time of night?' I says.

"'Going out to my—' He stopped. I s'pose the truth choked him. 'I was going to Provincetown,' he went on. 'Got any gasoline?'

"'What in the nation you starting to Provincetown in the middle of the night for?' I asks, innocent as could be.

"'Oh, thunder! I had business there, that's all. GOT ANY GASOLINE?'

"I made my skiff's painter fast to a cleat on the launch and climbed aboard. 'Gasoline?' says I. 'Gasoline? Why, yes; I've got some gasoline over on my power-boat out yonder. Has yours give out? Maybe the pipe's plugged or something. Have you looked?' And I caught hold of the handle of the cabin-door.

"He jumped and grabbed me by the arm. ''Tain't plugged,' he yells, sharp. 'The tank's empty, I tell you.'

"He kept pulling me away from the cabin, but I hung onto the handle.

"'You can't be too sure,' I says. 'This door's locked. Give me the key.'

"'I—I left the key at home,' he says. 'Don't waste time. Go over to your boat and fetch me some gasoline.

"Then I was sartin of what I suspicioned. The cabin was locked, but not with the key. THAT was in the keyhole. The door was bolted ON THE INSIDE.

"'All right,' says I. 'I'll sell you the gasoline, but you'll have to go with me in the skiff to get it. Get your anchor over or this craft'll drift to Eastham. Hurry up.'

"He didn't like the idee of leaving the launch, but I wouldn't hear of anything else. While he was heaving the anchor I commenced to talk to him.

"'I didn't know but what you'd started for foreign parts to meet that Newport girl you're going to marry,' I says, and I spoke good and loud.

"He jumped so I thought he'd fall overboard.

"'What's that?' he shouts.

"'Why, that girl you're engaged to,' says I. 'Miss—' and I yelled her name, and how she'd gone abroad with his folks, and all.

"'Shut up!' he whispers, waving his hands, frantic. 'Don't stop to lie.'

"''Tain't a lie. Oh, I know about it!' I hollers. He fairly shoved me into the skiff, after a spell.

"'Now,' he says, so mad he could hardly speak, 'stop your lying and row, will you!'

"I was willing to row then. I cal'lated I'd done some missionary work by this time.

"My plan had been to get him aboard the skiff and row somewheres—ashore, if I could. But 'twas otherwise laid out for me.

"Allie got more fidgety every minute. 'Ain't we 'most there?' he asks. And then he gives a screech. 'What's that ahead?'

"I turned to see, and as I done it the skiff's bow slid up on something. I give an awful yank at the port oar; she slewed and tilted; a wave caught her underneath, and the next thing I knew me and Allie and the skiff was under water, bound for the bottom. We'd run acrost one of the guy-ropes of my fish-weir.

"I hit sand with a bump and pawed up for air. When I got my head out I see a water-wheel doing business close along-side of me. It was Allie.

"'Help!' he howls. 'I'm drowning!'

"I got him by the collar, took one stroke and bumped against the weir-nets.

"'Help!' yells Allie, clawing the nets.

"It looked sort of dubious for a jiffy. Then I had an idee. I dragged him to the nighest weir- pole. 'Climb!' I hollers in his ear. 'Climb that pole.'

"He done it, somehow, digging his toes into the net and going up like a cat up a tree.

"'Hang on there!' says I. 'I'm going after the boat.' And I struck out. He yelled to me not to leave him, but the weir had give me my bearings, and I was bound for my power-boat.

"Soon's I got some breath I hauled anchor, started up my engine and headed back for the weir. I run along-side of it, keeping a good lookout for guy-ropes, and when I got abreast of that particular pole I looked for Allie. He was setting on the rope, a-straddle of the pole, and hanging onto the top of it like it owed him money.

He looked a good deal more comfortable than I was when he and Prince had treed me. And the remembrance of that time come back to me, and one of them things they call inspiration come with it.

"'Come here!' he yells. 'Come here, you fool, and take me aboard.'

"'Oh, I don't know,' says I. 'You're safe there, and, even if the yacht folks don't come hunting for you by and by—which I cal'late they will—the tide'll be low enough in five hours or so, so's you can walk ashore.'

"'What—what do you mean?' he says. 'Ain't you goin' to take me off?'

"'I was,' says I, 'but I've changed my plans. And, Mr. Allie Vander-what's-your-name Davidson, there's other things—low-down, mean things—planned for this night that ain't going to come off, either.'

"Then the beautiful tit for tat of the whole business come to me, and I couldn't help rubbing it in a little. 'As a sartin acquaintance of mine once said to me,' I says, 'you look a good deal handsomer up there than you do in a boat.'

"'You—you—etcetery and so forth, continued in our next!' says he, or words to that effect.

"'That's all right,' says I. 'You've got no kick coming. I allow you to—er—ornament my weir-pole, and 'tain't every dude I'd let do that.'

"I went back to the launch, pulled up her anchor and took her in tow. I towed her in to her pier, made her fast and then left her for a while. When I come back the little cabin-door was open and the girl's jacket was gone.

"Then I walked up the path to the Saunders house and it done me good to see a light in Barbara's window. And in the morning the yacht was gone and the weir-pole was vacant, and Cap'n Eben Saunders come on the first train.

"So's that's all there is of it. Allie hasn't come back to Bayport sence, and the last I heard he'd married that Newport girl; she has my sympathy, if that's any comfort to her.

"And Barbara? Well, for a long time she'd turn white every time I met her. But, of course, I kept my mouth shut, and she went to sea next v'yage with her dad. And now I hear she's engaged to a nice feller up to Boston.

"Oh, yes—one thing more. When I got back to my shanty that morning I wiped the chalkmark off the door. I kind of figgered that I'd paid that debt, with back interest added."

The Antiquers
(Abridged)

We've all got a crazy streak in us somewheres, I cal'late, only the streaks don't all break out in the same place, which is a mercy, when you come to think of it. I take summer boarders maybe, and you collect postage stamps. Oh, we're all looney, more or less, every one of us.

Speaking of collecting reminds me of the "Antiquers"—that's what Peter T. Brown called 'em. They put up at the Old Home House—summer before last. There was the Dowager and the Duchess and "My Daughter" and "Irene dear." Likewise there was Thompson and Small, but they, being nothing but husbands and fathers, didn't count for much first along, except when board was due or "antiques" had to be settled for.

The Dowager fetched port first. She hove alongside the Old Home one morning early in July, and she had "My Daughter" in tow. The names, as entered on the shipping list, was Mrs. Milo Patrick Thompson and Miss Barbara Millicent Thompson, but Peter T. Brown he had 'em re-entered as "The Dowager" and "My Daughter" almost as soon as they dropped anchor. Thompson himself come poking up to the dock on the following Saturday night; Peter didn't christen him, except to chuck out something about Milo's being an "also ran."

The Dowager was skipper of the Thompson craft, with "My daughter"—that's what her ma always called her—as first mate, and Milo as general roustabout and purser.

Mamma Small was built on the lines of old lady Thompson, only more so, and her daughter flew pretty nigh as many pennants as Barbara. Peter T. had 'em labeled the "Duchess" and "Irene dear" in a jiffy. He didn't nickname Small any more'n he had Thompson, and for the same reasons. Me and Cap'n Jonadab called Small "Eddie" behind his back, 'count of his wife's hailing him as "Edwin."

Well, the Dowager and the Duchess sized each other up, and, recognizing I jedge, that they was sister ships, set signals and agreed to cruise in company and watch out for pirates—meaning young men without money who might want to talk to their daughters.

In a week the four women was thicker than hasty-pudding and had thrones on the piazza where they could patronize everybody short of the Creator, and criticize the other boarders. Milo and Eddie got friendly too, and found a harbor behind the barn where they could smoke and swap sympathy.

'Twas fair weather for pretty near a fortni't, and then she thickened up. The special brand of craziness in Wellmouth that season was collecting "antiques," the same being busted chairs and invalid bureaus and sofys that your great grandmarm got ashamed of and sent to the sickbay a thousand year ago. I don't know who fetched the disease to the Old Home House. First along it seemed as if the Thompson-Small syndicate had been vaccinated—they didn't develop a symptom. But one noon the Dowager sails into the dining-room and unfurls a brown paper bundle.

"I've captured a prize, my dear," says she to the Duchess. And she dives under the brown paper hatches and resurrects a pink plate, with the picture of a pink boy, wearing curls and a monkey-jacket, holding hands with a pink girl with pointed feet.

"Ain't it perfectly lovely?" says she. "A ginuwine Hall nappy! And in SUCH condition!"

"Why," says the Duchess, "I didn't know you were interested in antiques."

"I dote on 'em," comes back the Dowager, and "my daughter" owned up that she "adored" 'em.

"If you knew," continues Mrs. Thompson, "how I've planned and contrived to get this treasure. Oh, no! I can't tell even you where I got it. All's fair in love and collecting, you know, and there are more gems where this came from."

She laughed and "my daughter" laughed, and the Duchess and "Irene dear" laughed, too, and said the plate was "SO quaint," and all that, but you could fairly hear 'em turn green with jealousy. It didn't need a spyglass to see that they wouldn't ride easy at their own moorings till THEY'D landed a treasure or two.

And sure enough, in a couple of days they bore down on the Thompsons, all sail set and colors flying. They had a pair of plates that for ugliness and price knocked the "ginuwine Hall nappy" higher 'n the main truck.

Well, you can see how a v'yage would end that commenced that way. The Dowager and Barbara would scour the neighborhood and capture more prizes, and the Duchess and her tribe would get busy and go 'em one better. That's one sure p'int about the collecting business—it'll stir up a fight quicker'n anything I know of.

One evening me and Cap'n Jonadab and Peter T. was having a confab by the steps of the billiard-room, when Milo beats up from around the corner.

"Hello!" hails Peter T. cordial. "You look as if you'd had money left you.

Milo laughed all over. "Well, well," says he, "I AM feeling pretty good. Made a ten-strike with Mrs. T. this afternoon for sure.

"That so?" says Peter. "What's up? Hooked a prince?"

"No," says Milo, laughing again. "Nothing like that. But I have got hold of that antique davenport she's been dying to capture."

One of the boarders at the hotel over to Harniss had been out antiquing a week or so afore and had bagged a contraption which answered to the name of a "ginuwine Sheriton davenport." The dowager heard of it, and ever since she'd been remarking that some people had husbands who cared enough for their wives to find things that pleased 'em.

So we was glad for Milo and said so. Likewise we wanted to know where he found the davenport.

"Why, up here in the woods," says Milo, "at the house of a queer old stick, name of Rogers."

"Not Adoniram Rogers?" says Cap'n Jonadab.

"That's him," says Thompson.

Now, I knew Adoniram Rogers. His house was old enough, Lord knows; but that a feller with a nose for a bargain like his should have hung on to a salable piece of dunnage so long as this seemed 'most too tough to believe.

"Well, I swan to man!" says I. "Adoniram Rogers! Have you seen the—the davenport thing?"

"Sure I've seen it!" says Milo. "I ain't much of a jedge, and of course I couldn't question Rogers too much for fear he'd stick on the price. But it's an old davenport, and it's got Sheriton lines and I've got the refusal of it till to-morrow, when Mrs. T's going up to inspect."

"Told Small yet?" asked Peter T.

Milo looked scared. "Goodness! No," says he. "And don't you tell him neither. His wife's davenport hunting too."

"You say you've got the refusal of it?" says I. "Well, I know Adoniram Rogers, and if I was dickering with him I'd buy the thing first and get the refusal of it afterwards."

"Is that so?" repeats Milo. "I'll take my wife up there first thing in the morning."

He walked off looking worried, and his tops'ls hadn't much more'n sunk in the offing afore who should walk out of the billiard room behind us but Eddie Small.

"Brown," says he to Peter T., "I want you to have a horse and buggy harnessed up for me right off. Mrs. Small and I are going for a little drive to—to—over to Orham," he says.

'Twas a mean, black night for a drive as fur as Orham and Peter looked surprised. He started to say something, then swallered it down, and told Eddie he'd see to the harnessing. When Small was out of sight, I says: "You don't cal'late he heard what Milo was telling, do you, Peter?" says I.

Peter T. shook his head and winked, first at Jonadab and then at me.

And the next day there was the dickens to pay because Eddie and the Duchess had driven up to Rogers' the night afore and had bought the davenport, refusal and all, for twenty dollars more'n Milo offered for it.

Adoniram brought it down that forenoon and all hands and the cook was on the hurricane deck to man the yards. 'Twan't nothing but a ratty old cripple of a sofy, with one leg carried away and most of the canvas in ribbons, but four men lugged it up the steps and the careful way they handled it made you think the Old Home House was a receiving tomb and they was laying in the dear departed.

'Twas set down on the piazza and then the friends had a chance to view the remains. The Duchess and "Irene dear" gurgled and gushed and received congratulations. Eddie stood around and tried to look modest as was possible under the circumstances. The Dowager sailed over, tilted her nose up to the foretop, remarked "Humph'" through it and come about and stood at the other end of the porch. "My daughter" follers in her wake, observes "Humph!" likewise and makes for blue water. Milo comes over and looks at Eddie.

"Well?" says Small. "What do you think of it?"

"Never mind what I think of IT," answers Thompson, through his teeth. "Shall I tell you what I think of YOU?"

I thought for a minute that hostilities was going to begin, but they didn't. Milo and Eddie just glared at each other and sheered off, and the "ginuwine Sheriton" was lugged into the sepulchre, meaning the trunk-room aloft in the hotel.

The "antiquing" went on harder than ever. Every time the Thompsons landed a relic, they'd bring it out on the veranda or in to dinner and gloat over it loud and pointed, while the Smalls would pipe all hands to unload sarcasm. And the same vicy vercy when 'twas t'other way about.

Adoniram Rogers had been mighty scurce 'round the Old Home sense the davenport deal. But one morning he showed up unexpected. A boarder had dug up an antique somewheres in the shape of a derelict plate, and was displaying it proud on the piazza. All of a sudden Rogers walks up the steps and reaches over and makes fast to the plate.

Adoniram grunted. "Huh!" says he. "'Tain't nothing but a blue dish. I've got a whole closet full of them."

All hands started for that poor, helpless plate owner as if they was going to swoop down on him like a passel of gulls on a dead horse-mack'rel. Everybody wanted to get Adoniram one side and talk with him, and everybody else was determined they shouldn't. Wherever he moved the "Antiquers" moved with him. Rogers got scared.

"Look here," says he. "What ails you folks? Are you crazy?"

I don't know how 'twould have ended if Peter T. Brown, cool and sassy as ever, hadn't come on deck just then and took command.

"See here, Rogers," he says, "let's understand this thing. Have you got a set of dishes like that?"

Adoniram looked at him. "Will I get jailed if I say yes?" he answers.

"Maybe you will if you don't," says Peter. "Now, then, ladies and gentlemen, this is something we're all interested in, and I think everybody ought to have a fair show. Now my idea is this; Rogers will bring those dishes down here tomorrer and we'll put 'em on exhibition in the hotel parlor. Next day we'll have an auction and sell 'em to the highest cash bidder. And, provided there's no objection, I'll sacrifice my reputation and be auctioneer."

So 'twas agreed to have the auction. Next day Adoniram heaves alongside with the dishes in a truck wagon, and they was strung out on the tables in the parlor. That auction was the biggest thing that ever happened at the Old Home. We had it on the lawn out back of the billiard room and folks came from Harniss and Orham and the land knows where.

But there wa'n't any real bidding except from the Smalls and Thompsons. A few of the boarders and some of the out-of-towners took a shy long at first, but their bids was only ground bait. The price went up and up. She went up to a hundred, then to one hundred and twenty-five, and with every raise Adoniram Roger's smile lengthened out. After the one-twenty-five mark the tide rose slower. Milo'd raise it a dollar and Eddie'd jump him fifty cents.

And just then two things happened. One was that a servant girl come running from the Old Home House to tell the Duchess and "Irene dear" that some swell friends of theirs from the hotel at Harniss had driven over to call and was waiting for 'em in the parlor. The female Smalls went in, though they wa'n't joyful over it. They give Eddie his sailing orders afore they went, too.

The other thing that happened was Bill Saltmarsh's arriving in port. Bill is an "antiquer" for revenue only. He runs an antique store over at Ostable and the prices he charges are enough to convict him without hearing the evidence.

Saltmarsh busts through the crowd and makes for the pulpit. He nods to Peter T. and picks up one of the plates. He looks at it first ruther casual; then more and more careful, turning it over and taking up another.

"Hold on a minute, Brown," says he. "Are THESE the dishes you're selling?"

"Sure thing," comes back Peter. "One thirty-two fifty, I'm bid. Now, Saltmarsh!"

But Bill only laughed. Then he picks up another plate, looks at it, and laughs again. "Good day, Brown," says he. And off he puts towards his horse and buggy.

Eddie Small was watching him. Milo, being on the other side of the pulpit, hadn't noticed so partic'lar.

"Who's that?" asks Eddie, suspicious. "Does he know antiques?"

I remarked that if Bill didn't, then nobody did.

"Look here, Saltmarsh!" says Small, catching Bill by the arm as he shoved through the crowd. "What's the matter with those dishes—anything?"

Bill turned and looked at him. "Why, no," he says, slow. "They're all right—of their kind."

But Eddie wa'n't satisfied. He turns to me. "By George!" he says. "What is it? Does he think they're fakes?"

I didn't know, so I shook my head. Small fidgetted, looked at Peter, and then run after Saltmarsh. Milo had just raised the bid.

"One hundred and thirty-three" hollers Peter. "One thirty-four do I hear? Make it one thirty-three fifty. Fifty cents do I hear? Come, come! this is highway robbery, gentlemen. Mr. Small—where are you?"

But Eddie was talking to Saltmarsh. In a minute back he comes, looking more worried than ever. Peter T. bawled and pounded and beckoned at him with the mallet, but he only fidgetted—didn't know what to do.

"One thirty-three!" bellers Peter. "One thirty-three! One thirty-three—once! One thirty-three—twice! Third and last call! One—thirty—"

Then Eddie begun to raise his hand, but 'twas too late.

"One thirty-three and SOLD! To Mr. Milo Thompson for one hundred and thirty-three dollars!"

And just then come a shriek from the piazza; the Duchess and "Irene dear" had come out of the parlor.

Well! Talk about crowing! The way that Thompson crowd rubbed it in on the Smalls was enough to make you leave the dinner table. They had the servants take in them dishes, piece by piece, and every single article, down to the last butter plate, was steered straight by the Small crowd.

As for poor Eddie, when he come up to explain why he hadn't kept on bidding, his wife put him out like he was a tin lamp.

"Don't SPEAK to me!" says she. "Don't you DARE speak to me."

He didn't dare. He just run up a storm sail and beat for harbor back of the barn. And from the piazza Milo cackled vainglorious. Me and Cap'n Jonadab and Peter T. felt so sorry for Eddie, knowing what he had coming to him from the Duchess, that we went out to see him. He was setting on a wrecked hencoop, looking heart-broke but puzzled.

"'Twas that Saltmarsh made me lose my nerve," he says. "I thought when he wouldn't bid there was something wrong with the dishes. And there WAS something wrong, too. Now what was it?"

"Maybe the price was too high," says I.

"No, 'twa'n't that. I b'lieve yet he thought they were imitations. Oh, if they only were!"

And then, lo and behold you, around the corner comes Adoniram Rogers. I'd have bet large that whatever conscience Adoniram was born with had dried up and blown away years ago. But no; he'd resurrected a remnant.

"Mr. Small," stammered Mr. Rogers, "I'm sorry you feel bad about not buying them dishes. I—I thought I'd ought to tell you—that is to say, I— Well, if you want another set, I cal'late I can get it for you—that is, if you won't tell nobody."

"ANOTHER set?" hollers Eddie, wide-eyed. "Anoth— Do you mean to say you've got MORE?"

"Why, I ain't exactly got 'em now, but my nephew John keeps a furniture store in South Boston, and he has lots of sets like that. I bought that one off him."

Peter T. Brown jumps to his feet.

"Why, you outrageous robber!" he hollers. "Didn't you say those dishes were old?"

"I never said nothing, except that they were like the plate that feller had on the piazza. And they was, too. YOU folks said they was old, and I thought you'd ought to know, so—"

Eddie Small threw up both hands. "Fakes!" he hollers. "Fakes! AND THOMPSON PAID ONE HUNDRED AND THIRTY-THREE DOLLARS FOR 'EM! Boys, there's times when life's worth living. Have a drink."

"Fellers," said Eddie, "drink hearty. I'm going in to tell my wife. Fake dishes! And I beat Thompson on the davenport."

He went away bubbling like a biling spring. After he was gone Rogers looked thoughtful.

"That's funny, too, ain't it?" he says.

"What's funny?" we asked.

"Why, about that sofy he calls a davenport. You see, I bought that off John, too," says Adoniram.

His Native Heath
(Abridged)

I never could quite understand why the folks at Wellmouth made me selectman. I s'pose likely 'twas on account of Jonadab and me and Peter Brown making such a go of the Old Home House and turning Wellmouth Port from a sand fleas' paradise into a hospital where city folks could have their bank accounts amputated and not suffer more'n was necessary. Anyway, I was elected unanimous at town meeting, and Peter was mighty anxious for me to take the job. So I finally agreed to serve, and the very first meeting I went to, the question of Asaph Blueworthy and the poorhouse comes up. Zoeth Tiddit—he was town clerk—he puts it this way:

"Gentlemen," he says, "we have here the usual application from Asaph Blueworthy for aid from the town. 'Suffering from lumbago and rheumatiz'—um, yes. 'Out of work'—um, just so. 'Respectfully begs that the board will'—etcetery and so forth. Well, gentlemen, what's your pleasure?"

Darius Gott, he speaks first. "Out of work, hey?" says Darius. "Mr. Chairman, I should like to ask if anybody here remembers the time when Ase was IN work?"

Nobody did, and Cap'n Benijah Poundberry—he was chairman at that time—he fetches the table a welt with his starboard fist and comes out emphatic.

"Feller members," says he, "I don't know how the rest of you feel, but it's my opinion that this board has done too much for that lazy loafer already. He ain't sick—except sick of work. Now, it's my idea that, long's he's bound to be a pauper, he might's well be treated as a pauper. Let's send him to the poorhouse."

"But," says I, "he owns his place down there by the shore, don't he?"

All hands laughed—that is, all but Cap'n Benijah. "Own nothing," says the cap'n. "The whole rat trap, from the keel to maintruck, ain't worth more'n three hundred dollars, and I loaned four hundred on it years ago, and the mortgage fell due last September. Whether he goes to the poorhouse or not, he goes out of that house of mine to-morrer. Nobody could help hearing him, unless they was deefer than the feller that fell out of the balloon and couldn't hear himself strike, so all hands agreed that sending Asaph Blueworthy to the poorhouse would be a good thing. 'Twould be a lesson to Ase, and would give the poorhouse one more excuse for being on earth.

Wellmouth's a fairly prosperous town, and the paupers had died, one after the other, and no new ones had come, until all there was left in the poorhouse was old Betsy Mullen, who was down with creeping palsy, and Deborah Badger, who'd been keeper ever since her husband died.

Well, we voted to send Asaph to the poorhouse, and then I was appointed a delegate to see him and tell him he'd got to go. I wasn't enthusiastic over the job, but everybody said I was exactly the feller for the place.

"To tell you the truth," drawls Darius, "you, being a stranger, are the only one that Ase couldn't talk over."

So, as there wa'n't no way out of it, I drove down to Asaph's that afternoon. He lived off on a side road by the shore, in a little, run-down shanty that was as no account as he was.

I knocked on the door, but nobody answered. After knocking three or four times, I tried kicking, and the second kick raised, from somewheres inside, a groan that was as lonesome a sound as ever I heard.

"Who's that?" wails Ase from 'tother side of the door. "Did anybody knock?"

"Knock!" says I. "I all but kicked your everlasting derelict out of water. It's me, Wingate—one of the selectmen. Tumble up, there! I want to talk to you."

Blueworthy didn't exactly tumble, so's to speak, but the door opened, and he comes shuffling and groaning into sight. His face was twisted up and he had one hand spread-fingered on the small of his back.

"Dear, dear!" says he. "I'm dreadful sorry to have kept you waiting, Mr. Wingate. I've been wrastling with this terrible lumbago, and I'm 'fraid it's affecting my hearing. I'll tell you—"

"Yes—well, you needn't mind," I says; "'cordin' to common tell, you was born with that same kind of lumbago, and it's been getting no better fast ever since. Jest drag your sufferings out onto this bench and come to anchor."

When he'd got planted on the bench he didn't let up any—kept on with the misery.

"Look here," says I, "when you get through with the Job business I'll heave ahead and talk. Now, you listen to me."

And then I told him just how matters stood. His house was to be seized on the mortgage, and he was to move to the poorhouse next day. You never see a man more surprised or worse cut up. Him to the poorhouse? HIM—one of the oldest families on the Cape? Well, the dignity didn't work, so he commenced on the lumbago; and that didn't work, neither. But do you think he give up the ship? Not much; he commenced to explain why he hadn't been able to earn a living and the reasons why he'd ought to have another chance. Well, if I hadn't been warned he'd have landed ME, all right. I never heard a better sermon nor one with more long words in it.

I actually pitied him. It seemed a shame that a feller who could argue like that should have to go to the poorhouse. Thinks I, "I'm an idiot, but I'll make him one more offer."

So I says: "See here, Mr. Blueworthy, I could use another man in the stable at the Old Home House. If you want the job you can have it. ONLY, you'll have to work, and work hard."

Well, sir, would you believe it?—his face fell like a cook-book cake. That kind of chance wa'n't what he was looking for. He shuffled and hitched around, and finally he says: "I'll—Ill consider your offer," he says.

"Well, I'll be yardarmed!" says I, and went off and left him "considering." I don't know what his considerations amounted to. All I know is that next day they took him to the poorhouse.

And from now on this yarn has got to be more or less hearsay. Seems that, while I was down notifying Blueworthy, Cap'n Poundberry had gone over to the poorhouse to tell the Widow Badger about her new boarder. The widow was glad to hear the news.

"He'll be somebody to talk to, at any rate," says she. "Poor old Betsy Mullen ain't exactly what you'd call company for a sociable body. But I'll mind what you say, Cap'n Benijah. It takes more than a slick tongue to come it over me."

So when Asaph arrived—per truck wagon—at three o'clock the next afternoon, Mrs. Badger was ready for him. She didn't wait to shake hands or say: "Glad to see you." No, sir! The minute he landed she sent him out by the barn with She waited till she heard the ax "chunk" once or twice, and then she went into the house, figgering that she'd gained the first lap, anyhow.

But in an hour or so it come over her all of a sudden that 'twas awful quiet out by the woodpile. She hurried to the back door, and there was Ase, setting on the ground in the shade, his eyes shut and his back against the chopping block, and one poor lonesome slab in front of him with a couple of splinters knocked off it.

She tip-toed out to the wood-pile, grabbed her new boarder by the coat collar and shook him till his head played "Johnny Comes Marching Home" against the chopping block.

"You lazy thing, you!" says she. "Wake up and tell me what you mean by sleeping when I told you to work."

"Sleep?" stutters Asaph. "I—I wa'n't asleep."

"You wa'n't hey?" says Deborah. "What WAS you doing, if 'tain't too personal a question?"

"I—I guess I must have fainted. You see, ma'am, I ain't been well for—"

"Yes, I know. I understand all about that. To-morrer morning you'll get up at five o'clock and chop wood till breakfast time. If I think you've chopped enough, maybe you'll get the breakfast. If I don't think so you'll keep on chopping. Now, march!"

Blueworthy, he marched, but 'twa'n't as joyful a parade as an Odd Fellers' picnic. He could see he'd made a miscue—a clean miss, and the white ball in the pocket. Deborah, she went out into the kitchen, but she ordered Ase to stay in the dining room and set the table; told him to get the dishes out of the closet.

All the time he was doing it he kept thinking about the mistake he'd made, and wondering if there wa'n't some way to square up and get solid with the widow. If he could only find out something that Deborah Badger was particular interested in, then he believed he could make a ten- strike. And, all at once, down in the corner of the closet, he see a big pile of papers and magazines. The one on top was the *Banner of Light*, and underneath that was the *Mysterious Magazine*.

Then he remembered, all of a sudden, the town talk about Debby's believing in mediums and spooks and fortune tellers and such. And he commenced to set up and take notice.

At the supper table he was as mum as a rundown clock; just set in his chair and looked at Mrs. Badger. She got nervous and fidgety after a spell, and fin'lly bu'sts out with: "What are you staring at me like that for?"

Ase kind of jumped and looked surprised. "Staring?" says he. "Was I staring?"

"I should think you was! Is my hair coming down, or what is it?"

He didn't answer for a minute, but he looked over her head and then away acrost the room, as if he was watching something that moved.

"Your husband was a short, kind of fleshy man, as I remember, wa'n't he?" says he.

"Course he was. But what in the world—"

"'Twa'n't him, then."

"HIM? My husband? What DO you mean?"

And then Asaph begun to put on the fine touches. He leaned acrost the table and says he, in a sort of mysterious whisper: "Mrs. Badger," says he, "do you ever see things? Not common things, but strange—shadders like?"

"Mercy me!" says the widow. "No. Do YOU?"

"Sometimes seems's if I did. Jest now, as I set here looking at you, it seemed as if I saw a man come up and put his hand on your shoulder."

Well, you can imagine Debby. "Good land!" she hollers. "Where? What? Who was it?"

"I don't know who 'twas. His face was covered up; but it kind of come to me—a communication, as you might say—that some day that man was going to marry you."

"Land of love! Marry ME? You're crazy! I'm scart to death."

Ase shook his head, more mysterious than ever. "I don't know," says he. "Maybe I am crazy. But I see that same man this afternoon, when I was in that trance, and—"

"Trance! Do you mean to tell me you was in a TRANCE out there by the wood-pile? Are you a MEDIUM?"

Well, Ase, he wouldn't admit that he was a medium exactly, but he give her to understand that there wa'n't many mediums in this country that could do business 'longside of him when he was really working. 'Course he made believe he didn't want to talk about such things, and, likewise of course, that made Debby all the more anxious TO talk about 'em. Particular she wanted to know more about that "man" that was going to marry her, but Asaph wouldn't say much about him.

"All I can say is," says Ase, "that he didn't appear to me like a common man. He was sort of familiar looking, and yet there was something distinguished about him, something uncommon, as you might say. But this much comes to me strong: He's a man any woman would be proud to get, and some time he's coming to offer you a good home. You won't have to keep poorhouse all your days."

So the widow went up to her room with what you might call a case of delightful horrors. As for Asaph, he waited till 'twas still, and then he crept downstairs to the closet, got an armful of *Banners of Light* and *Mysterious Magazines*, and went back to his room to study up. You can see how things went after that. Blueworthy was star boarder at that poorhouse. Mrs Badger was too much interested in spooks and fortunes to think of asking him to work, and if she did hint at such a thing, he'd have another "trance" and see that "man," and 'twas all off.

One evening, just after the Fourth, Deborah and Asaph was in the dining room, figgering out fortunes with a pack of cards, when there comes a knock at the door. The widow answered it, and there was an old chap, dressed in a blue suit, and a stunning pretty girl in what these summer women make believe is a sea-going rig.

It turned out that the man's name was Lamont, with a colonel's pennant and a million-dollar mark on the foretop of it, and the girl was his daughter Mabel. They'd been paying six dollars a day each for sea air and clam soup over to the Wattagonsett House, in Harniss, and either the soup or the air had affected the colonel's head till he imagined he could sail a boat all by his ownty-donty.

Well, he'd sailed one acrost the bay and got becalmed, and then the tide took him in amongst the shoals at the mouth of Wellmouth Crick, and there, owing to a mixup of tide, shoals, dark, and an overdose of foolishness, the boat had upset and foundered and the Lamonts had waded half a mile or so to shore. Once on dry land, they'd headed up the bluff for the only port in sight, which was the poorhouse—although they didn't know it.

The widow and Asaph made 'em as comfortable as they could; rigged 'em up in dry clothes which had belonged to departed paupers, and got 'em something to eat. The Lamonts was what they called "enchanted" with the whole establishment.

"This," says the colonel, "is delightful, really delightful. The New England hospitality that we read about. So free from ostentation and conventionality."

When you stop to think of it, you'd scurcely expect to run acrost much ostentation at the poorhouse, but, of course, the colonel didn't know, and he praised everything so like Sam Hill, that the widow was ashamed to break the news to him. As for Mabel, she was one of them gushy, goo-gooey kind of girls, and she was as struck with the shebang as her dad.

And after supper they paired off and got to talking, the colonel with Mrs. Badger, and Asaph with Mabel. Now, I can just imagine how Ase talked to that poor, unsuspecting young female. He was a man with a hidden sorrer, and the way he'd sigh and change the subject when it come to embarrassing questions was enough to bring tears to a graven image, let alone a romantic girl just out of boarding school.

Then, after a spell of this, Mabel wanted to be shown the house, so as to see the "sweet, old-fashioned rooms." And she wanted papa to see 'em, too, so Ase led the way. And the way them Lamonts agonized over every rag mat, and corded bedstead was something past belief. When they was saying good-night—they HAD to stay all night because their own clothes wa'n't dry and those they had on were more picturesque than stylish—Mabel turns to her father and says she: "Papa, dear," she says, "I believe that at last we've found the very thing we've been looking for."

And the colonel said yes, he guessed they had. Next morning they was up early and out enjoying the view. When breakfast was done the Lamonts takes Asaph one side and the colonel says: "Mr. Blueworthy," he says, "my daughter and I am very much pleased with the Cape and the Cape people. Some time ago we made up our minds that if we could find the right spot we would build a summer home here. We are—ahem!—well, frankly, your place here suits us exactly."

"We adore it," says Mabel, emphatic.

"Mr. Blueworthy," goes on the colonel, "will you sell us your home? I am prepared to pay a liberal price."

Poor Asaph was kind of throwed on his beam ends, so's to speak. He hemmed and hawed, and finally had to blurt out that he didn't own the place. The colonel wanted to know if it belonged to Mrs. Badger.

"Why, no," says Ase. "The fact is—that is to say—you see—"

And just then the widow opened the kitchen window and called to 'em.

"Colonel Lamont," says she, "there's a sailboat beating up the harbor, and I think the folks on it are looking for you."

The colonel excused himself, and run off down the hill toward the back side of the point, and Asaph was left alone with the girl. So he fetched a sigh that sounded as if 'twas racking loose the foundations and commenced.

He asked Mabel if she was prepared to hear something that would shock her turrible, something that would undermine her confidence in human natur'. So then he told her that her dad and her had been deceived, that that house wa'n't his nor Mrs. Badger's; 'twas the Wellmouth poor farm, and he was a pauper.

She was shocked, all right enough, but afore she had a chance to ask a question, he begun to tell her the story of his life. He told her how him and his sister had lived in their little home, their own little nest, over there by the shore, for years and years. He led her out to where she could see the roof of his old shanty over the sand hills, and he wiped his eyes and raved over it. Then, he said, he was took down with an incurable disease. He tried and tried to get along, but 'twas no go. He mortgaged the shanty to a grasping money lender and that money was spent. Then his sister passed away and his heart broke; so they took him to the poorhouse.

"Miss Lamont," says he, "good-by. Sometimes in the midst of your fashionable career, in your gayety and so forth, pause," he says, "and give a thought to the broken-hearted pauper who has told you his life tragedy."

Well, now, you take a green girl, right fresh from novels and music lessons, and spring that on her—what can you expect? Mabel, she cried and took on dreadful.

"Oh, Mr. Blueworthy!" says she. "I'm SO glad you told me. Cheer up," she says. "I respect you more than ever, and my father and I will—"

Just then the colonel comes puffing up the hill. He looked as if he'd heard news. "My child," he says in a kind of horrified whisper, "can you realize that we have actually passed the night in the—in the ALMSHOUSE?"

Mabel held up her hand. "Hush, papa," she says. "I know all about it. Come away, quick; I've got something very important to say to you."

And she took her dad's arm and went off down the hill, mopping her pretty eyes with her handkerchief and smiling back, every once in a while, through her tears, at Asaph.

Now, it happened that there was a selectmen's meeting that afternoon at four o'clock. Zoeth was as happy as a clam at high water; he'd sold the poorhouse property that very day to a Colonel Lamont, from Harniss, who wanted it for a summer place.

"And I got the price we set on it, too," says Zoeth. "But that wa'n't the funniest part of it. Seems's old man Lamont and his daughter was very much upset because Debby Badger and Ase Blueworthy would be turned out of house and home 'count of the place being sold. The colonel was hot foot for giving 'em a check for five hundred dollars to square things; said his daughter'd made him promise he would. Says I: 'You can give it to Debby, if you want to, but don't lay a copper on that Blueworthy fraud.' Then I told him the truth about Ase. He couldn't hardly believe it, but I finally convinced him, and he made out the check to Debby. I took it down to her myself just after dinner."

And as Zoeth was telling this, in comes Cap'n Benijah. "I cal'late the Lamonts must be buying all the property alongshore," he says when he heard the news. "I sold that old shack that I took from Blueworthy to that Lamont girl to-day for three hundred and fifty dollars. She wouldn't say what she wanted of it, neither, and I didn't care much."

"I can tell you what she wanted of it," says somebody behind us.

We turned round and 'twas Gott; he'd come in. "I just met Squire Foster," he says, "and the squire tells me that that Lamont girl come into his office with the bill of sale for the property you sold her and made him deed it right over to Ase Blueworthy, as a present from her."

"WHAT?" says all hands.

"That's right," said Darius. "She told the squire a long rigamarole about what a martyr Ase was, and how her dad was going to do some thing for him, but that she was going to give him his home back again with her own money. The squire tried to tell her what a no-good Ase was, but she froze him quicker'n—Where you going, Cap'n Benije?"

"I'm going down to that poorhouse," hollers Poundberry. "I'll find out the rights and wrongs of this thing mighty quick."

We all said we'd go with him, and we went. As we hove in sight of the poorhouse a buggy drove away from it, going in t'other direction.

"That looks like the Baptist minister's buggy," says Darius.

As we run alongside the poorhouse door, Ase Blueworthy stepped out, leading Debby Badger.

"By time, Ase Blueworthy!" hollers Cap'n Benijah, "what do you mean by—Debby, what are you holding that rascal's hand for?"

But Ase cut him short. "Cap'n Poundberry," says he, "I might pass over your remarks to me, but when you address my wife—"

"Your WIFE?" hollers everybody—everybody but the cap'n; he only sort of gurgled.

"My wife," says Asaph. "When you men sold the house over her head, I'm proud to say that I, having a home once more, was able to step for'ard and ask her to share it with me. We was married a few minutes ago," he says.

"And, oh, Cap'n Poundberry!" cried Debby, "oh, Cap'n Poundberry!" she says, "we've known for a long time that some man—an uncommon kind of man—was coming to offer me a home some day, but even Asaph didn't know 'twas himself; did you, Asaph?"

We selectmen talked the thing over going home, but Cap'n Benijah didn't speak till we was turning in at his gate.

"A house and lot for nothing," he says, "a wife to do the work for him, and five hundred dollars to spend! Sometimes the way this world's run gives me moral indigestion."

Jonesy
(Abridged)

'Twas Peter T. Brown that suggested it, you might know. And, as likewise you might know, 'twas Cap'n Jonadab that done the most of the growling.

"They ain't no sense in it, Peter," says he. "Education's all right in its place, but 'tain't no good out of it. Why, one of my last voyages in the schooner *Samuel Emory*, I had a educated cook, feller that had graduated from one of them correspondence schools.

Why, say! one of the fo'mast hands ate half a dozen of that cook's saleratus biscuit and fell overboard. If he hadn't been tangled up in his cod line, so we could haul him up by that, he'd have been down yet. Now, what good was education to that cook? Why—"

"Cut it out!" says Peter T.. "Who's talking about cooks? These fellers ain't cooks—they're—"

"I know. They're waiters. When I give an order and there's any back talk, I want to understand it. You take a passel of college fellers, like you want to hire for waiters. S'pose I tell one of 'em to do something, and he answers back in Greek or Hindoo, or such. What's the matter with the waiters we had last year? They talked Irish, of course, but I understood the most of that, and when I didn't 'twas safe to roll up my sleeves and begin arguing. But—"

"Oh, ring off!" says Peter.

I didn't say nothing. I knew how 'twould end. If Peter T. Brown thought 'twas good judgment to hire a mess of college boys for waiters, fellers who could order up the squab in pigeon-English and the ham in hog-Latin, I didn't care, so long as the orders and boarders got filled and the payroll didn't have growing pains. I had considerable faith in Brown's ideas, and he was as set on this one as a Brahma hen on a plaster nest-egg.

"It'll give tone to the shebang," says he, referring to the hotel; "and we want to keep the Old Home House as high-toned as a ten-story organ factory. And as for education, that's a matter of taste. When it comes to tone and tin, Cap'n, you tr ust your Uncle Pete."

So it went his way finally, as I knew it would, and when the Old Home opened up on June first, the college waiters was on hand. And they was as nice a lot of boys as ever handled plates and wiped dishes for their board and four dollars a week. And they made a hit with the boarders, especially the women folks. Before June was over the Old Home was full up and we had to annex a couple of next-door houses for the left-overs.

I was skipper for one of them houses, and Jonadab run the other. Each of us had a cook and a waiter, a housekeeper and an up-stairs girl. My housekeeper was the boss prize in the package. Her name was Mabel Seabury, and she was young and quiet and as pretty as the first bunch of Mayflowers in the spring. She was city born and brought up, but she wa'n't one of your common "He! he! ain't you turrible!" lunch-counter princesses, with a head like a dandelion gone to seed and a fish-net waist. Her dad had had money once, afore he tried to beat out Jonah and swallow the stock exchange whale. After that he was skipper of a little society library up to Cambridge, and she kept house for him. Then he died and left her his blessing, and some of Peter Brown's wife's folks, that knew her when she was well off, got her the job of housekeeper here with us.

The only trouble she made was first along, and that wa'n't her fault. I thought at one time we'd have to put up a wire fence to keep them college waiters away from her. She was nice to 'em, too, but when you're just so nice to everybody and not nice enough to any special one, the prospect ain't encouraging. So they give it up, but there wa'n't a male on the place, from old Dr. Blatt, mixer of Blatt's Burdock Bitters and Blatt's Balm for Beauty, down to the boy that emptied the ashes, who wouldn't have humped himself on all fours and crawled eight miles if she'd asked him to.

Jonadab took a special interest in her. It pretty nigh broke his heart to think she was running my house instead of his. He thought she'd ought to be married and have a home of her own.

"Well," says I, "why don't she get married then? She could drag out and tie up any single critter of the right sex in this neighborhood with both hands behind her back."

"Humph!" says he. "I s'pose you'd have her marry one of these soup-toting college chaps, wouldn't you? No, sir! a girl hasn't no right to get married unless she gets a man with money. There's a deck-load of millionaires comes here every summer, and I'm goin' to help her land one of 'em. It's my duty as a Christian," says he.

One evening, along the second week in July 'twas, I got up from the supper-table and walked over toward the hotel. And, in the shadder of the big bunch of lilacs by the gate, I see a feller standing, a feller with a leather bag in his hand, a stranger.

"Good evening," says I. "Looking for the hotel, was you?"

He swung round, kind of lazy-like, and looked at me. Then I noticed how big he was. Seemed to me he was all of seven foot high and broad according.

"Good evening," says the seven-footer. "Is this the Old Ladies' Home—the Old Home House, I should say?"

"Yes, sir," says I.

"Right," he says. "Will you be good enough to tell me where I can find the proprietor?"

"Well," says I, "I'm him; that is, I'm one of him. But I'm afraid we can't accommodate you, mister, not now."

"I'm not looking for a room," says he. "I'm looking for a job."

"A job!" I sings out.

"Yes. I understand you employ college men as waiters."

"A waiter?" I says. "Be you a waiter?"

"I don't know. I've been told so. Our coach used to say I was the best waiter on the team. At any rate I'll try the experiment."

Soon's ever I could gather myself together I reached across and took hold of his arm.

"Son," says I, "you come with me and turn in. You'll feel better in the morning. I don't know where I'll put you, unless it's the bowling alley, but I guess that's your size."

He laughed a big, hearty laugh. "It's straight," he says. "I mean it. I want a job."

"But what for? You ain't short of cash?"

"You bet!" he says.

"Then," says I, "you come with me to-night and to-morrer morning you go somewheres and sell them clothes you've got on. You'll make more out of that than you will passing pie, if you passed it for a year."

He laughed again, but he said he was bound to be a waiter and if I couldn't help him he'd have to hunt up the other portion of the proprietor. So I told him to stay where he was, and I went off and found Peter T. You'd ought to seen Peter stare when we hove in sight of the candidate.

I done the polite, mentioning Brown's name, hesitating on t'other chap's.

"Er-Jones," says the human lighthouse. "Er-yes; Jones."

"Glad to meet you, Mr. Jones," says Peter. "So you want to be a waiter, do you? For how much per?"

"Oh, I don't know. I'll begin at the bottom, being a green hand. Twenty a week or so; whatever you're accustomed to paying."

Brown choked. "The figure's all right," he says, "only it covers a month down here."

"Right!" says Jones, not a bit shook up. "A month goes."

Peter stepped back and looked him over, beginning with the tan shoes and ending with the whirligig hat.

"Jonesy," says he, finally, "you're on."

A little later, when I had the chance and had Brown alone, I says to him:

"Peter," says I, "for the land sakes what did you hire the emperor for? A blind man could see HE wa'n't no waiter. And we don't need him anyhow; no more'n a cat needs three tails. Why—"

But he was back at me before I could wink. "Need him?" he says. "He puts all the rest of the Greek statues ten miles in the shade. If I could only manage to get his picture in the papers we'd have all the romantic old maids in Boston down here inside of a week; and there's enough of THEM to keep one hotel going till judgment. Need him? Whew!"

Next morning we was at the breakfast-table in my branch establishment, me and Mabel and the five boarders. All hands was doing their best to start a famine in the fruit market, and Dr. Blatt was waving a banana and cheering us with a yarn about an old lady that his Burdock Bitters had h'isted bodily out of the tomb.

He was at the most exciting part, the bitters and the undertaker coming down the last lap neck and neck, and an even bet who'd win the patient, when the kitchen door opens and in marches the waiter with the tray full of dishes of "cereal." Seems to me 'twas chopped hay we had that morning—either that or shavings; I always get them breakfast foods mixed up.

But 'twa'n't the hay that made everybody set up and take notice. 'Twas the waiter himself. Our regular steward was a spindling little critter with curls and eye-glasses who answered to the hail of "Percy." This fellow clogged up the scenery like a pet elephant, and was down in the shipping list as "Jones."

"Well, Mr. Jones," says I, "this is kind of unexpected, ain't it? Thought you was booked for the main deck."

"Yes, sir," he says, "I was, but Percy and I have exchanged. Cereal this morning, madam?"

Mrs. Bounderby took her measure of shavings and Jones's measure at the same time. But I wa'n't watching her just then. I was looking at Mabel Seabury—looking and wondering.

The housekeeper was white as the tablecloth. She stared at the Jones man as if she couldn't believe her eyes, and her breath come short and quick. I thought sure she was going to cry. And what she ate of that meal wouldn't have made a lunch for a hearty humming-bird.

When 'twas finished I went out on the porch to think things over. The dining room winder was open and Jonesy was clearing the table. All of a sudden I heard him say, low and earnest:

"Well, aren't you going to speak to me?"

The answer was in a girl's voice, and I knew the voice. It said:

"You! YOU! How COULD you? Why did you come?"

"You didn't think I could stay away, did you?"

"But how did you know I was here?"

"It took me a month, but I worked it out finally. Aren't you glad to see me?"

She burst out crying then, quiet, but as if her heart was broke. "Oh!" she sobs. "How could you be so cruel! And they've been so kind to me here."

I went away then, thinking harder than ever. At dinner Jonesy done the waiting, but Mabel wa'n't on deck. She had a headache, the cook said, and was lying down. 'Twas the same way at supper, and after supper Peter Brown comes to me, all broke up, and says he:

"There's merry clink to pay," he says. "Mabel's going to leave."

"No?" says I.

"She says she's going to-morrer. She won't tell me why, and I've argued with her for two hours. What'll we do?" says he.

I couldn't help him none, and he went away, moping and miserable. All round the place everybody was talking about the "lovely" new waiter, and to hear the girls go on you'd think the Prince of Wales had landed. Jonadab was the only kicker, and he said 'twas bad enough afore, but now that new dude had shipped, 'twa'n't the place for a decent, self-respecting man.

"How you goin' to order that Grand Panjandrum around?" he says. "I'd as soon think of telling the Pope of Rome to empty a pail of swill as I would him. Why don't he stay to home and be a tailor's sign or something?"

Well, most of that was plain jealousy, so I didn't contradict. Besides I was too busy thinking. By eight o'clock I'd made up my mind and I went hunting for Jones. I found him, after a while, standing by the back door and staring up at the chamber winders as if he missed something. I asked him to come along with me. So he fell into my wake, looking puzzled, and in a jiffy we was planted in the rocking chairs up in my bedroom.

"Look here," says I, "Mr.—Mr.—"

"Jones," says he.

"Oh, yes—Jones. It's a nice name."

"I remember it beautifully," says he, smiling.

"All right, Mr. Jones. It's Miss Seabury," says I.

He was surprised, I guess, but he never turned a hair. "Indeed?" he says. "She is the—the housekeeper, isn't she?"

"She was," says I, "but she leaves to-morrer morning."

"No?" he sings out. "Not really?"

"You bet," I says. "Now down in this part of the chart we've come to think more of that young lady than a cat does of the only kitten left out of the bag in the water bucket. Let me tell you about her."

So I went ahead, telling him how Mabel had come to us, why she come, how well she was liked, how much she liked us, and a whole lot more. I guess he knew the most of it, but he was too polite not to act interested.

"And now, all at once," says I, "she gives up being happy and well and contented, and won't eat, and cries, and says she's going to leave. There's a reason, as the advertisement folks say, and I'm going to make a guess at it. I believe it calls itself Jones."

His under jaw pushed out a little and his eyebrows drew together. But all he said was, "Well?"

"Yes," I says. "And now, Mr. Jones, I'm old, and nosey maybe, but I like that girl. Perhaps I might come to like you, too; you can't tell. Under them circumstances, and with the understanding that it didn't go no farther, maybe you might give me a glimpse of the lay of the land. Possibly I might have something to say that would help. What do you think about it?"

He didn't answer right off; seemed to be chewing it over. After a spell he spoke.

"Mr. Wingate," says he, "with the understanding that you mentioned, I don't mind supposing a case. Suppose you was a chap in college. Suppose you met a girl in the vicinity that was—well, was about the best ever. Suppose you came to find that life wasn't worth a continental without that girl. Then suppose you had a dad with money, lots of money. Suppose the old fo—the gov'nor, I mean—without even seeing her or even knowing her name or a thing about her, said no. Suppose you and the old gentleman had a devil of a row, and broke off for keeps. Then suppose the girl wouldn't listen to you under the circumstances. Talked rot about 'wasted future' and 'throwing your life away' and so on. Suppose, when you showed her that you didn't care a red for futures, she ran away from you and wouldn't tell where she'd gone. Suppose—well, I guess that's enough supposing."

I pulled at my pipe a minute or so and then says I:

"Hum!" I says, "I presume likely it's fair to suppose that this break with the old gent is for good?"

He didn't answer, but he didn't need to; the look on his face was enough.

"Yes," says I. "Well, it's likewise to be supposed that the idea—the eventual idea—is marriage, straight marriage, hey?"

He jumped out of his chair. "Why, damn you!" he says. "I'll—"

"All right. Set down and be nice. I was fairly sure of my soundings, but it don't do no harm to heave the lead. I ask your pardon. Well, what you going to support a wife on—her kind of a wife? A summer waiter's job at twenty a month?"

He set down, but he looked more troubled than ever. I was sorry for him; I couldn't help liking the boy.

"Suppose she keeps her word and goes away," says I. "What then?"

"I'll go after her."

"Suppose she still sticks to her principles and won't have you? Where'll you go, then?"

"To the hereafter," says he.

"Oh, well, there's no hurry about that. Most of us are sure of a free one-way pass to that port some time or other, 'cording to the parson's tell. See here, Jones. You don't want to keep chasing that girl from pillar to post, making her more miserable than she is now. And you ain't in no position to marry her. The way to show a young woman like her that you mean business and are going to be wuth cooking meals for is to get the best place you can and start in to earn a living and save money. Now, Mr. Brown's father-in-law is a man by the name of Dillaway, Dillaway of the Consolidated Cash Stores. He'll do things for me if I ask him to, and I happen to know that he's just started a branch up to Providence and is there now. Suppose I give you a note to him, asking him, as a favor to me, to give you the best job he can. This is, of course, providing that you start for Providence to-morrer morning. What d'you say?"

He was thinking hard. "Suppose I don't make good?" he says. "I never worked in my life. And suppose she—"

"Oh, suppose your granny's pet hen hatched turkeys," I says, getting impatient, "I'll risk your making good. And as for her, it seems to me that a girl who thinks enough of a feller to run away from him so's he won't spile his future, won't like him no less for being willing to work and wait for her. You stay here and think it over."

When I come back Jonesy was ready for me.

"Mr. Wingate," says he, "it's a deal. I'm going to go you, though I think you're plunging on a hundred-to-one shot. Now I'm going to take your advice and the position. I'll do my best, and I must say you're a brick. Thanks awfully."

"Good enough!" I says. "Now you go and tell her, and I'll write the letter to Dillaway."

So the next forenoon Peter T. Brown was joyful all up one side because Mabel had said she'd stay, and mournful all down the other because his pet college giant had quit almost afore he started.

I went up to the depot with Jonesy to see him off.

"Good-by, old man," he says. "You'll write me once in a while, telling me how she is, and—and so on?"

"Bet you!" says I. "I'll keep you posted up. And let's hear how you tackle the Consolidated Cash business."

July and the first two weeks in August moped along and everything at the Old Home House kept about the same. Mabel was in mighty good spirits, for her, and she got prettier every day. I had a couple of letters from Jones, saying that he guessed he could get bookkeeping through his skull in time without a surgical operation, and old Dillaway was down over one Sunday and was preaching large concerning the "find" my candidate was for the Providence branch. So I guessed I hadn't made no mistake.

I had considerable fun with Cap'n Jonadab over his not landing a rich husband for the Seabury girl.

"Aw, belay!" says he. "The season ain't over yet."

One morning he comes to me, excited as a mouse at a cat show, and says he:

"Ah, ha! what did I tell you? I've got one!"

"I see you have," says I. "Want me to send for the doctor?"

"Stop your foolishing," he says. "I mean I've got a millionaire. One of the biggest big-bugs there is in New York. Ah, ha! what did I tell you?"

He was fairly boiling over with gloat, but from between the bubbles I managed to find out that the new boarder was a big banker from New York, name of Van Wedderburn, with a barrel of cash and a hogshead of dyspepsy.

"And I've fixed it that he's to stop at your house, Barzilla," crows Jonadab. "And when he sees Mabel—well, you know what she's done to the other men folks," he says.

"Humph!" says I, "maybe he's got dyspepsy of the heart along with the other kind. She might disagree with him. What makes you so cock sartin?"

"'Cause he's a widower," he says. "Them's the softest kind."

"Well, you ought to know," I told him. "You're one yourself. But, from what I've heard, soft things are scarce in Wall Street. Bet you seventy-five cents to a quarter it don't work."

He wouldn't take me, having scruples against betting—except when he had the answer in his pocket. But he went away cackling joyful, and that night Van Wedderburn arrived.

Van was a substantial-looking old relic, built on the lines of the Boston State House, broad in the beam and with a shiny dome on top. But he could qualify for the nervous dyspepsy class all right, judging by his language to the depot-wagon driver. When he got through making remarks because one of his trunks had been forgot, that driver's quotation, according to Peter T., had "dropped to thirty cents, with a second assessment called."

However, 'twas up to me, and I towed him in and made him acquainted with Mabel. She wa'n't enthusiastic until I mentioned his name. Then she gave a little gasp like. She took me by the arm and says she:

"WHAT did you say his name was, Mr. Wingate?"

"Van Wedderburn," says I.

"Not of Van Wedderburn & Hamilton, the bankers?" she asks, eager.

"That's him," says I. "Why? Do you know him?"

She laughed, but her face was all lit up and her eyes fairly shone.

"Oh, no," she says, "I don't know him, but I know of him—everybody does."

Well, everybody did, that's a fact, and the way Marm Bounderby and Maizie was togged out at the supper-table was a sin and a shame. But what surprised me was Mabel Seabury. She was dressed up, too; not in the Bounderbys' style—collar-bones and diamonds—but in plain white with lace fuzz. And she was as nice to Van as if he was old Deuteronomy out of the Bible. He set down to that meal with a face on him like a pair of nutcrackers, and afore 'twas over he was laughing and eating apple pie and telling funny yarns about robbing his "friends" in the Street.

And I understood it less and less as the days went by. If she'd been Maizie Bounderby, with two lines in each hand and one in her teeth, she couldn't have done more to hook that old stock-broker.

And Jonadab! he wa'n't fit to live with. Finally I owned up to myself that I'd made a mistake; the girl was a whitewashed tombstone and the whitewash was rubbing thin. That night I dropped a line to poor Jonesy at Providence, telling him that, if he could get a day off, maybe he'd better come down to Wellmouth, and see to his fences; somebody was feeding cows in his pasture.

The next day was Labor Day, and what was left of the boarders was going for a final picnic over to Baker's Grove at Ostable. We went, three catboats full of us, and Van and Mabel Seabury was in the same boat. When the dinner dishes was washed I went off by myself to a quiet bunch of bayberry bushes half a mile from the grove and laid down to rest, being beat out.

I guess I fell asleep, and what woke me was somebody speaking close by.

"Oh, no!" says Mabel Seabury, "oh, no! Mr. Van Wedderburn, please don't say any more. I can't listen to you, I'm so sorry."

"Do you mean that—really mean it?" asks Van. "My dear young lady, I realize that I'm twice your age and more, and I suppose that I was an old fool to hope; but I've had trouble lately, and I've been very lonely, and you have been so kind that I thought—I did hope—I— Can't you?"

"No," says she, more nervous than ever, and shaky, too, but decided. "No! Oh, NO! It's all my fault. I wanted you to like me; I wanted you to like me very much. But not this way. I'm—I'm—so sorry."

She walked on then, fast, and toward the grove, and he followed, slashing at the weeds with his cane, and acting a good deal as if he'd like to pick up his play-things and go home.

That night as I passed the lilac bushes by the gate, somebody steps out and grabs my arm. I jumped, looked up, and there, glaring down at me out of the clouds, was friend Jones from Providence, R. I.

"Wingate," he whispers, fierce, "who is the man? And where is he?"

"Easy," I begs. "What man?"

"That man you wrote me about. Who is he?"

"Oh, it's all right now," says I. "There was an old rooster from New York who was acting too skittish to suit me, but I guess it's all off. He's a hundred years old or so; name of Van Wedderburn."

"WHAT?" he says. " Stop joking. I'm not funny to-night."

"It's no joke," says I. "Van Wedderburn is his name. 'Course you've heard of him. Why! there he is now."

Sure enough, there was Van, standing like a statue of misery on the front porch of the main hotel, the light from the winder shining full on him. Jonesy stared and stared.

"Is that the man?" he says, choking up. "Was HE sweet on Mabel?"

"Sweeter'n a molasses stopper," says I. "But he's going away in a day or so."

He commenced to laugh, and I thought he'd never stop.

"What's the joke?" I asks.

He stopped long enough to ask one more question. "Tell me, for the Lord's sake!" says he. "Did she know who he was?"

"Sartin," says I. "So did every other woman round the place. You'd think so if—"

He walked off then, laughing himself into a fit. "Good night, old man," he says. "No, I don't think I shall worry much."

If he hadn't been so big I cal'lated I'd have risked a kick. A man hates to be made a fool of and not know why.

A whole lot of the boarders had gone on the evening train, and at our house Van Wedderburn was the only one left. He and Mabel and me was the full crew at the breakfast-table the follering morning.

I done all the talking there was; every time the broker and the housekeeper looked at each other they turned red.

Finally 'twas "chopped-hay" time, and in comes the waiter with the tray. And again we had a surprise, just like the one back in July. Percy wa'n't on hand, and Jonesy was.

But the other surprise wa'n't nothing to this one. The Seabury girl was mightily set back, but old Van was paralyzed.

"Cereal, sir?" asks Jones.

"Why! why, you—you rascal!" hollers Van Wedderburn. "What are you doing here?"

"I have a few days' vacation from my position at Providence, sir," answers Jones. "I'm a waiter at present."

"Why, ROBERT!" exclaims Mabel Seabury.

Van swung around like he was on a pivot. "Do you know HIM?" he pants, wild as a coot, and pointing.

'Twas the waiter himself that answered.

"She knows me, father," he says. "In fact she is the young lady I told you about last spring; the one I intend to marry."

Did you ever see the tide go out over the flats? Well, that's the way the red slid down off old Van's bald head and across his cheeks. But it came back again like an earthquake wave. He turned to Mabel once more, and if ever there was a pleading "Don't tell" in a man's eyes, 'twas in his.

"Cereal, sir?" asks Robert Van Wedderburn, alias "Jonesy."

Van Senior took it enough sight more graceful than you'd expect, under the circumstances. He went straight up to his room and never showed up till suppertime. Then he marches to where Mabel and his son was, on the porch, and says he:

"Bob," he says, "if you don't marry this young lady within a month I'll disown you, for good this time. You've got more sense than I thought."

Jonadab ain't paid me the quarter yet. He says the bet was that she'd land a millionaire, and a Van Wedderburn, afore the season ended, and she did; so he figgers that he won the bet. Him and me got wedding cards a week ago, so I suppose "Jonesy" and Mabel are on their honeymoon now. I wonder if she's ever told her husband about what I heard in the bayberry bushes. Being the gamest sport, for a woman, that ever I see, I'll gamble she ain't said a word about it.

Cap'n Dan's Daughter
(Abridged)

CHAPTER I

The Metropolitan Dry Goods and Variety Store at Trumet Centre was open for business. Sam Bartlett, the boy whose duty it was to take down the shutters, sweep out, dust, and wait upon early-bird customers, had performed the first three of these tasks and gone home for breakfast. The reason he had not performed the fourth—the waiting upon customers—was simple enough; there had been no customers to wait upon. There should have been. This was August, the season of the year when, if ever, Trumet shopkeepers should be beaming across their counters at the city visitor, male or female, and telling him or her, that "white duck hats are all the go this summer," or "there's nothin' better than an oilskin coat for sailin' cruises or picnics."

Captain Daniel Dott, proprietor of the Metropolitan Store, bending over his own ledger spread on the little desk by the window at the rear of his establishment, was realizing this fact. The Dott ledger, instead of showing a profit of a thousand or fifteen hundred dollars, as it had the first summer after Daniel bought the business, showed but a meager three hundred and fifty, over and above expenses.

Through the window the sun was shining brightly. From the road in front of the store—Trumet's "Main Street"—came the rattle of wheels and the sound of laughter and conversation in youthful voices.

A big two-horsed vehicle had stopped before the door. Two of the masculine members of the party descended from the "barge" and entered the store. Daniel, smiling his sweetest, stepped forward to meet them.

"Good mornin', good mornin'," he said. "A fine mornin', ain't it?"

The greeting was acknowledged by both of the young fellows, and one of them added that it was a fine morning, indeed.

"Don't know as I ever saw a finer," observed Daniel. "Off on a cruise somewhere, I presume likely; hey?"

"Picnic down at the Point."

"Well, you've got picnic weather, all right."

"Is—is Miss Dott about?" inquired one of the callers.

"Miss Dott? Oh, Gertie! No, she ain't. Be back pretty soon, I shouldn't wonder."

"Humph! Well, I'm afraid we can't wait. We hoped she might go with us on the picnic."

"That so? I'm sorry, but I'm afraid she couldn't go, even if she was here. You see, it's her last day at home, and—we—her mother and I—that is, I don't believe she'd want to leave us to-day."

"No; no, of course not. Well, tell her we wish she might have come, but we understand. Well, good by, Captain Dott."

"Er—good by. Er—er—don't want anything to take along, do you? A nice box of candy, or—or anything?"

"No, I think not. We stopped at the Emporium just now, and loaded up with candy enough to last a week. Good morning."

"How are you fixed for sun hats and things? I've got a nice line of hats and—well, good by."

"Good by."

The "barge" moved off. Daniel, standing dejectedly in the door, remembered his manners.

"Hope you have a nice time," he shouted. Then he turned and moved disconsolately back to the desk. He might have expected it. The Emporium, Mr. J. Cohen, proprietor, was his undoing in this instance as in so many others. The Emporium got the trade and he got the good bys. Mr. Cohen bought cheap and sold cheap, and the Emporium flourished like a green bay tree, while the Metropolitan Store was rapidly going to seed. Daniel thought of the past, of the days when, as commander and part owner of the three masted schooner *Bluebird*, he had been free and prosperous and happy. Then he considered the future, which was bluer than the sea, and sighed again. Why had he not been content to stick to the profession he understood, instead of retiring from the sea to live on dry land and squander his small fortune in a business for which he was entirely unfitted?

And yet the answer was simple enough. Mrs. Dott—Mrs. Serena Dott, his wife—was the answer, she and her social aspirations. It was Serena who had coaxed him into giving up seafaring; who had said that it was a shame for him to waste his life ordering foremast hands about when he might be one of the leading citizens in his native town.

The side door of the store opened, and Azuba Ginn appeared. Azuba had been the Dott maid of all work for eighteen years, ever since Gertrude was a baby.

Azuba entered the store in the way in which she did most things, with a flurry and a slam. Her sleeves were rolled up, she wore an apron, and one hand dripped suds, demonstrating that it had just been taken from the dishpan. In the other, wiped more or less dry on the apron, she held a crumpled envelope.

"Well!" she exclaimed, excitedly. "If some human bein's don't beat the Dutch then I don't know, that's all. If the way some folks go slip-slop, hit or miss, through this world ain't a caution then—Tut! tut! tut! don't talk to ME!"

Captain Dan looked up from the ledger. "What?" he asked absently.

"I say, don't talk to ME!"

"We—ll," with deliberation, "I guess I shan't, unless you stop
talkin' yourself, and give me a chance. What's the matter now, Zuba?"

"Matter! Carelessness is the matter! Here's a man that calls himself a man and goes mopin' around pretendin' to BE a man, and what does he do?"

"I don't know. I'd tell you better, maybe, if I knew who he was."

"Who he was! I'll tell you who he was—is, I mean. He's Balaam Hambleton, that's who he is."

"Humph! Bale Hamilton, hey? Then it's easy enough to say what he does—nothin', most of the time. Is that letter for me?"

"Course it's for you! And it's a week old, what's more. One week ago that letter come in the mail and the postmaster let that—that Hambleton thing take it, 'cause he said he was goin' right by here and could leave it just as well as not. And this very mornin' that freckle-faced boy of his rung the front door bell and yanked me right out of the dish water, and he says his ma found the letter in Balaam's other pants and would I please excuse his forgettin' it 'cause he had so much on his mind lately."

"Let's see the letter."

He bent forward and took the letter from her hand. It was of the ordinary business size and was stamped with the Boston postmark, and a date a week old. On the flap was printed "Shepley and Farwell, Attorneys, ------ Devonshire Street."

The captain drew a long breath; he leaned back in his chair and sat staring at the envelope.

"Well?" observed Azuba.

The captain started. "Hey?" he exclaimed.

"I said 'Well?'."

"'Well?' Well what?"

"Oh, nothin'! I was just wonderin'—"

"Wonderin' what?"

"I was wonderin' if that letter was anything important. Ain't you goin' to open it?"

"Hey? Open it? I gen'rally open my letters. It's a funny habit I have."

"Humph! Well, all right, then. Course, 'tain't none of my business what's in other folks's letters. Nobody can accuse me of—"

"Nobody can accuse you of anything, Zuba. Not even dish washin' just now."

Azuba drew herself up. "Well!" she exclaimed; "Here I leave my work to do folks favors, to fetch and carry for 'em, and this is what I get. Cap'n Dott, I want you to understand that I ain't dependent on nobody for a job. If you ain't satisfied—"

"There, there, Zuba! I was only jokin'. Don't get mad!"

"Mad! Who's mad, I'd like to know? It takes more'n that to make me mad, I'd have you understand."

"That's good; I'm glad of it. Well, I'm much obliged to you for bringin' the letter."

"You're welcome. I don't mind doin' errands, only I like to have 'em appreciated. And I like jokes well as anybody, but when you tell me—"

"Hold on! don't get het up again. Think of that dish water; it's gettin' cooler every minute."

The answer to this was an indignant snort followed by the bang of the door. Azuba had gone. Captain Daniel looked after her, smiled faintly, shook his head, and again turned his attention to the letter in his hand.

He was sure, perfectly sure, what he should find when he did open it. A letter from the legal representatives of Smith and Denton, the Boston hat manufacturers and dealers, stating that, unless the latter's account was paid within the next week, suit for the amount due would be instituted in the courts.

He did not blame Smith and Denton; they had been very kind, very lenient indeed. The thirty-day credit originally given him had been extended to sixty and ninety. They had written him many times, and each time he had written in reply that as soon as collections were better he should be able to pay in full; that he had a good deal of money owed him, and as soon as it came in they should have it. But it did not come in. The more recent letters from the hat dealers had been sharper and less kindly. They had ceased to request; they demanded. At last they had threatened. And now the threat was to be fulfilled.

His fingers shook as he tore the end from the envelope. They shook still more as he drew forth the enclosure. He read it through to the end. Then, with a loud exclamation, he rushed to the side door, flung it open and darted across the yard, the letter fluttering from his fingers like a flag.

He stumbled up the steps into the kitchen. Azuba, was, to say the least, startled.

"What—what—what—" stammered Azuba.

"Where's Serena?" demanded Captain Daniel.

"Hey? Oh, what IS it? Is the store afire?"

"No, no! Where's Serena?"

"She—she—what—"

"Where's SERENA, I ask you?"

"In her room, I cal'late. For mercy sakes, what—"

But the captain did not answer. Through dining-room, sitting-room, and parlor he galloped, and up the front stairs to the bedroom occupied by himself and wife. Mrs. Dott was standing before the mirror, red-faced and panting, both arms behind her and her fingers busily engaged. She caught a glimpse of him in the mirror, and heaved a sigh of relief.

"Oh, it's you, is it!" she panted. "My, I'm glad! For mercy sakes fasten those last three hooks; I'm almost distracted with 'em."

But the hooks remained unfastened for the time. Captain Dan threw himself into a chair and waved the letter.

"Serena," he cried. "What—WHAT do you suppose has happened? Aunt Laviny is dead."

Serena turned. "Dead!" she repeated. "Your Aunt Lavinia Dott? The rich one?"

"Yes, sir; she's gone. Died in Italy a fortnight ago. The letter says she was taken sick on a Friday, and died Sunday, so 'twas pretty sudden. I—"

But Mrs. Dott interrupted. "What else does it say?" she asked excitedly. "Who is if from?"

"It's from her lawyers up to Boston. What made you think it said anything else?"

"Because I'm not blind and I can see your face, Daniel Dott. What else does it say? Tell me! Has she—did she—?"

Captain Dan nodded solemnly. "She didn't forget us, Serena. The letter says her will gives us that solid silver teapot and sugar-bowl that was presented to Uncle Jim by the Ship Chandlers' Society, when he was president of it. She willed that to us. She knew I always admired that tea-pot and—"

His wife interrupted once more. "Tea-pot!" she repeated strongly. "Do you mean to say that all she left us was a TEA-POT? If you do I—"

"No, no, Serena. Hush! She's left us three thousand dollars besides."

His voice shook as he said it. He spoke as if three thousand dollars was an unheard-of sum, a fortune. Mrs. Dott had no such illusion.

"Three thousand dollars!" she exclaimed. "Is that all? Three thousand dollars!"

"All! My soul, Serena! Why, ONE thousand dollars just now is like—"

"Hush! Do be still! A lone woman, without a chick or a child or a relation except you, and that precious young swell of a cousin of hers she thought so much of. I suppose he gets the rest of it. Oh, how can anybody be so stingy!"

"Sh-sh, sh-h, Serena. Don't speak so of the dead. Why, we ought to be mournin' for her, really, instead of rejoicing over what she left us. I'm ashamed of myself—or I ought to be. But, you see, I thought sure the letter was from those hat folks's lawyers, sayin' they'd started suit. When I found it wasn't, I was so glad I forgot everything else."

His wife shook her head.

"Daniel," she said, "I—I declare I try not to lose patience with you, but it's awful hard work.Mourn for her! What did she ever do to make you sorry she was gone? Did she ever come near us when she was alive? Did she ever offer to give you, or even lend you, a cent? And she knew you needed it, for I wrote her."

"You DID? Serena!"

"Yes, I did. I wrote her six months ago, telling her how bad your business was, and that Gertie was at school, and we were trying to give her a good education, and how much money it took and—oh, everything. When your Uncle Jim's business was bad, in the hard times back in '73, who was it that helped him out and saved him from bankruptcy? Why, his brother—your own father. And he never got a cent of it back. I reminded her of that, too."

Daniel sprang out of his chair.

"You did!" he cried again. "Serena, how could you?"

"Somebody in this family must be practical and worldly-minded, and I seem to be the one. YOU wouldn't ask her for a cent. You wouldn't ask anybody for money, even if they owed it a thousand years."

Captain Dan looked very grave.

"I guess you're right, Serena," he admitted. "I ain't much good, I'm afraid."

Mrs. Dott's expression changed. She rose, walked over, and kissed him. "You're too good, that's the main trouble with you," she said. "Well, I won't scold any more. I'm glad we've got the three thousand anyway—and the tea-pot."

"It's a lovely tea-pot, all engravin' and everything. And the sugar-bowl's almost as pretty."

"Well, there's one good thing about it—Gertie can keep on with her college. This is her last year."

"Yes; I thought of that. Say, Serena, you've never told Gertie anything about how trade was or how hard-up we've been?"

"Of course not."

"No, I knew you wouldn't. She's such a conscientious girl; if she thought we couldn't afford it she wouldn't think of keepin' on with that college, and I've set my heart on her havin' the best start in life we can give her."

"I know. Ah hum! I wish she could have the start some people's daughters have. Mrs. Black was with me at the lodge room yesterday—we are decorating for the men's evening to-morrow night, you know—and Mrs. Black has been helping me. You'd think she belonged here in Trumet, instead of being rich and living in Scarford and being way up in society there. She and her husband are just like common folks."

"Humph! Barney Black IS common folks. HE needn't put on airs with me."

"He doesn't. And yet, if he was like some people, he would. So successful in his big factory, and his wife way up in the best circles of Scarford; she's head of the Ladies of Honor there as I am here, and means to get a national office in the order. But there! that reminds me that I was going to meet her at the lodge room at ten, and it's half-past nine now. Do help me with these hooks."

"Why didn't you call Zuba? She'd have hooked 'em for you."

"Azuba! Heavens and earth! She's worse than nobody; her fingers are all thumbs. Besides, she would talk me deaf, dumb and blind. She doesn't know her place at all; thinks she is one of the family, I suppose."

"Well, she is, pretty nigh."

"I don't care. She isn't one of the family; she's a servant, or ought to be. Oh dear! when I hear Annette Black telling about her four servants and all the rest it makes me so jealous, sometimes."

"Don't make ME jealous. I'd rather have you and Gertie and this place than all Barney Black owns."

"Daniel, I keep telling you not to call Mr. Black 'Barney.' He is B. Phelps Black now. Mrs. Black always calls him 'Phelps.'"

"He was Barney Black when he lived here regular. Havin' a summer cottage here and a real house in Scarford must make a lot of difference. By the way, speakin' of Scarford, that's where Aunt Laviny used to live afore she went abroad. She owned a big house there."

"Why, so she did! I wonder what will become of it. I suppose that cousin will get it, along with the rest. Oh dear! suppose—just suppose there wasn't any cousin. Suppose you and I and Gertie had that house and the money. Wouldn't it be splendid? WE could be in society then."

"Humph! I'd look pretty in society, wouldn't I?"

"Of course you would. And I—Oh, HOW I should love it! A real intelligent, ambitious woman has no chance in Trumet."

The captain shook his head. He recognized the last sentence as a quotation from the works of Mrs. Annette Black, self-confessed leader in society in the flourishing manufacturing city of Scarford, and summer resident and condescending patroness of Trumet.

"Well," he observed; "we've got more chance, even in Trumet, than we've had for the last year, thanks to Aunt Laviny's three thousand. If only trade in the store would pick up, I—Hey! I forgot the store altogether. Sam hadn't got back from breakfast and I left the store all alone."

He bolted from the room and down the stairs, the legacy forgotten for the moment, and in his mind pictures of rifled showcases and youthful Trumet regaling itself with chocolates at his expense.

Azuba shrieked another question as her employer once more rushed through the kitchen, but again her question was unanswered.

"Well!" she exclaimed, in alarmed soliloquy. "WELL, the next time I fetch that man a letter I'll fetch the doctor along with it. Has the world turned upside down?"

She might have made a worse guess. The Dott world was turning upside down; this was the beginning of the revolution.

CHAPTER II

Captain Dan's fears concerning the safety of his showcases were groundless. Even as he sprang up the steps to the side door of his place of business, he heard familiar voices in the store. Gertrude, his daughter, was seated in his chair by the desk, and John Doane was leaning upon the desk, talking with her. In the front of the store, Sam Bartlett, was doing nothing in particular, and doing it with his usual air of enjoyment.

Gertrude looked up as her father entered. John Doane, who had been looking at Gertrude, also changed the direction of his gaze. Captain Dan struggled with the breath and the composure.

"Why, Dad!" exclaimed Gertrude. "What is it?"

"What's the matter, Cap'n Dott?" asked Mr. Doane.

Daniel did his best to appear calm.

"Hey?" he panted. "Matter? Nothin's the matter. I left the store alone for a minute and I was in a kind of hurry to get back to it, that's all."

The explanation was not entirely satisfactory. Gertrude looked more puzzled than ever.

"A minute," she repeated. "Why, John and I have been here fifteen minutes, and Sam was here when we came."

The captain looked at his watch. "Well, maybe 'twas a little more'n a minute," he admitted.

Master Bartlett sauntered up to take part in the conversation.

"I got here twenty minutes ago," he observed, grinning, "and you wasn't here then, Cap'n Dan'l. I was wonderin' what had become of ye."

Daniel seized the opportunity to change the subject.

"Anybody been in since you came?" he asked, addressing Sam.

"No, nobody special. Abel Calvin was in to see if you wanted to buy some beach plums for puttin' up. He said he had about a bushel of first-rate ones, just picked."

"Beach plums! What in time would I want of beach plums? I don't put up preserves, do I? Why didn't he go to the house?"

Gertrude spoke again. "Don't mind that, Dad," she urged. "Why, how warm you are, and how excited you look. What is it? You haven't spoken a word to John."

Her father shook his head. "Mornin', John," he said. "I beg your pardon. I—I've had some news that's drivin' everything else out of my mind."

"News? Why, Dad! what do you mean? Bad news?"

"No, no! Good as ever was, and. . . . Humph! no, I don't mean that. It is bad news, of course. Your Great-aunt Laviny's dead, Gertie."

He told of the lawyer's letter, omitting for the present the news of the legacy. Gertrude was interested, but not greatly shocked or grieved. She had met her great-aunt but once during her lifetime, and her memory of the deceased was of a stately female, who sat bolt upright at the further end of a hotel room in Boston, and ordered Captain Dan not to bring "that child" any nearer until its hands were washed.

"She's gone, anyhow," he said. "It's liable to happen to any of us, bein' cut off that way. We ought to be prepared, I suppose."

"I suppose so. But, Daddy, Aunt Lavinia wasn't cut off exactly, was she? She was your aunt and she must have been quite old."

"No, Aunt Laviny was eighty-eight, or thereabouts. She wasn't exactly cut off, was she, come to think of it?"

Gertrude's brown eyes twinkled. "Not exactly—no," she said, gravely. "Well, Daddy, I'm sure I am sorry she has gone, but, considering that she has never deigned to visit us or have us visit her, or even to write you a letter for the past two years, I don't think we should be expected to mourn greatly. And," glancing at him, "I don't understand just what you meant by saying first that the news was good, and then that it was bad. There is something else, isn't there?" Her father smiled, in an embarrassed way. "Well, ye—es," he admitted, "there is somethin' else, but—but I don't know as I didn't do wrong to feel so good over it. Let me get sort of used to it first. I'll tell you pretty soon."

His daughter laughed, softly. "I know you will, Dad," she said. "You couldn't keep a secret in that dear old head of yours if you tried. Not from me, anyway; could you, dear?"

"I guess not," regarding her fondly. "Anyhow, I shan't try to keep this one. Well, this time to-morrow you'll be back at college again, in among all those Greek and Latin folks. Wonder she'll condescend to come and talk plain United States to us Cape Codders, ain't it, John."

John Doane admitted that it was a wonder. He seemed to regard Miss Dott as a very wonderful young person altogether. Gertrude glanced up at him, then at her father, and then at the blotter on the desk.

"Dad," she said, suddenly, "you are not the only one who has a secret."

The captain turned and looked at her. "Oh!" said Captain Daniel; and added, "I want to know!"

"Yes, you're not the only one. We—I—there is another secret. Daddy, dear, John wants to talk with you."

"Oh!" he said, again.

"Yes. I—I—" She rose and, putting her arms about her father's neck, kissed him. "I will be back before long, dear," she whispered, and hurried out. Mr. Doane cleared his throat.

"Well, sir," began the young man, and stopped. "Well, sir," began Mr. Doane, again, "I—I—" For one who, as Gertrude had declared, wished to talk, he seemed to be finding the operation difficult. "I—Well, sir, the fact is, I have something to say to you."

Captain Dan, who was looking very grave, observed that he "wanted to know." John Doane cleared his throat once more, and took a fresh start.

"Yes, sir," he said, "I have something to say to you—er—something that—that may surprise you."

A faint smile disturbed the gravity of the captain's face.

"May surprise me, hey?" he repeated. "Is that so?"

"Yes. You see, I—Gertie and I—have—are—"

Daniel looked up.

"Hard navigatin', ain't it, John?" he inquired. "Maybe I could help you over the shoals. You and Gertie think you'd like to get married sometime or other, I presume likely. Is that what you're tryin' to tell me?"

There was no doubt of it. The young man's face expressed several emotions, relief that the great secret was known, and surprise that anyone should have guessed it.

"Why, yes, sir," he admitted, "that is it. Gertie and I have known each other for years, ever since we were children, in fact; and, you see—you see—" he paused once more, began again, and then broke out impatiently with, "I'm making an awful mess of this. I don't know why."

Captain Dan's smile broadened.

"I made just as bad a one myself, once on a time," he observed. "Just as bad, or worse—and I didn't know why either."

"So you think you want Gertie, do you, John?" said the captain.

"I know it," was the emphatic answer.

"So. And she thinks she wants you?"

"She says so."

"Think she means it?"

"I'm trying to believe she does."

The tone in which this was uttered caused Captain Dan to chuckle.

"'Tis strange, I'll give in," he remarked, drily. "No accountin' for taste, is there—

Well," his gravity returning, "I suppose likely you realize that her mother and I think consider'ble of her."

"I realize that thoroughly."

"You don't realize it as much as you will some day, perhaps. Yes, we think Gertie's about right. She's a smart girl and, what's more, she's a good girl, and she's all the child we've got."

"Cap'n Dott," said the young man, "I know how you feel, I think. I know what Gertie is to you and how anxious you and her mother must be concerning her future. If I did not feel certain—practically certain—that I could give her a good home and all that goes with it, I should not have presumed to speak to her, or to you, concerning marriage. My business prospects are good, or I think they are. I—"

The captain held up his hand. "Er—er—John," he said, uneasily, "maybe you'd better tell about that part of it when Serena's around. She's the practical one of us two, I guess, far's money's concerned, anyway."

"I shall be glad to tell Mrs. Dott everything, of course. I have been with the firm now employing me for eight years, ever since I left high school. I have been steadily advanced, my salary is a fairly good one, and in another year I have the promise of a partnership. After that my progress will depend upon myself."

"And you're certain sure that you two care enough for each other?" he asked. "Not just care, but care enough?"

"Yes."

"Well, then, I guess I ain't got much to say. There's one thing, though. Gertie's young. She ain't finished her schoolin' yet, and—"

"And you think she should. So do I. She wishes to do it, herself, and I should be the last to prevent her, even if I could. We have agreed that she shall have the final year at college and then come back to you. After that—well, after that, the time of our marriage can be settled. Gertie and I are willing to wait; we expect to. I may never be a rich man, but Gertie's tastes and mine are modest. She does not care for society—"

The captain interrupted. "That's so," he said, hastily, "she don't. She don't care for 'em at all. Well, John, I—I—it'll come pretty hard to give her up to anybody. Wait till you have a daughter of your own and you'll know how hard. But, if I've got to give her up, I'd rather give her to you than anybody I know. All I can say is, God bless you and—and take good care of my girl, that's all."

He extended his hand and John seized it.

At dinner, a meal at which Mrs. Dott, still busy with the lodge room decorations, was not present, Gertrude and her father talked it over.

"It comes kind of hard, Gertie," he admitted, "but, Lord love you, there's a heap of hard things in this world. John's a good fellow and—and, well, we ain't goin' to lose you just yet, anyhow."

Gertrude rose and, coming around the table, put her arms about his neck.

"Indeed you're not, dear," she said. "If I supposed my marriage meant giving you up, I shouldn't think of it."

"Wouldn't think of John, either, I suppose, hey?"

"Well, I—I might think of him a little, just a tiny little bit."

"I shouldn't wonder. That's all right. You can't get rid of me so easy. There! let's go into the sittin'-room a few minutes and give Zuba a chance to clear off."

In the sitting-room they spoke of many things, of Gertrude's departure for school, of the engagement, of course, and of the three thousand dollar windfall from Aunt Lavinia.

"What is that cousin's name?" asked Gertrude. "The one who inherits all of your aunt's fortune?"

"Let's see. His name? I ought to know it well's I know my own. Hungerford, Percy Hungerford, that's it!"

Gertrude looked surprised. "Not Percy Hungerford—of Scarford!" she cried. "What sort of a man is he? What does he look like?"

"Looked like a picked chicken, last time I saw him. Kind of a spindlin' little critter, with sandy complexion and hair, but dressed—my soul! there wasn't any picked chicken look about his clothes."

Gertrude nodded. "I believe it is the same one," she said. "Yes, I am sure of it. He came out to the college at one of our commencements. He danced with me—once. They said he was very wealthy."

"Humph! All the wealth he had come from Aunt Laviny, far's I ever heard. He was her pet and the only thing she ever spent money on, except herself. Like him, did you?"

"No," said Gertrude, and changed the subject.

Before her father departed for the store and she went to her room to finish packing, she sat upon the arm of his chair and, bending down, said:

"Daddy, if you hadn't got this money, this three thousand dollars, do you know what I had very nearly made up my mind to do?"

"No, I'm sure I don't."

"I had almost decided not to stay at college, but to come back here and live with you and mother."

"For the land sakes! Why?"

"Because I was sure you needed me. You never told me, of course—being you, you wouldn't—but I was sure that you were troubled about—about things."

"Me? Troubled? What put that into your head? I don't get troubled enough. Ask your mother if that ain't so."

"I shall not ask anybody but you. Tell me truly: Weren't you troubled; about the business, and the store?"

Captain Dan rubbed his chin. He wished very much to deny the allegation, or at least to dodge the truth. But he was a poor prevaricator at any time, and his daughter was looking him straight in the eye.

"Well," he faltered, "I—I—How in time did you guess that? I—Humph! why, yes, I was a little mite upset. You see, trade ain't been first rate this summer, and collections were awful slow. I hate to drive folks, especially when I know they're hard up. I was a little worried, but it's all right now. Aunt Laviny's three thousand fixed that all right. It'll carry me along like a full sail breeze. You go back to school, like a sensible girl, and don't you worry a mite. It's all right now, Gertie."

"Honest?"

"Honest to Betsy!"

He meant it; he really thought it was all right. The fact that he owed a thousand already and that the remaining two would almost certainly be swept into the capacious maw of the Metropolitan Store did not occur to him then.

"Then you're sure you can afford to have me go back for my last year?"

"Course I am. I couldn't afford to do anything else."

His absolute certainty stifled his daughter's doubts for the time, but she asked another question.

"And there's nothing that troubles you at all?"

"No-o." The captain's answer was not quite as emphatic this time.

Gertrude smiled, and patted his shoulder. "Daddy, dear," she said, "you're as transparent as a window pane, aren't you. Well, don't worry any more. That will be all right pretty soon, too. Mrs. Black doesn't stay in Trumet all the year."

Her father gasped. That this child of his should dive into the recesses of his soul and drag to light its most secret misgivings was amazing.

"What on earth?" he demanded.

"You know what I mean. Mother is just a little carried away. She has heard so much about big houses and servants and society and woman's opportunity, and all the rest of it, that she has been swept off her feet. But it won't last, I'm sure. She isn't really discontented; she only thinks she is."

Daniel sighed. "I know," he said. "Fact is, I ain't up-to-date enough, myself, that's what's the matter. She's a mighty able, ambitious woman, your mother is, Gertie, and I don't wonder she gets to thinkin', sometimes, that Trumet is a kind of one-horse town. I like it. But she ain't satisfied to be satisfied, like me. It's a good thing she ain't, I guess. Somebody's got to live up to the responsibilities of life, and—"

Gertrude laughed. "She said that, didn't she," she interrupted.

"Why, yes, she did. How did you know?"

"I guessed. But there, Dad, be patient and. . . . Sh-sh! here's Mother now."

It was Serena, sure enough, breathless from hurrying, but full of energy and impatience.

"I suppose you've had dinner," she exclaimed. "Well, all right, I don't care. I couldn't help being late, there was so much to do at the lodge rooms and nobody to do it right, except me. If Mrs. Black hadn't helped and superintended and—and everything, I don't know where we should have been. I must get a bite and hurry back. She was rushing in the direction of the kitchen, but her husband detained her.

"Hold on, Serena," he shouted. "Goin' back! What do you mean? You ain't goin' back to that lodge this afternoon, are you? Why, Gertie's goin' on the up-train!"

"I know, but I must go back, Daniel. Goodness knows what would happen if I didn't. If you had seen some of the decorations those other women wanted to put up, you would think it was necessary for someone with respectable taste to be there. Gertie, I shall be at the depot to say good by, but I must be at that lodge room first. I MUST. You understand, don't you?"

Gertrude said she understood perfectly and her mother hurried to the kitchen, where she ate lukewarm fried fish and apple pie, while Azuba washed the dishes and prophesied darkly concerning "dyspepsy." Gertrude went to her room to put the last few things in her trunks, and Captain Dan returned to the store, where he found the Bartlett boy pacifying a gnawing appetite with chocolate creams abstracted from stock.

At a quarter to three the captain was at the railway station, where he was joined by John Doane, who, his vacation over, was returning to Boston. After a five-minute wait Serena and Gertrude appeared.

The latter had called at the lodge room for her mother and, during the walk to the station, had broken the news of her engagement. Farewells were harder to say than usual, although Gertrude tried her best to seem cheerful, and the captain swallowed the lump in his throat and smiled and joked in a ghastly fashion all through the ceremony. Just before the train started, his daughter led him to one side and whispered:

"Now, Daddy, remember—you are not to worry. And, if you need me at any time, you will tell me so, and I shall surely come. You'll promise, won't you? And you will write at least once a week?"

The captain made both promises. They kissed, Serena and Gertrude exchanged hugs, and John Doane solemnly shook hands once more. Then the train moved away from the station.

Daniel and Serena walked homeward, Mrs. Dott wiping her eyes with a damp handkerchief, and her husband very grave and silent. As they passed the lodge building the lady said:

"I ought to go right back in there again. I ought to, but I just can't, not now. I—I want to be with you, Daniel, a time like this."

"Goodness knows I want you, Serena; but—but for mercy sakes don't call it a 'time like this.' Sounds as if we'd just come from the cemetery instead of the depot."

In spite of this philosophical declaration the remainder of that afternoon was rather funereal for Captain Dan. He moped about the store, waiting half-heartedly upon the few customers who happened in, and the ring of the supper bell was welcome, as it promised some company other than his thoughts.

But the promise was not fulfilled. He ate his supper alone. Mrs. Dott had gone back to the lodge room, so Azuba said.

"I don't think she was intendin' to," remarked the latter, confidentially. "She said she guessed she'd 'lay down a spell'; said she was 'kind of tired.' But afore she got upstairs scarcely, along comes that Black automobile with that Irish 'shover man' drivin' it and her in the back seat, and he gets out and comes and rings the front door bell, and when I answer it he said that she said she wanted to see her and—"

"Here! hold on, Zuba!" interrupted her bewildered employer. "'Vast heavin' a second, will you? You ought to run that yarn of yours through a sieve and strain some of the 'hes' and 'shes' out of it. 'He said that she said she wanted to see her.' Who wanted to see what?"

"Why, Barney Black's wife. She wanted to see Serena. So in she came, all rigged up in her best clothes and—"

"How do you know they were her best ones?"

"Hey? Well, they would have been MY best ones, if I owned 'em, I tell you that. I never see such clothes as that woman has!"

"Hi! steady there, Zuba. Keep your eye on the compass. You're gettin' off the course again. Annette—Mrs. Black, I mean—came to see Mrs. Dott; that's plain sailin' so far. What happened after that?"

"Why, they went off together in the automobile and Serena said to tell you she had to go to lodge, and she'd be back when she could and not to wait supper. That's all I know."

The captain finished his lonely meal and returned to the store, where he found Abel Blount's wife and their twin boys, aged eight, waiting to negotiate for rubber boots.

At nine o'clock he and Sam locked up, extinguished the lamps, and closed the Metropolitan Store for the night. Crossing the yard to the house, which he entered by the front door, he found Serena in the sitting-room.

"Oh, dear!" she exclaimed, acknowledging her husband's greeting with a nod, "I am just about worn out, Daniel."

"I should think you would be, Serena. You've been makin' tracks between here and that lodge room all to-day and yesterday, too."

"It isn't that. I don't mind the work. It's the thanklessness of it all that breaks me down. I give my time and effort to help the lodge, and what does it amount to?"

"Well, I—I give in that it don't seem to me to amount to much, 'cordin' to my figurin'. I don't care much for lodge meetin's and sociables and such, myself. I'd rather have one evenin' at home with you than the whole cargo of 'em."

This statement was frank, but it was decidedly undiplomatic. Serena sniffed contempt.

"Of course you would!" she said. "I don't get a bit of encouragement here at home, either. I should think you'd be proud to have your wife the head of the Chapter, presiding at meetings and welcoming the visiting delegates and—and all."

"I am," hastily. "I'm proud of you, Serena. Always have been, far's that goes. But I'm just as proud of you here in this sittin'-room as I am when you're back of that pulpit, poundin' with your mallet and tellin' Alphy Ann Berry to 'come to order.'"

Mrs. Dott did not chuckle. "You think it's a joke," she said. "I don't. It is the Berry woman and her kind that make me disgusted. I'm tired of them all.

I'm tired of Trumet. I wish we were somewhere where I had an opportunity; somewhere where I might be appreciated."

"I appreciate you, Serena."

Serena ignored the remark. "I wish we had never settled here," she went on. "I'd leave in a minute, if I could. I'd like to be in with nice people, cultivated people, intelligent, up-to-date society, where I could have a chance to go on and be somebody. Annette says I would be in a city like Scarford. She says I 'have the faculty of the born leader.' All I lack is the opportunity."

Her husband sighed. Inwardly he wished Mrs. Black at Scarford, or China, or anywhere, provided it was not Trumet.

His wife heard the sigh. "There, Daniel," she said; "I won't be complaining. But," she hesitated, "there is one thing I'd like to ask, now that we've got your Aunt Lavinia's three thousand: Don't you suppose I could have some new clothes; I need at least two dresses right away."

"Why—why, I guess likely you could, Serena. Yes, course you can. You go see Sarah Loveland right off."

"I don't want Sarah to make them, Daniel," she said. "Mrs. Black says the things she makes are awful old-fashioned; 'country,' she calls them."

Daniel snorted. " Country, huh! Scarford ain't any Paris, is it? I never heard it was."

"Well, it isn't Trumet. No, Daniel, if we could afford it, I'd like to have these dresses made up in Boston, where Gertie gets hers. Mrs. Black often speaks of Gertie's gowns; she says they are remarkably stylish, considering."

"CONSIDERIN'! What does she mean by that?"

"Don't be cross. I suppose she meant considering that they were not as expensive as her own. DO you suppose I could go to that Boston dressmaker, Daniel?"

Captain Dan's reply was slow in coming. He hated to say no; in fact, he said it so seldom that he scarcely knew how. So he temporized.

"Well, Serena," he began, "I—I'd like to have you; you know that. If 'twasn't for the cost I wouldn't hesitate a minute."

"But we have that three thousand dollars."

"Well, we ain't got all of it. Or we shan't have it long. I was footin' up what I owed—what the store owes, I mean—just now, and it come to a pretty high figure. Over twelve hundred, it was. That's GOT to be paid. Then there's Gertie's schoolin' and her board. Course, I never tell her we ain't so well off as we were. You and I agreed she shouldn't know. But it takes a lot of money and—"

Mrs. Dott sat up on the couch. "Oh!" she cried; "money! money! money! It's always money! If only just once I had all the money I wanted, I should be perfectly happy. If I wouldn't GO IT!"

Steps sounded on the front porch, and the patent door bell clicked and clanged.

CHAPTER III

Next morning an astonishing rumor began to circulate through Trumet. The Dotts had inherited money! The Dotts were rich! The Dotts were millionaires! Captain Daniel's brother had died and left him fifty thousand dollars! His brother's wife had died and left him a hundred thousand! It was not his brother's wife, but Serena's uncle who had died, and the inheritance was two hundred and fifty thousand at least. By the time the story reached Trumet Neck it seemed to be fairly certain that all the Dott relatives on both sides of the house had passed away, leaving the sole survivors of the family all the money and property in the world, with a few trifling exceptions.

Captain Dan, coming into the house for dinner, expressed his opinion of Trumet gossip mongers.

"My heavens and earth, Serena!" he cried, sinking into his chair at the table, "am I me, or somebody else? Do I know what I'm doin' or what's happened to me, or don't I?"

Serena, a transformed, flushed, excited Serena, beamed at him across the table. "I should hope you did, Daniel," she answered.

"Well, if I do, then nobody else does, and if THEY do, I don't. I've heard of more dead relations this forenoon than I ever had alive. And yarns about 'em! and about you and me! Say, did you know you had a cousin-in-law in Californy?"

"I? In California? Nonsense!"

"No nonsense about it. You had one and he was a lunatic or a epileptic or an epizootic or somethin', and lived in a hospital or a palace or a jail, and he was worth four millions or forty, I forget which, and fell out of an automobile or out of a balloon or out of bed—anyhow, it killed him—and—"

"Daniel Dott! DON'T talk so idiotic!"

"Humph! that's nothin' to the idiocy that's been talked to me this forenoon. I've done nothin' for the last hour but say 'No' to folks that come tearin' in to unload lies and ask questions. My head's kind of wobbly this mornin', after the shock that hit it last night, but it's a regular Dan'l Webster's alongside the general run of heads in this town. Aunt Laviny's will has turned Trumet into an asylum, and the patients are all runnin' loose."

"But WHAT foolishness was that about a cousin in California?"

"'Twa'n't foolishness, I tell you. You ask any one of a dozen folks you meet outside the post-office now, and they'll all tell you you had one. They might not agree whether 'twas a cousin or a grandmother or a step-child, or whether it lived in Californy or the Cape of Good Hope, but they all know it's dead now, and we've got anywheres from a postage stamp to a hogshead of diamonds."

"Daniel, I never saw you so worked up. You must expect people to be excited. I'm excited myself."

The captain wiped his forehead with his napkin. "I ain't exactly a graven image, now that you mention it," he admitted. "But you and I have got some excuse and they ain't. Haven't they been in to see you; or did you lock the doors?"

"I have had callers, of course. Mrs. Berry was here, and Mrs. Tripp, and the Cahoon girls, and Issachar Eldredge's wife. Daniel, HOW do you suppose the news got out so soon? I didn't tell a soul and you promised you wouldn't."

"I didn't, neither. Probably that lawyer man dropped a hint down at the Manonquit House, and that set things goin'."

"But you didn't tell anyone how much your Aunt Lavinia left us?"

"You bet I didn't. I told 'em I didn't know yet. What did you tell your gang?"

"I simply said," Serena unconsciously drew herself up and spoke with a gracious dignity; "I said they might quote me as saying it was NOT a million."

Yes, something had happened to the Dotts, something vastly more wonderful and surprising than falling heir to three thousand dollars and a silver tea-pot. When Serena bewailed her fate and expressed a desire for an opportunity, he was almost at the front gate, and the ring of the bell which interrupted her conversation with her husband was the signal that Opportunity, in the person of Mr. Glenn Farwell, Junior, newest member of the firm of Shepley and Farwell, attorneys, of Boston, was at the door.

Shown into the Dott sitting-room by Azuba, who, as usual, had neglected to remove her kitchen apron, he bowed politely and inquired if he had the pleasure of addressing Captain and Mrs. Daniel Abner Dott. The captain assured him that he had.

"Won't you—won't you sit down, Mr. er—er—" began the captain.

"Captain Dott," he said, "you received a letter from our firm about a week ago, did you not?"

Captain Dan, who had scarcely recovered from his surprise at his caller's identity, shook his head. "As a matter of fact," he stammered, "I—I only got it to-day. It came all right, that is, it got as far as the post-office, but the postmaster, he handed it over to Balaam Hamilton, to bring to me. Well, Balaam his top riggin' is kind of lackin' in spots. You'd understand if you knew him. He put the letter in his pocket and—"

"Mercy!" cut in Serena, impatiently, "what do you suppose Mr. Farwell cares about Balaam Hamilton? He forgot the letter, Mr. Farwell, and we only got it this morning. That is why it hasn't been answered. What about the letter?"

The visitor did not answer directly. "I see," he said. "That letter informed you that Mrs. Lavinia Dott—your aunt, Captain,—was dead, and that we, her legal representatives, having, as we supposed, her will in our possession, and being in charge of her affairs—"

Mrs. Dott interrupted. Her excitement had been growing ever since she learned the visitor's name and, although her husband did not notice the peculiar phrasing of the lawyer's sentence, she did.

"As you supposed?" she repeated. "You did have the will, didn't you?"

"We had a will, one which Mrs. Dott drew some eight or nine years ago. But we received word from Italy only yesterday that there was another, a much more recent one, which superseded the one in our possession. Of course, that being the case, the bequests in the former were not binding upon the estate."

Serena gasped. "Then we—then she didn't leave us the three thousand dollars?" she cried.

"Or—or the tea-pot?" faltered Captain Dan.

Mr. Farwell smiled. He was having considerable fun out of the situation. "She left you a great deal more than that," he said. "In the former will, her cousin, Mr. Percy Hungerford of Scarford, was the principal legatee. But last February it appears that he and she had a falling out. Under the new will he receives twenty thousand dollars in cash. The balance—" Mr. Farwell now spoke with impressive solemnity,—"the balance," he said, "one hundred thousand in money and securities, and the house at Scarford, which is valued, I believe, at thirty-five thousand more, she leaves to you, as her only other relative, Captain Dott. I am here to congratulate you and to offer you my services and those of the firm, should you desire legal advice."

Having sprung his surprise, Mr. Farwell leaned back in his chair to enjoy the effect of the explosion. The first effect appeared to be the complete stupefaction of his hearers. Those which followed were characteristic.

"My soul and body!" gasped Captain Dan. "I—I—my land of love! And only this mornin' I was scared I couldn't pay my store bills!"

"A hundred thousand dollars!" cried Serena. "And that beautiful house at Scarford!"

Mr. Farwell crossed his knees. "A very handsome little windfall," he observed.

"We get a hundred thousand!" murmured the captain. "My! I wish Father was alive to know about it. But, say, it's kind of rough on that young Hungerford, after expectin' so much, ain't it now!"

"A hundred thousand!" breathed his wife, her hands clasped. "And that lovely house! Why, we could move to Scarford to-morrow if we wanted to! Yes, and live there! Oh—oh, Daniel! I—I don't know why I'm doing it, but I—I believe I'm going to cry."

Her husband rushed over to the couch and threw his arm about her shoulder.

"Go ahead, old lady," he commanded. "Cry, if you want to. I—I'm goin' to do SOMETHIN' darn ridiculous, myself!"

Thus it was that Fortune and Opportunity came to the Dott door, and it was the news of the visitation, distorted and exaggerated, which set all Trumet by the ears next day.

Azuba's clam fritters were neglected that noon, just as breakfast had been. Neither Captain Dan nor his wife had slept, and they could not eat. They pretended to, they even tried to, but one or the other was certain to break out with an exclamation or a wondering surmise, and the meal was, as the captain said, "all talk and no substantials." They had scarcely risen from the table when the doorbell rang.

Azuba heard it and made her entrance from the kitchen. She had remembered this time to shed the offending apron, but she carried it in her hand.

She started for the sitting-room, but the captain stepped in front of her.

"You stay right where you are," he ordered. "I'll answer that bell myself this time."

"Daniel," cried his wife, "what are you going to do?"

"Do? I'm goin' to head off some more fools, that's what I'm goin' to do. They shan't get in here to pester you to death with questions, not if I can help it."

"But, Daniel, you mustn't. You don't know who it may be."

"I don't care."

"Oh, dear me! What are you going to say? You mustn't insult people."

"I shan't insult 'em. I'll tell 'em—I'll tell 'em you're sick and can't see anybody."

"But I'm not sick."

"Then, I am," said Captain Dan. "They make me sick. Shut up, will you?" addressing the bell, which had rung the second time. "I'll come when I get ready."

He seemed to be quite ready that very moment. At all events he strode from the room, and his anxious wife and the flushed Azuba heard him tramping through the front hall.

"What—WHAT is he going to do?" faltered Serena; "or say?" Azuba shook her head. "Land knows!" she exclaimed. "I ain't seen him this way since the weasel got into the hen-house."

But no riot or verbal explosion followed the opening of the door. The anxious listeners in the dining-room heard voices, but they were subdued ones. A moment later Captain Dan returned. He looked troubled. "It's Barney Black and his wife," he answered. "I couldn't tell THEM to go to thunder. They're in the front room, waitin'. I suppose we'll have to see 'em, won't we?"

Mrs. Dott was hurriedly shaking the wrinkles out of her gown and patting her hair into presentable shape.

"See 'em!" she repeated. "Of course we'll see them. I declare! I think it's real kind of 'em to call. Daniel, do fix your necktie. It's way round under your ear."

They entered the parlor, Serena, outwardly calm, in the lead and her husband following, and tugging at the refractory tie.

Mrs. and Mr. Black rose as they appeared. Annette swept forward. "Oh, my dear Mrs. Dott," she gushed. "We've just heard the news, Phelps and I, and we couldn't resist dropping in to congratulate you. Isn't it wonderful!"

Serena admitted that it was wonderful. "We can hardly believe it yet, ourselves," she said. "But it was real nice of you to come. Do sit down again, won't you? Daniel, get Mr. Black a chair."

Captain Dan and Mr. Black shook hands. "Sit down anywhere, Barney," said the former. "Anywhere but that rocker, I mean; that's got a squeak in the leg."

Mr. Black, who had headed for the rocker, changed his course and sank into an arm chair. The shudder with which his wife heard the word "Barney," and the glare with which Serena favored her husband, were entirely lost upon the latter.

"We had that rocker up in the attic till last month," he observed; "but Serena found out 'twas an antique, and antiques seem to be all the go now-a-days, though you do have to be careful of 'em. I suppose it's all right. We'll be antiques ourselves before many years, and we'll want folks to be careful of us. Hey? Ha! ha! . . . Why, what's the matter, Serena?"

Mrs. Dott replied, rather sharply, that "nothing was the matter."

"The rocker isn't very strong," she explained, addressing Mrs. Black. "But it belonged to my great—that is, it has been in our family for a good many years and we think a great deal of it."

Mrs. Black condescendingly expressed her opinion that the rocker was a "dear." "I love old-fashioned things," she said. "So does Mr. Black. Don't you, Phelps?"

"Yes," replied that gentleman.

"But do tell us about your little legacy," went on the lady. "Of course we have heard all sorts of ridiculous stories, but we know better than to believe them. Why, we even heard that you were worth a million. Naturally, THAT was absurd, wasn't it? Ha! ha!"

Captain Dan opened his mouth to reply, but his wife flashed a glance in his direction, and he closed it again.

"Yes," said Serena, addressing Mrs. Black, "that was absurd, of course."

"So I told Phelps. I said that the way in which these country people exaggerated such things was too funny for anything. Why, we heard that your cousin had died—that is, I heard it was a cousin; Phelps heard it was an uncle. An uncle was what you heard, wasn't it, Phelps?"

"Yes," said Phelps.

"So," went on Mrs. Black, "we didn't know which it was." She paused, smilingly expectant. Again Captain Dan started to speak, and again a look from his wife caused him to change his mind. Before he had quite recovered, Mrs. Black, who may have noticed the look, had turned to him.

"Wasn't it funny!" she gushed. "Here was I saying it was a cousin and Phelps declaring it was an uncle. It was so odd and SO like this funny little town. Do tell us; which was it, really, Captain Dott?"

Daniel, staggering before this point blank attack, hesitated. "Why," he stammered, "it was—it was—" He looked appealingly at Serena.

"Why don't you answer Mrs. Black?" inquired his wife, rather sharply.

"It was my Aunt Laviny," said the captain.

Mrs. Black nodded and smiled. "Oh! your aunt!" she exclaimed. "There! isn't that funny! What did you say her name was?"

"Laviny?"

"Yes, I know. Laviny—what an odd name!"

Serena, who had been fidgeting in her chair, cut in here. "It wasn't Laviny at all," she said. "That is only Daniel's way of pronouncing it. It is what he used to call her when he was a child. A—a sort of pet name, you know."

"Why, Serena! how you talk! She never had any pet name, far's I ever heard."

"Hush! it doesn't make any difference. Her name, Mrs. Black, was Lavinia. She was Mrs. Lavinia Dott, and her husband was James Dott, Daniel's father's brother."

This statement caused a marked sensation. Mrs. Black gasped audibly, and leaned back in her chair. B. Phelps evinced his first sign of interest.

"What!" he exclaimed. "Mrs. Lavinia Dott, of Scarford? You don't say! Her place is one of the finest in town."

Serena bowed. Life, for her, had not offered many sweeter moments than this.

"Yes," she said, calmly, "so we understand. The place—er—that is, the estate—is a PART—" she emphasized the word—"a PART of what she left to my husband."

"Great Scott!" exclaimed Mr. Black. Captain Dan crossed his knees.

"I remember seein' that place after Uncle Jim first built it," he observed, reminiscently. "I tell you it looked big enough to me! Ho! ho! when I got inside and was sittin' in the front parlor, I declare I was all feet and hands! didn't know what to do with 'em. . . . Hey? did you speak, Serena?"

"I was only going to say," replied his wife, "that that was a good while ago, of course. Things look different after we grow up, don't they, Mrs. Black?"

Annette's composure, a portion of it, had returned by this time. Nevertheless, there was an odd note in her voice. "They do, indeed," she said. "I remember the Dott house, of course. It was very fine, I believe, in its day."

Her husband interrupted. "In its day!" he repeated. "Humph! there's nothing the matter with it now, that I can see. I wish I had as good. Why—"

"Phelps!" snapped Annette, "don't be silly. Mrs. Dott understands what I meant to say. The place is very nice, very attractive, indeed. Perhaps some might think it a bit old-fashioned, but that is a matter of taste."

"Humph! it's on the best street in town. As for being old-fashioned—I thought you just said you loved old-fashioned things. That's what she said, wasn't it, Dan?"

Mrs. Black's gloved fingers twitched, but she ignored the remark entirely. Daniel, too, did not answer, although he smiled in an uncertain fashion. It was Serena who spoke.

"I haven't any doubt it is lovely," she said. "We're just dying to see it, Daniel and I. I hope you can be with us when we do, Mrs. Black. You might suggest some improvements, you know."

"Improvements!" the visitor repeated the word involuntarily. "You're not going to LIVE there, are you?"

"I don't know. We may. Now, Daniel, don't argue. You know we haven't made up our minds yet what we shall do. And Scarford is a beautiful city. What were you going to say, Mrs. Black?"

The lady addressed looked as if she would like to say several things, particularly to her husband, who was grinning maliciously. But what she did was to smile, a smile of gracious sweetness, and agree that Scarford was beautiful.

"And so is the place, my dear Mrs. Dott," she added. "A very charming, quaint old house. But don't you think it might prove rather expensive for you to maintain?"

Serena's armor was not even dented. "Oh," she said, "that wouldn't trouble us, I'm sure. The Scarford place wasn't ALL that Aunt Lavinia left us, Mrs. Black."

"Indeed!" rather feebly, "wasn't it?"

"My goodness, no! But there! I mustn't talk about ourselves and our affairs any more. Have you seen the lodge rooms to-day? I must find time to run down there this afternoon for a last look around. I want this open meeting to go off nicely. Who knows—well, I may not have the care of the next one."

Azuba appeared in the doorway. "The minister and his wife's comin'," she announced.

Mrs. Dott turned. "The minister and his wife?" she repeated. "How do you know they're coming here?"

"See 'em through the window," replied Azuba, cheerfully. "Here they be," as the callers' footsteps sounded on the porch. "Shall I let 'em in?"

"Let them in! Why, of course! Why shouldn't you let them in?"

"Well, I didn't know. The way the cap'n was talkin' when you was havin' dinner, I thought—oh, that reminds me," addressing the horror stricken Daniel, "Sam was in just now and wanted you to come right out to the store. Ezra Taylor's there and he wants another pair of them checkered overalls, same as he had afore."

That evening when the captain and his wife were on their way to the lodge meeting, Daniel voiced a feeling of perplexity which had disturbed his mind ever since the Blacks' call.

"Say, Serena," he asked, "ain't you and Barney Black's wife friends any more?"

"Why, of course we're friends. What a question that is."

"Humph! didn't seem to me you acted much like friends this afternoon. Slappin' each other back and forth—"

"Slappin' each other! Have you lost your brains altogether? What DO you mean?"

"I don't mean slappin' each other side of the head. But the way you talked to each other—and the way you looked. And when 'twa'n't her it was me. She as much as asked you four or five times who it was that had died and you wouldn't tell, so, of course, I supposed you didn't want to. And yet, when she asked me and I was backin' and fillin', tryin' to get off the shoals, you barked out why didn't I 'answer her'? That may be sense, but I don't see it, myself."

Serena laughed and squeezed his arm with her own. "Did I bark?" she asked. "I'm sorry; I didn't mean to. But it did make me cross to have her come sailing in, in that high and mighty way—"

"It's the same way she always sails. I never saw her when she didn't act as if she was the only clipper in the channel and small craft better get out from under her bows."

"I know, you never did like her, although she has been so kind and nice to me and to Gertrude."

The captain muttered that he knew it but that THAT didn't make him like her any better. His wife continued. "I was a little put out by her to-day," she admitted. "You see, she was SO anxious to find out things, and SO sure we couldn't be very rich, and SO certain we couldn't keep up Aunt Lavinia's big house, that—that I just had to give her as good as she sent."

Daniel chuckled. "You did that all right," he said.

"But I wouldn't hurt her feelings—really hurt them—for the world. I like her and admire her, and I am sure she likes me."

"Humph! All right; only next time you get to admirin' each other I'm goin' out. That kind of admiration makes me nervous. I heard you admirin' Zuba out in the kitchen just before we left."

"Azuba makes me awfully out of patience. Just think what she said about you when the minister called. That's it—laugh! I expected you'd think it was funny."

"Well, I give in that it does seem kind of funny to me, now, though it didn't when she started to say it. But you can't stop Zuba talkin' any more than you can a poll parrot. She means well; she's awful good-hearted—yes, and sensible, too, in her way."

"I can't help it. She's got to learn her place. Just think of having her up there at Scarford, behaving as she does."

The captain caught his breath. "Scarford!" he repeated. "You didn't mean what you said to that Black woman about our goin' to Scarford to live?"

"I don't know that I didn't. There! there! don't get excited. I don't say I do mean it, either. Aunt Lavinia's left us that lovely house, hasn't she? We've got it on our hands, haven't we? What are we going to do with it?"

"Why—why, I—I was cal'latin' we'd probably sell it, maybe. We've got our own place here in Trumet. We don't want two places, do we?"

"We might sell this one, at a pinch. No, Daniel, I don't know what we shall do yet awhile. But, one thing I AM sure of—you and I will go to Scarford and LOOK at that house, if nothing more. Now, don't argue, please. We're almost at the meeting. Be sure you don't tell anyone how much money we've got or anything about it. They'll all ask, of course, and they'll all talk about us, but you must expect that. Our position in life has altered, Daniel, and rich folks are always looked at and talked over."

Daniel Dott, as has been intimated, did not share his wife's love for lodge meetings. He attended them because she did, and wished him to, but he was not happy while they were going on. At this one he was distinctly unhappy. He was thinking, and thinking hard. Aunt Lavinia's will had changed their position in life, so Serena had said. She had said other things, also, and he was beginning, dimly, to realize what they might mean.

CHAPTER IV

"SCARFORD!" screamed the brakeman, throwing open the car door. "Scarford!"

Mrs. Dott was already in the aisle. Captain Dan, standing between the seats, was struggling to get the suitcase down from the rack above. It was a brand-new suitcase. Her umbrella, silk with a silver handle, was new also. So was her hat, her gown and her shoes. So, too, was the captain's hat, and his suit and light overcoat.

The suitcase, the buckle of which had caught in the meshes of the rack, giving way, came down unexpectedly and with a thump on the seat. A stifled laugh from the occupants of adjacent seats reached Serena's ears.

"What is it?" she demanded impatiently. "Aren't you coming?"

"I—I'm comin'," stammered her husband. "I'm comin'. Go ahead! I'll be right along."

Through the crowd on the platform they passed, through the waiting room and out to the sidewalk. "Lively place, ain't it, Serena?" he observed. "Whew! that valise is heavy. Well, where's the next port of call?"

"We'll go to the hotel first. Oh, dear, it's a shame things happened so we had to come now. In another fortnight the Blacks would have been here and we could have gone right to their house."

The captain made no answer. Picking up the suitcase, he stepped forward to the curb.

"Where are you going?" demanded his wife.

"Why, to the hotel. That's where you wanted to go, wasn't it?"

"Certainly; but how were you going? You don't know where it is."

"No, so I don't. But I can hail one of those electrics and ask the conductor to stop when he got to it. He'd know where 'twas, most likely."

"Electric" is the Down East term for trolley car, lines of which were passing and repassing the station. Daniel waved his disengaged hand to the conductor of the nearest. The car stopped.

"Wait a minute," said Serena quickly. "How do you know that car is going the right way?"

"Hey? Well, of course I don't know, but—"

"Of course you don't. Besides, we don't want to go in an electric. We must take a carriage."

"A carriage? A hack, you mean. What do we want to do that for?"

"Because it's what everyone does."

“No, they don’t. Look at all the folks on that electric now. Besides, we—”

“Hi there!” shouted the conductor of the car angrily. “Brace up! Get a move on, will you?”

Mrs. Dott regarded him with dignity. “We’re not coming,” she said. “You can go right along.”

The car proceeded, the conductor commenting freely and loudly, and the passengers on the broad grin.

“Now, Daniel,” said Serena, “you get one of those carriages and we’ll go as we ought to. I know we’ve always gone in the electrics when we were in Boston, but then we didn’t feel as if we could afford anything else. Now we can. And don’t stop to bargain about the fare. What is fifty cents more or less to US?”

The captain shook his head, but he obeyed orders. A few minutes later they were seated in a cab and were moving toward the Palatine House, the hostelry recommended by Mrs. Black as the finest in Scarford.

The Palatine House was new and gorgeous; built in the hope of attracting touring automobilists, it was that dreary mistake, a cheap imitation of the swagger metropolitan article. However, to the Dotts, its marble-floored lobby and gilded pillars and cornices were grand and imposing. Their room on the third floor looked out upon the street below, and if the view of shops and signs and trucks and trolleys was not beautiful it was, at least, distinctly different from any view in Trumet.

They had left Trumet the previous evening, spending the night at Centreboro and taking the early morning train for Scarford. Two weeks had passed since the fateful visit of young Mr. Farwell, and, though the wondrous good fortune which had befallen the Dott family was still wonderful, they were beginning to accept it as a real and established fact. All sorts of things had happened during those two weeks. They had gone to Boston, where they spent the better part of two days with the lawyers, going over the lists of securities, signing papers, and arranging all sorts of business matters. Serena and the attorneys did the most of the arranging.

Captain Dan looked on, understanding very little, saying “Yes” or “No” as commanded by his wife, and signing his name whenever and wherever requested.

After another day, spent in the Boston shops, where the new clothes were purchased or ordered, a process which Serena enjoyed hugely and her husband endured with a martyr’s patience, they had paid a flying visit to the college town and Gertrude. They found the young lady greatly excited and very happy, but her happiness was principally on their account.

“I’m so glad for you both, Daddy,” she told her father. “When I got Mother’s letter with the news the very first thing I thought was: ‘There! now Father won’t have to worry any more about the old store or anything else. He can be comfortable and carefree and happy, as he deserves to be.’ And you won’t worry, will you, Dad?”

The captain seemed oddly doubtful. “I shan’t if I can help it,” he said. “When the business was so I had to worry about it all the time I used to set up nights wishin’ I didn’t own it. Now that we’re fixed so it don’t make much difference whether I get a profit or not, I find myself frettin’ and wonderin’ how Nathaniel and Sam are gettin’ along. I wake up guessin’ how much they’ve sold since I’ve been away, and whether we’re stuck on those canvas hats and those middy blouses and one thing or ‘nother, same as I was afraid we’d be. I’ve only been away three days altogether, but it seems about a year.”

Gertrude smiled and shook her head. “Why don’t you sell out?” she asked. “Or would no one buy? I presume that’s it.”

"No-o, that ain't it. Cohen—the fellow that owns the Emporium—was in only the day afore we left, hintin' around about my retirin' and so on. He didn't make any real bid for the business, but he as much as said he'd consider buyin' me out if I'd sell. Your mother, she'd give me fits if she knew it. She wants me to sell; but—but somehow I can't make up my mind to. I've been so used to goin' out to that store every mornin' and—and havin' it on my mind that somehow I hate to give it up. Seems like cuttin' my anchor rope, as you might say."

"I understand. I shall feel much the same, I know, when I graduate and my college work is over. I shall be lost for a time without it; or I should be if it were not for John and—and my other plans. But, whether you keep the store or not, you mustn't worry any more, Daddy dear. Nathaniel is a clever, able fellow; every one says so. Why don't you engage him permanently? With his experience, he might make a real success of the business."

He could not possibly make less of a success than the captain had made, that was fairly certain, although she did not say so. Nathaniel Bangs was a Trumet young man who had been getting on well with a little business of his own in Brockton, but who, owing to ill health, had been obliged to return to the Cape the year before. Then, health much improved, he was very glad of the opportunity to take charge of the Metropolitan Store during its owners' short absence. Serena had thought of him, and Serena had hired him.

Captain Dan's real reason for not selling out to the astute Mr. Cohen he had kept to himself. His wife's hints concerning Scarford and her discontent in Trumet were his reasons. He liked Trumet; he liked its quiet, easy-going atmosphere; he liked the Trumet people, and they liked him. He had never been in Scarford, but he was certain he should not like the life there, the kind of life lived by the B. Phelps Blacks, at any rate. The Metropolitan Store was, he felt, an anchor holding him fast to the Cape Cod village.

On the very day of their return from the Boston trip Serena had begun to discuss the visit to Scarford, the visit of inspection to Aunt Lavinia's "estate." To all Daniel's feeble objections and excuses she was deaf. Of course they could leave the house. Azuba would take care of that, just as she always did when they were away. As for the store, Nathaniel would be glad to remain as manager indefinitely if they wanted him. Surely he had done splendidly with it while they were in Boston.

Mr. Bangs' services were retained, "for a spell, anyhow," and the captain's principal excuse for not visiting Scarford was knocked in the head. To Scarford they went, and at the Palatine Hotel in Scarford they now were.

The next feature of Mrs. Dott's program was the visit to the Aunt Lavinia homestead. There was a caretaker in charge, so the Boston lawyers told them, and Serena had written him announcing the coming of the new owners. In spite of her husband's protestations, another carriage was hired for the journey. Daniel was strongly in favor of walking or going by trolley.

"Walkin'll be cheaper, Serena," he declared, "and pretty nigh as fast, to say nothin' of bein' more cheerful. Let's walk, will you?"

But Serena would not walk. "We must get used to carriages," she said. "We may ride in them a great deal from now on. And, besides, we needn't take a horse carriage. Get one of those new kind, the automobile ones. What is it they call them? Oh, yes—taxis."

The taxi gave no opportunity for complaint as far as slowness was concerned. After the first quarter of a mile dodge up the crowded street Captain Dan shouted through the window. "Hi!" he hailed, addressing the driver. "Hi, you! You've made a mistake, ain't you? You thought we wanted to fly. We don't. Just hit the ground once in a while, so we'll know it's there."

After this the cab moved at a more reasonable speed and its occupants had an opportunity to observe the streets through which they were passing. The business district was being left behind and they were entering the residential section.

Mrs. Dott seized her husband's arm. "Look!" she cried. "Look, Daniel, quick! Do you see that? That building there!"

"I see it. Some kind of a hall or somethin', ain't it?"

"Yes. And I'm quite sure, from what Mrs. Black said, that it is the hall where the Scarford Guild meets. Yes, it's just as she said it was. I'm SURE that's it. Yes, and Mrs. Black said they lived not very far from the hall. Daniel! Daniel! ask the man if he knows where the Blacks live and if he can show us their house."

Captain Dan obediently made the inquiry. "Who?" grunted the driver. "Black and Cobb, the Wee Waist Corset feller? Sure! I know where he lives."

A few moments later the cab slackened its speed. "There you are!" said the driver, pointing. "That's Black's house. Built two years ago, 'twas."

Serena and Daniel looked. The house was new and commodious, a trifle ornate in decoration, perhaps, and a bit mixed in architecture, owing to Mrs. Black's insisting upon the embodiment of various features which she had seen in magazines; but on the whole a rather fine house. To the Dotts, of course, it was a mansion.

"My!" said Serena, "to think of our knowing, really knowing, people who live in a house like that! Oh, dear!" with a sigh, "I almost wish I hadn't seen it until after we'd seen our own. We must try not to be disappointed, mustn't we?"

Captain Dan was surprised. "Disappointed?" he said. "Why, what do you mean? As I recollect Aunt Laviny's place, 'twas just as good as that, if not better. You said so yourself. You used to call it a regular palace."

"I know, but don't you think that was because we hadn't seen many fine houses then? You know Mrs. Black said it was old-fashioned."

"Humph! Barney—What's his name? Phelps, I mean—he said he wished his was as good. Don't you remember he did?"

"Probably he didn't mean it. I'm going to try and think of it as just a nice old place, and then I shan't feel bad when I see it. I'm not going to get my expectations up or be a bit excited."

In proof of the sincerity of this determination, she sat bolt upright on the seat and looked straight before her. Her husband, however, was staring out of the window with all his might.

"Say!" he exclaimed, "this is a mighty nice street, anyhow."

"Is it? Is it really?" For a person not excited, Mrs. Dott's breathing was short and her fingers were trembling.

"You bet it is! Hey! Why, we're slowin' up! We're stoppin'."

The cab drew up at the curb and came to a standstill. "Here you are," said the driver. "This is Number 180."

Daniel made no reply. Leaning from the window, he was staring with all his might. Serena's impatience got the better of her.

"Well? WELL?" she burst forth. "What does it look like?"

The captain drew back into the carriage. "My—soul!" he exclaimed presently. "Look, Serena."

Serena looked, and her look was a long one. "Oh! Oh, Daniel!" she gasped. "It's as good as the Blacks', isn't it? I—I do believe it's better! Get out, quick!"

The caretaker, a middle-aged man with dark hair and mutton-chop whiskers, met them at the top of the stone steps leading to the front door. He bowed low. "Good afternoon, ma'am," he said. "Good afternoon, sir. Mr. Dott, ain't it, sir? And Mrs. Dott, ma'am. My name is 'Apgood, sir. I was expecting you. Will you be so good as to walk in?"

He threw open the door and, bowing once more, ushered them into the hall, a large, old-fashioned hall with lofty ceiling and a mahogany railed staircase.

"I presume, sir," he said, addressing the captain, "that you and the madam would wish to 'ave me show you about a bit. I was Mrs. Dott's—the late Mrs. Dott's—butler when she resided 'ere, sir, and she was good enough to make me 'er caretaker when she went away, sir."

Captain Dan, rather overawed by Mr. Hapgood's magnificent manner, observed that he wanted to know, adding that he had heard about the caretaking from the lawyers "up to Boston." After an appraising glance at the speaker, Mr. Hapgood addressed his next remark to Serena. "Shall I show you about the establishment, madam?" he asked.

Serena's composure was a triumph. "Yes," she said loftily, "you can show us."

Mr. Hapgood was a person of wide experience; however, he merely bowed and led the way. Serena followed him, and Captain Dan followed Serena.

A large drawing-room, a library, a very large dining-room, five large bedrooms—"owners' and guest rooms," Mr. Hapgood grandly termed them, to distinguish from the servants' quarters at the rear—billiard room, bathroom, and back to the hall again.

"You would wish to see the kitchens, I suppose, ma'am," said Mr. Hapgood. "Doubtless Mr. Dott wouldn't care for those, sir. Most gentlemen don't. Perhaps, sir, you'd sit 'ere while the lady and I go through the service portion of the 'ouse, sir."

Daniel, who was rather curious to see the "service portion," partly because he had never heard of one before, hesitated. His wife, however, settled the question. She was conscious of a certain condescension in the Hapgood tone.

"Of course," she said lightly, "Cap'n Dott will not go to the—er—service portion. Sit here, Daniel, and wait. Now—" cutting off just in time the "Mister" that was on the tip of her tongue and remembering how butlers in novels were invariably addressed—"Now—er—Hapgood, you can take me to the—ahem—kitchens."

It was somewhat disappointing to find that the plural was merely a bit of verbal embroidery on the caretaking butler's part, and that there was but one kitchen, situated in the basement. However, it was of good size and well furnished with closets, the contents of which stirred Serena's housekeeping curiosity. The inspection of the kitchen and laundry took some time.

Meanwhile, upstairs in the dim front hall, Captain Dan sat upon a most uncomfortable carved teak-wood chair and looked about him. Through the doorway leading to the drawing-room—"front parlor," he would have called it—he could see the ebony grand piano, the ormolu clock, and the bronze statuettes on the marble mantel, the buhl cabinet filled with bric-a-brac, the heavy mahogany-framed and silk-covered sofa. Captain Dan felt strangely out of place alone amid this oppressive grandeur. Again, as on the memorable occasion of his first visit to the house, he was conscious of his hands and feet. Mrs. Dott and the caretaker reentered the hall.

"Thank you, Mr.—er—Thank you, Hapgood," said the lady. "That will be all for to-day, I think. We will go now. Come, Daniel."

Hapgood bowed. "You would wish me to stay 'ere as I've done, ma'am?" he asked.

"Yes. You may stay, for the present. Cap'n Dott and I will pay your regular wages as long as we need you."

"Thank you kindly, ma'am. And might I take the liberty of saying that if you decide to stay 'ere permanently, ma'am, and need a butler or a manservant about the place, I should be glad to 'ave you consider me for the position."

"Well," said the captain, with surprising promptness for him, "you see, Mr. Hapgood, as far as that goes we ain't intendin' to—"

"Hush, Daniel. We don't know what we intend. You know that our plans are not settled as yet. We will consider the matter, Hapgood. Good day."

"Good day, ma'am," said Hapgood. "Good day, sir."

He opened the big front door, bowed them out, and stood respectfully waiting as they descended the steps. The taxi driver, whom the captain had neglected to discharge or pay, was still there at the curb with his vehicle. Serena addressed him.

"The Palatine Hotel," she said, with great distinctness. "Come, Daniel."

As the cab whizzed through the streets Serena gloated over the splendors of their new possessions. The house was finer than she expected, the furniture was so rich and high-toned, the pictures—did Daniel notice the pictures?

"And the location!" she cried ecstatically. "Right on the very best street in town, and yet, so the Hapgood man said, convenient to the theaters and the clubs and the halls. We saw the Ladies of Honor hall on the way up, Daniel, you remember."

Daniel nodded. "Yes," he admitted, "it's fine and convenient and all. We"—with a sidelong glance at his wife's face—"we ought to get a good rent for it if we decide not to sell; hey, Serena?"

Serena did not answer. When they reached the hotel she left her husband to settle with the driver and took the elevator to their room. A few minutes later the captain joined her. He looked as if suffering from shock.

"My heavens and earth, Serena!" he exclaimed, "what do you suppose that tax hack feller had the cheek to—"

"Sshh! shh!" interrupted the lady, who was reclining upon the couch. "Don't bother me now, Daniel. I don't want to be bothered with common every-day things now; I want to think."

"Common! Everyday! My soul and body! if what that pirate charged me was everyday, I'd be in the poorhouse in a fortni't. Why—"

"Oh, don't! Please don't! Can't you see I am trying to realize that it's true and not a dream. Please don't talk. Do go away, can't you? Just go out and take a walk, or something; just for a little while. I want to be alone."

Captain Dan slowly descended the stairs. The elevator, of course, would have been quicker, but he was in no hurry. He descended the stairs to the ground floor of the hotel and wandered aimlessly about through the lobby into the billiard room, and finally to a plate glass door upon which was lettered the word "Rathskeller."

What a Rathskeller might be he did not know, but, as there was another set of letters on the door and those spelled "Push," he pushed. The Rathskeller was a large room, with a bar at one end and many little tables scattered about. At these tables men were eating, drinking and smoking.

The captain looked about him, selected one of three chairs at an unoccupied table, and sat down. A waiter drifted alongside. "What'll you have, sir?" inquired the waiter.

"Hey? Oh, I don't know. Give me a cup of coffee."

"Coffee? Yes, sir. Anything to eat?"

"No, I guess not."

"Smoke?"

"Well, you might bring me a ten-cent cigar."

The coffee and cigar were brought. This was not taking a walk exactly, but, so far as leaving his wife alone was concerned, it answered the purpose.

The room, already well tenanted, gradually filled. Several times the two vacant chairs at the captain's table were on the point of being taken, but each time the prospective occupants went elsewhere.

At length, however, two young men, laughing and talking rather loudly, sauntered through the room. One of them paused.

"Here are a couple," he said, indicating the chairs. His companion, an undersized, dapper individual, whose raiment might comprehensively be described as a symphony in brown, paused also, turned and looked at the chairs, then at the table, and finally at the captain.

"Yes," he drawled, regarding the latter fixedly, "so I see. Well, perhaps we can't do better. This place is getting too infernally common, though. If it wasn't that they put up the best cocktail in town I should have quit before."

He seated himself in one of the chairs. His friend followed suit. The watchful waiter was on hand immediately. "Good afternoon, gentlemen," he said, bowing obsequiously.

Neither of the young men acknowledged the bow or the greeting, although it was evident that the waiter was an old acquaintance. The symphony in brown did not even turn his head.

"Two dry Martinis," he said. "And mind that they ARE dry."

"Yes, sir. All right, sir. Will you have a bit of lunch with them, sir? Caviare sandwich or—"

"No."

"Shall I bring cigars, sir?"

"Lord, no! Get the cocktails and be lively about it."

The waiter departed. The young gentleman drew a gold cigarette case from his pocket.

"Here you are," he drawled, proffering the case. "Cigars!" with a contemptuous laugh. "They buy their cigars by the yard, at the rope walk. Fact, Monty; take my word for it."

"Monty" laughed. "That's pretty rough, Tacks," he declared.

"Oh, but it's so. You can actually smell the hemp. Eh? By gad, you can smell it now, can't you?"

Captain Dan was relighting the stump of his "ten-center" which had gone out. He had scarcely noticed the newcomers; his thoughts were far away from Scarford and the Palatine Hotel. Now, however, he suddenly became aware that his tablemates were regarding him and the cigar with apparent amusement. He smiled good naturedly.

"Been runnin' her too low," he observed. "Have to get up steam if I want to be in at the finish."

This nautical remark was received with blank stares. "Monty" turned his shoulder toward the speaker. "Tacks" did not even turn; he continued to stare. The arrival of the cocktails was the next happening of importance.

"I say, Tacks," observed Monty, "how are you getting on? Made up your mind what to do?"

"No," shortly.

"Going to fight, are you?"

"No use. The confounded lawyers say I wouldn't have a show."

"Humph! Low-down trick of the old woman's, wasn't it, giving you the shake that way? Everybody thought you were her pet weakness. Did you get the go-by altogether?"

"Pretty near. Got a little something, but it was precious little."

"Can you pull through on it?"

"'Twill be a devilish hard pull."

"Too bad, old man. But cheer up! You'll come out on top."

More Martinis were ordered. "Monty" and his friend lit fresh cigarettes. The former asked another question.

"Who are the lucky winners?" he inquired. "Some country cousins or other, I know that; but who are they?"

"Oh, I don't know. Yes, I know; but what difference does it make?"

"Isn't there a girl somewhere in the crowd?"

"Yes, but—" He broke off. Captain Dan was regarding him intently.

"Is there anything I can do to make you more comfortable, Uncle?" drawled "Tacks," with bland sarcasm.

Daniel was taken aback. "Why," he stammered, "I—I don't know's there is."

"Shall I speak a little louder? Possibly that might help. Delighted to oblige, I'm sure."

This was plain enough, certainly. The captain colored. His confusion increased. "I—I hope you don't think I was listenin' to you and your friend's talk," he protested hastily. "You see, I was thinkin'—when you spoke to me—I was thinkin' there was somethin' familiar about your face. Seemed as if I'd seen you somewhere before, that's all; and—"

The young gentleman in brown interrupted him. "You're mistaken," he said, "I was never there." Then, turning to his friend, he added, with an elaborate "Josh Whitcomb" accent: "Monty, 'taters must be lookin' up. All aour folks have come to town to spend their money."

Monty, upon whom, like his companion, the second cocktail seemed to be having some effect, laughed uproariously. Even the joker himself deigned to smile. Captain Dan did not smile. He had risen, preparatory to leaving the table; now he slowly sat down again.

"I guess I WAS mistaken," he said gravely. "I guess you're right about my not havin' seen you before. If I had I wouldn't have forgot where."

Monty evidently thought it his turn to be funny. "You have a good memory, haven't you, Deacon?" he observed.

The captain looked at him. "That don't necessarily follow, young man," he said. "There's some things you CAN'T forget."

There was a choking sound at the next table; a stout man there seemed to be having trouble in swallowing. Those with him looked strangely happy, considering.

"Tacks" frowned, pushed back his chair and stood up. "Come on, Monty," he growled. "This place is going to the dogs. They let ANYTHING in here now."

Daniel turned to the stout man and his party. "That's strange, ain't it?" he said in a tone of grave surprise. "I was just thinkin' that myself."

Then, his cigar smoked to the bitter end, he, too, rose, and, he walked out of the Rathskeller and took the elevator to the third floor. He opened the door of the room gently and entered on tiptoe, for he thought it likely that Serena was taking a nap. She was not, however; on the contrary, she was very wide awake.

"Where have you been?" she demanded.

Daniel chuckled. "I've been down below in a place they call the Rat Cellar, or some such name," he said. "The rats was there, two of 'em, anyhow. And I'd met one of 'em before. I know I have. I wish I could think who he was. A sort of—"

But Serena was not listening. "Daniel," she interrupted, "it is all settled. I have made up my mind."

Her voice was tremulous with excitement. Captain Dan looked at her.

"Made up your mind?" he repeated. "What about?"

"About our plans and our future, Daniel; my opportunity has come, the opportunity I was wishing for. Daniel, you and I must move to Scarford."

The captain gasped. "Why—why, Serena," he faltered. "What are you talkin' about? DON'T talk so! Move to Scarford! Give up Trumet and—"

"Don't mention Trumet to me. Daniel Dott, you'll never get me back to Trumet again—to live there, I mean—never, never, NEVER!"

CHAPTER V

Captain Dan said—Well, it does not matter much what he said. He said a great deal, of course, during that evening and the next morning, and would have kept on saying it all the way to Trumet if his wife had not declined to listen.

"It is no use, Daniel," she declared. "I have thought it all out and I KNOW it is the right thing for us to do. You will think so, too, one of these days."

"Durned if I will! I tell you, Serena—"

"Hush! you're telling everybody in the car, and THAT isn't necessary, at any rate. Now we won't argue any more until we get home. Then you can say your say; but"—with discouraging candor—"it won't change my decision a single mite. My mind is made up. We are going to Scarford to live, and we will go just as soon as we can get ready."

And go they did. The captain fought a stubborn battle, surprisingly stubborn and protracted for him, but he surrendered at last. Serena drove him from one line of entrenchments after the other, and, at length, when she had him in the last ditch, where, argument and expostulation unavailing, he could only say, "No! no, I won't, I tell you!" over and over again, she used her most effective weapon, tears, and brought him to terms.

"You don't care," she sobbed. "You don't care for me at all. All you care about is just yourself. You're willing to stay here in this awful place, you're willing to plod along just as you always have; and it doesn't make any difference about my wishes or my hopes, or anything. If you were like most husbands you'd be proud and glad to see me getting on in the world; you'd be glad to give me the chance to be somebody; you'd—"

"There! there! Serena, don't talk so. I'd do anything in this world to please you."

Sobs and more sobs, frantic clutchings at the sofa pillows and declarations that she had better die; it would be better for her and ever so much better for everyone else if she were dead. No one would care.

Poor Daniel, distressed and remorseful, vaguely conscious that he was right, but conscience stricken nevertheless, hoisted the white flag.

"Hush, hush, Serena!" he pleaded. "Land sakes, don't say such things—please don't. I'll go to Scarford, if you say so. I was just—"

"I don't ask you to go there forever. I only ask you to go there and live a while and just see how we like it. But you won't! you won't!"

"Why, yes I will, too. I'll go—go next week, if you say so. I—I just—"

He got no further. Mrs. Dott, wet-eyed but radiant, lifted her head from the sofa pillow and threw her arms about his neck.

"Will you?" she cried ecstatically. "Will you, Daniel? I knew you would. We will be so happy. You see if we aren't."

The captain was no less doubtful of the happiness than he had ever been, but he tried to smile and to find comfort in the thought that she was happy if he was not.

He had written Gertrude telling of her mother's new notion and asking for advice and counsel. The reply, which came by return mail, did not cheer him as much as he had hoped.

"It was inevitable, I suppose," Gertrude wrote. "I expected it. I was almost certain that Mother would want to live in Scarford. Perhaps it is just as well. Mother won't be satisfied until she has tried it, and perhaps, after she has tried it, she may be glad to come back to Trumet. My advice is to let her find out for herself, but, of course, if you feel sure it is wrong, then you must put your foot down, say no, and stick to it. No one can do that for you; you must do it yourself."

Which was perfectly true, as true as the other fact—namely, that Captain Dan could not "stick to it" in a controversy with his wife, having lost the sticking faculty years before.

But, oddly enough, there was one point upon which he did stick and refused to budge: That point was Azuba's going to Scarford with them. Mrs. Ginn's attitude when she was told of the family exodus was a great surprise. Serena, who broke the news to her, expected grief and lamentations; instead Azuba was delighted.

"Well, now!" she exclaimed. "Ain't that fine! I always wanted to go somewhere's besides Trumet, and now I'm goin'. Say, it's a good thing you've got me to help in the goin' and the settlin', ain't it, Sereny—Mrs. Dott, I mean."

In the face of this superb confidence Serena, who had intended leaving Azuba behind, lacked the courage to mention the fact. And when she sought her husband in the store and asked him to do it, he flatly refused.

"What!" he said. "Tell Zuba Ginn we're goin' to cast her adrift! I should say not!"

"But what can we do with her, Daniel? We might leave her here to take care of the place, I suppose, but that would only be for a time, until we find somebody to buy it."

Daniel, to whom the idea of selling the home of which he had been so proud was unthinkable, ignored the question.

"You couldn't leave her here," he declared. "She wouldn't stay. She'd know right off you were tryin' to get rid of her."

"Then what can we do with her?"

"Take her with us. She can do housekeepin' in Scarford same as she can here, can't she?"

"Take her with us! Why, Daniel Dott! the very idea! Think of Azuba in a place like that Scarford mansion! Think of her and that dignified, polite Hapgood man together!"

The captain seemed to find the thought amusing. "Say, that would be some fun, wouldn't it?" he chuckled. "I'd risk Zuba, though. He wouldn't do the Grand Panjandrum over her more'n once."

"What do you think the B. Phelps Blacks would say if they saw Azuba trotting through the grand front hall with her kitchen apron on?"

The mention of the name had an odd effect upon the captain. "I don't care what they say," he declared. "I don't care what the Blacks would say, nor the Yellows nor the Blues either. If they don't like it they can stay in their own front halls and lock the door. Look here, Serena: Zuba Ginn has been with us ever since Gertie was born. She may be queer and hard to keep in her place, as you call it, and a regular walkin' talkin' machine, and all that. What I do say is she's been good enough for us all these years and she's good enough for me now. She ain't got any folks; her husband is as queer as she is, and only shows up once in two or three years, when he happens to think of it. She ain't got any home but ours, and nobody else to turn to, and I won't cast her adrift just because I've got more money than I did have. No, sir! if Zuba Ginn wants to go to Scarford, along with us, she goes, or I don't go myself."

He struck the desk a violent blow with his clenched fist. Serena regarded him with astonishment. "Why—why, Daniel," she faltered, "I didn't mean to make you cross. I—I only thought. . . . Of course, she can go with us if you feel that way."

"That's the way I feel," said her husband shortly. Then, as if suddenly awakening and with a relapse into his usual manner, he added, "Was I cross? I'm real sorry, Serena."

So, upon the fateful day when, preceded by a wagonload of trunks and bags and boxes, the Dotts once more drove through Scarford's streets to the mansion which was to be their home—permanently, according to Serena; temporarily, so her husband hoped—Azuba accompanied them.

That night, as they sat down for the first meal in the new abode, Serena voiced the exultation she felt. "There, Daniel," she observed, "now you begin to appreciate what it means, don't you. NOW you begin to see the difference."

There was no doubt that the captain noticed the difference. He noticed it more the following day, and more still on each succeeding one.

The next evening the Blacks called—called in state. A note from Mrs. Black, arriving by the morning's post, announced their coming. Serena noted the Black stationery, its quality and the gilded monogram, and resolved to order a supply of her own immediately. Also she bade her husband don his newest and best. She did the same, and when Captain Dan, painfully conscious of a pair of tight shoes, entered the drawing-room he found her already there.

"My!" he exclaimed, "you do look fine, Serena. Is that the one the Boston dressmaker made?"

"Yes. I'm glad you like it."

"Couldn't help likin' it. Whew! I always said you looked ten years younger than you are. THAT rig don't spell forty-five next January, Serena."

Mrs. Dott sniffed. "Don't remind me of my age, Daniel," she protested."

"All right. Nobody'd guess it, anyhow. But how funny you walk. What makes you take such little short steps?"

"I can't help it. This dress—gown, I mean—is so tight I can hardly step at all."

"Have to shake out a reef, won't you? How in the world did you get downstairs—hop?"

"Hush! Don't be foolish. The gown is no tighter than anyone else's. It's the style, Daniel, and you and I must get used to it. Are those your new shoes?"

"They certainly are. I walk about the way you do, Serena. Bein' in style ain't all joy, is it?"

"It's better than being out of it. And, Daniel, please remember not to say 'ain't.' I've asked you so many times. We have our opportunity now and so must improve ourselves. You are a man of means, living among cultivated society people, and you must try to behave like the ladies and gentlemen you will be called upon to associate with."

"Humph!" doubtfully. "I don't know as I could behave like a lady if I tried. As for the gentleman, if you mean Barney Black—"

"I mean B. Phelps Black. Don't you dare call him Barney to-night. Hush! Here they are."

Even Serena's new gown, fine as it was and proud as she had been of it, lost something of its glory and sank into a modest second place when Annette appeared. Mrs. Black had dressed for the occasion. Also, she had insisted upon her husband's dressing.

"What in blazes must I climb into a dress suit for?" demanded that gentleman grumpily. "Going to call on Dan Dott and his wife. You don't expect Dan to be wearing a dress suit, do you? He never wore one in his life."

"It doesn't make any difference what he wears. I want you to go in evening dress."

"But, confound it, Annette, we've been calling on those people all summer."

"THAT was in the country; this is not. Those Dotts have come here to live. I did all I could to prevent it, but—"

"WHAT?" Mr. Black interrupted with an amazed protest. "Did all you could to prevent it! Why, you used to preach Scarford to Serena Dott from morning till night. I don't believe she would ever have thought of coming here if it hadn't been for you."

Annette stamped her foot impatiently. "Don't you suppose I know it?" she demanded. "That was when I never imagined there was any chance of their really coming. That is why I want them to see how people of our class dress. I can't TELL her that her clothes are a sight and she's clever enough to understand. And you can show her husband."

Mrs. Black had another reason for making this call upon the Dotts in their new home a ceremonial occasion. It was true that they would be obliged to associate with these acquaintances from the country more or less. But she meant there should be no misunderstanding of the relations between the families. In Trumet she had made Mrs. Dott her protegee because it was her nature to patronize, and Serena had not resented the patronage. Now circumstances were quite different; now the Dotts possessed quite as much worldly wealth as the Blacks, but Annette did not intend to let Serena presume upon that. She intended, not only by the grandeur of her raiment and that of her husband, but by her tone and manner, to make perfectly plain the fact that the acquaintanceship was still a great condescension on her part and did not imply equality in the least.

But this lofty attitude was destined to be shaken before the evening was over. The first shock came at the very beginning, and Mr. Hapgood was responsible for it. Annette had referred, during the Trumet acquaintanceship, to her "staff of servants," and had spoken casually of her cook and second girl and laundress and "man," as if the quartette were permanent fixtures in the Black establishment. As a matter of fact, the only fixtures were the cook and second girl.

So when the door of the Dott mansion was opened by a butler—and such a dignified, polite, imposing butler—Mrs. Black's soul was shaken by a twinge of envy. The second shock was Serena's appearance and the calm graciousness of her demeanor. The Boston gown was not as grand, as prodigal of lace and embroidery, as was the visitor's, but it was in the latest fashion and Serena wore it as if she had been used to such creations all her life. Neither was she overawed or flurried when her callers entered. Serena had read a good deal, had observed as much as her limited opportunities would allow, and was naturally a clever woman in many ways.

"Why, how do you do, Mrs. Black?" she said. "It's so good of you to come. And to bring Mr. Black, too. You must take off your things. Yes, you must. Hapgood, take the lady's wraps."

"I had such a time to get Phelps to come," declared Annette, sinking, with a rustle, into the next best chair. "He wanted to see you both, of course, and to welcome you to Scarford, but he is SO busy and has so many engagements. If it isn't a directors' meeting it is a house committee at the club, or—or something. It was a club meeting to-night, wasn't it, Phelps, dear?"

"'Twas a stag dinner," observed Mr. Black. "Say, Dan, I'll have to take you to one of 'em some time. It's a good bunch of fellows and we have some of the cleverest vaudeville stunts afterward that you ever saw. Last week there were a couple of coons that—"

"Phelps!" Annette interrupted tartly, "you needn't go into details. I don't imagine Captain and Mrs. Dott will be greatly interested. What a charming old room this is, isn't it? SO quaint! Everything looks as if it had been here a hundred years."

Before Serena could frame a reply to this back-handed compliment the unconscious B. Phelps removed the greater part of its sting by observing: "That butler of yours looks as if he had been here a thousand. He's a star, all right. Did he come with the place?"

Mrs. Dott explained that Hapgood was one of Aunt Lavinia's old servants. "She thought the world of him. He is pretty expensive, his wages, I mean, but he is worth it all. Don't you think so?"

Yes, Mrs. Black found it much more difficult to patronize than she expected, and Serena was correspondingly happy. But the crowning triumph came later. The doorbell rang, and Hapgood entered the drawing-room bearing a tray upon which were several cards. He bent and whispered respectfully.

Mrs. Dott was evidently surprised and startled. "Who?" she asked.

Hapgood whispered again.

Serena rose. "Yes, of course," she said nervously. "Yes, certainly. I declare, I—"

"What's up?" asked her husband, his curiosity aroused. "Nothin' wrong, is there?"

His wife, who had caught a glimpse of Mrs. Black's face, fought down her nervousness and announced with dignified composure. "Some more callers, that's all, Daniel," she said. "Oh, you mustn't go, Mrs. Black. You know them, I'm sure. I've heard you speak of 'em—of them often. It's"—referring to the cards—"the Honorable Oscar Fenholtz and Mrs. Fenholtz. Ask them right in, Hapgood. Daniel, get up!"

Daniel hurriedly obeyed orders. Mr. Black also rose. "The Fenholtzes!" he observed in a tone of surprise. "Say, Dan, I didn't know you knew them. Annette didn't say anything about it."

Annette hadn't known of it; her expression showed that. The Honorable and Mrs. Fenholtz were Scarford's wealthiest citizens. Mr. Fenholtz was proprietor of a large brewery and was an ex-mayor. His wife was prominent socially; as prominent as Mrs. Black hoped to be some day.

Hapgood reappeared, ushering in the new arrivals. The Honorable Oscar was plump and florid and good-natured. He wore a business suit and his shoes were not patent leathers. Mrs. Fenholtz was likewise plump. Her gown, in comparison with Annette's, or even Serena's, was extremely plain and old-fashioned.

"How do you do, Mrs. Dott?" she said pleasantly. "Welcome to Scarford. You and I have never met, of course, but I used to know Mrs. Lavinia Dott very well indeed. And this is Mr. Dott, I suppose. How do you do? And here is my husband. Oscar, these are our new neighbors."

Mr. Fenholtz and the captain shook hands. Captain Dan felt his embarrassment disappearing under the influence of that hearty shake.

"I suppose you scarcely expected callers—or calls from strangers—so soon," went on Mrs. Fenholtz. "But, you see, I hope we shan't be strangers after this. I couldn't bear to think of you all alone here in this great house in a strange place, and so I told Oscar that he and I must run in. We live near here, only on the next corner."

"I said you would be having your after-dinner smoke, Mr. Dott," explained the Honorable, with a smile and a Teutonic accent. "I said you would wish we was ouid instead of in; but Olga would not have it so. And, when the women say yes, we don't say no. Eh; what is the use?" He chuckled.

Captain Dan grinned. "That's right," he said. "No use for the fo'mast hand to contradict the skipper."

Mrs. Black stepped forward. "How do you do, Mrs. Fenholtz?" she said with unction.

"Dear me!" exclaimed Serena. "I—I'm forgetting everything. But you know Mr. and Mrs. Black, don't you, Mrs. Fenholtz?"

Mrs. Fenholtz turned. "How do you do, Mrs. Black?" she said. Her tone lacked the enthusiasm of Annette's.

"Hello, Black," said her husband. "What are you doing here? I thought you would be at the club, listening to the—what is it?—the cabaret."

Before B. Phelps could answer, Mrs. Black spoke. "He wanted to go, Mr. Fenholtz," she declared. "But he felt, as I did, that our first duty was here. Captain and Mrs. Dott are old friends of ours. We meet them every year at the Cape; we have a summer home there, you know."

Fenholtz seemed interested. "That is so," he said. "I forgot. Dott, are you one of those Cape Cod skippers they tell me about? I am glad of it. I have got a boat myself down in Narragansett Bay. But this one is like the women, it will gruise only where and when it wants to, and not where I want to at all. There is something the matter with the engine always. I wish you could see it."

Captain Dan was interested, too. "Well," he said, "I'd like to, first rate. I've got a boat of my own back home; that is, I used to have her. She was a twenty-five foot cat and she had a five-horsepower auxiliary in her. I had consider'ble experience with that engine. Course, I ain't what you'd call an expert."

"I am glad of that. Now I will explain about this drouble of mine."

He went on to explain. In five minutes he and the captain were head over heels in spark plugs and batteries and valves and cylinders. Mr. Black endeavored to help out with quotations from his experience as a motorist, but his suggestions, not being of a nautical nature, were ignored for the most part. After a time he lost interest and settled back in his chair.

Meanwhile the three ladies were engrossed in other matters. Mrs. Fenholtz asked to be shown the house; she had not seen it for a long time, she said, and was much interested. Annette suddenly remembered that, she also was "mad" to see it. So Serena led a tour of inspection, in which Mr. Hapgood officiated as assistant pilot and superintendent of lighting.

After the tour was at an end, and just before the party descended to the drawing-room, Mrs. Fenholtz turned to Serena and said: "Mrs. Dott, are you interested in club matters; in women's clubs, I mean?"

Serena's answer was a prompt one. "Indeed I am," she said. "I have always been interested in them. In fact, I am president of the Trumet Chapter; that is, I was; of course, I resigned when I came here."

Mrs. Fenholtz looked puzzled. "Trumet Chapter?" she repeated. "Why, yes, the Chapter of the Guild of the Ladies of Honor."

"Oh!" in a slightly different tone. "Oh, yes, I see."

"I'm terribly interested in THAT," declared Serena enthusiastically. "If you knew the hours and hours I have put in working for the Guild. It is a splendid movement; don't you think so?"

"Why—why, I have no doubt it is. I don't belong to it myself. I was thinking of our local club, our Scarford women's club, when I spoke. I thought perhaps you might care to attend a meeting of that with me."

"I should love—" began Serena, and stopped.

Mrs. Black, who was standing behind Mrs. Fenholtz, was shaking her head. The last-named lady noticed her hostess' hesitation.

"But of course," she went on, "if you are interested in the Ladies of Honor you would no doubt prefer visiting a meeting of theirs. In that case Mrs. Black could help you more than I. She is vice-president of the Scarford Branch, I think. You are vice-president, aren't you, Mrs. Black?"

Annette colored slightly.

"Why—why, yes," she admitted; "I am."

Serena was surprised. "Vice-president?" she repeated. "Vice-president—I—I—must have made a dreadful mistake. I introduced you as president at that Trumet meeting. I certainly thought you were president."

Now, as a matter of fact, if Mrs. Black had not specifically said that she was president of the Scarford Chapter, she had led her acquaintances in Trumet to infer that she was.

"Oh, no!" she said. "I noticed that you made a mistake when you introduced me, but, of course, I could hardly correct you publicly, and, when it was all over, I forgot. I am only vice-president, just as Mrs. Fenholtz says."

Mrs. Fenholtz smiled. "Well, I am not even an officeholder in our club," she said, "although I was at one time. I have no doubt you will prefer to be introduced by a vice-president rather than a mere member; and I am sure Mrs. Black is planning for you to attend one of the Guild meetings, so I mustn't interfere."

Annette was visibly flurried. The Scarford Chapter was the one subject which she had carefully avoided that evening. But between it and the Woman's Club there was a bitter rivalry, and, although she had not been at all anxious to act as sponsor for her friend from the country, now that Mrs. Fenholtz had offered to do so and had placed the responsibility squarely on her shoulders, she could not dodge.

"Why—why, of course," she said. "That was understood. We have had so many things to talk about this evening that I had really forgotten it, my dear Mrs. Dott. When," she hesitated, "when could you make it convenient to attend one of our meetings? Of course I know how busy you are just now in your new home, and I shall not be unreasonable. I shouldn't, of course, expect you to attend the NEXT meeting."

"Oh," said the unconscious Serena, "I'm not so busy as all that. I could go to the next meeting just as well as not. I should love to."

They entered the drawing-room, to find Captain Dan and the Honorable Oscar still deep in the engine discussion and Mr. Black sound asleep in his chair. Roused by his indignant wife, he drowsily inquired if it was time to get up, and then, becoming aware of the realities of the situation, hastily explained that he had been thinking about business affairs and had forgotten where he was.

"Going, Annette, are you?" he asked.

Annette tartly observed that she was going, and added that she judged it high time to do so. Mrs. Fenholtz said that she and her husband must be going, also.

"But we shall hope to see a great deal of you and Mr.—I should say Captain Dott," she said. "You must dine with us very soon. I will set an evening and you mustn't say no."

"That is right," said Mr. Fenholtz heartily. "Captain, some of these days you and I will take a gouple of days and go down and look at that boat."

Altogether, it was a wonderful evening. The only fly in the ointment was Azuba, who appeared just as the visitors were at the door, to announce that "that foolhead of a grocer's boy" hadn't brought the things she ordered and what they was going to do for breakfast she didn't know.

On the way home Mrs. Black divided her discourse into two parts, one a scorching of her husband for falling asleep and making her ridiculous before the Fenholtzes, and the other a sort of irritated soliloquy concerning "those Dotts" and the way in which they had been loaded upon her shoulders.

"I did my best to keep the Guild out of the conversation," she said, "but that Fenholtz woman had to drag it in, and now, of course, I've got to take that Dott person to the next meeting and introduce her to everybody, and I suppose I shall have to see that she is made a member. Oh, dear! I almost wish I had never seen Trumet."

B. Phelps grunted. "Humph!" he said. "If the Fenholtzes take them up I don't see what you've got to kick about. You've been trying to get in the Fenholtz set yourself for the last three years. Maybe you can do it now."

CHAPTER VI

The Scarford Chapter of the Guild of the Ladies of Honor was not as large a body as Mrs. Black in the exuberance of her Trumet conversation had led Serena to think. It was formed in the beginning by a number of seceders from the local Women's Club, who, disappointed in their office-seeking ambitions and deeming the club old-fashioned and old-fogyish in its ideas, had elected to form an organization of their own. They had affiliated with the national order of the Ladies of Honor, chiefly because of the opportunity which such a body offered for office holding and notoriety. The members were not drawn from the oldest families of Scarford nor from those whose social position was established. They were chiefly the wives and daughters of men who had made money rather suddenly; would-be geniuses whose genius had not been recognized as yet; women to whom public speaking and publicity were as the breath of their nostrils; extravagants and social climbers of all sorts. The purposes of the organization, outside those specified in the constitution of the parent body, were rather vague.

The ladies of the Scarford Chapter made it a point to be always abreast of the times. Their motto was "Advancement." Just what sort of advancement seemed to make little difference.

The next meeting—that is, the meeting to which Serena had been invited—was one of the few at which men were permitted to be present. The Blacks called at the Dott mansion with the car, Mr. Black not acting as driver this time, and the journey to the hall was made in that vehicle. It was not a lively journey, so Captain Dan thought. He and B. Phelps occupied the folding seats facing the two ladies and Mr. Black maintained a gloomy silence all the way. As for Annette and Serena, they talked and talked upon subjects miles above the head of the captain. Mrs. Black did most of the talking; Serena was content to listen and pretend to understand.

The Chapter building proved to be not quite up to Serena's expectation. It was a building, of course, but the Chapter occupied only two or three rooms on the third floor, the other floors being occupied by offices of various sorts. The largest room, that which Mrs. Black dignified by the title of "Assembly Hall," was partially filled when they entered. Some sixty women of various ages, with a sprinkling of men among them, occupied the chairs on the floor. Upon the speakers' platform half a dozen ladies in radiant attire were chatting volubly with another, an imposing creature in crimson silk, who surveyed the audience through a gold lorgnette, and whose general appearance reminded Daniel of one of the stuffed armchairs in the parlor of their new home.

"That is Mrs. Cornish, the speaker of the evening," whispered Annette. "She is one of our most brilliant members."

"Yes," replied Dan'l, "yes, she—she does look sort of—sort of brilliant."

"But I thought the Chapter was larger than this," said the puzzled Mrs. Dott. "I thought Scarford had one of the largest Chapters."

"Oh, no, not the largest, merely one of the best. Our motto always has been quality not quantity. And now will you excuse me? They are waiting for me on the platform. I will see you when the open meeting is over. Phelps, find good seats for Mr. and Mrs. Dott."

She bustled away to the platform. The gloomy B. Phelps found seats for the guests and himself and sank heavily down beside them. Daniel, who had been gazing about him with curiosity, whispered a question.

"What do they do at these things, Barney—Phelps, I mean?" he asked."This is my first trip here, you know."

"Humph!" grunted his companion. "You're in luck."

"Talk, don't they?"

"Talk! Good Lord! Say, Dan, if I get to sleep and you notice Annette looking this way, nudge me, that's a good fellow."

He settled himself in his chair and closed his eyes.

The Chapter president, a Mrs. Lake, advanced to the desk, smote it fiercely with a gavel and demanded order. Then Mrs. Lake opened the meeting. She delivered a short speech. Mrs. Black, in lieu of the secretary, who was absent, read the minutes. Then there were motions and amendments and excited calls for recognition from "Madam President." It was livelier than Daniel had expected.

But soon the woman in crimson silk was introduced. Mrs. Cornish bowed in recognition of the gloved applause, and proceeded to talk . . . and talk . . . and talk. . . .

At first Captain Dan endeavored to pay strict attention to the address. Its title was "The Modern Tendency," and the tendency in this case seemed to be to say as much as possible about nothing in particular.

Daniel found his attention wandering and his eyes closing. They opened at intervals as the applause burst forth, but they closed between bursts. The tremendous enthusiasm at the end, however, awoke him for good, and he remained awake until the close of the "open meeting," a marked contrast to Mr. Black, who slumbered to the finish.

When it was over Annette descended from the platform and came hurrying to them. "How did you enjoy it, Captain Dott?" she purred.

Daniel rather dubiously admitted that he guessed 'twas first rate, far's he could make it out. His wife was enthusiastic; she affirmed that it was splendid.

"I'm sure we couldn't help enjoying it, Mrs. Black," she said. "Everyone of us. Didn't you enjoy it, Mr. Black?"

"Sure!" replied Phelps promptly. "Great stuff!"

His wife swooped upon him like a swallow on a fly. "You?" she snorted contemptuously. "You didn't hear a word of it. I only hope Mrs. Cornish wasn't watching you, as I was. And now," she added, turning to Serena, "comes the other part, the important part. Captain Dott, there is to be a short business meeting in a few minutes, and men are, of course, excluded. Phelps, will you have James drive Captain Dott home? You had better go with him, and then come back again and wait for us. Captain Dott, I am going to borrow your wife for a short time."

Daniel, not knowing exactly what to say, said nothing. Phelps seized his arm and led him down to the carriage. The driver received his instructions and the homeward ride began.

"I say, Barney," observed Daniel, after waiting for his escort to volunteer a word or two, "are all their meetings like that?"

Mr. Black snorted. "No," he declared; "some are a sight worse." It was after eleven when Serena returned. Her face was flushed and shining with excitement. She did not wait to remove her hat, but rushed into the parlor where her husband sat in lonely magnificence.

"Oh, Daniel!" she cried. "What do you think? I've been made a member of the Chapter!"

Captain Dan should perhaps have been enthusiastic. If he was, he suppressed his feelings wonderfully. "Have you, Serena?" he observed. "I want to know!"

He listened while his wife dilated upon the wonderful happenings at the meeting and the glorious consequences which she felt sure were to follow. Just before putting out the light he asked one more question.

"That—that Mrs. Lake?" he said. "She's a grass widow, ain't she—isn't she, I mean?"

"Yes, what of it?"

"Oh, nothing. Only I thought you were kind of prejudiced against—against—"

"I've had a good many prejudices, I suppose. But Mrs. Lake's husband was a brute; Mrs. Black told me so. He must have been, for she is perfectly lovely. I've met them all, and they are ALL lovely. They're going to call and—and everything. Oh, Daniel, this means so much to us!"

Captain Dan turned out the gas. "Yes, Serena," he said slowly. "I shouldn't wonder if it did."

The calls began the very next afternoon. Mrs. Black, having made up her mind that the taking of the Dotts under her wing was a necessity, made a virtue of that necessity and explained to her fellow members of Scarford Chapter that Serena and Daniel were really very nice people. "A little countrified, of course. You must expect that. But they are very kind hearted and immensely wealthy—oh, immensely." She was kind enough to add that Serena was quite an exceptional person and an advanced thinker, considering her opportunities. "The club people were going to take them up, and so I felt that we should get in first," she explained. "If they should prove to be impossible we can drop them at any time, of course."

In making this explanation she did not mention the Fenholtzes, and yet if it had not been for the call of the Honorable Oscar and his wife it is extremely doubtful if Serena would have become a member of Scarford Chapter so soon. Also it is doubtful if the little dinner given by the Blacks to Mr. and Mrs. Dott would have taken place within the week. At that dinner Captain Dan wore his first dress suit. He bought it ready made at one of the Scarford shops and it fitted him remarkably well, considering. What he could not do, however, was to feel at ease in it.

"Good land, Serena!" he said, when the dressing was completed and they were about to start for the dinner, "don't pick at me so everlastin'ly. I'm doin' my best, so don't keep remindin' me what I look like all the time."

"I don't care what you say, Daniel," declared his wife. "The clothes are just what you ought to wear, and if you would only forget them for a little while you would look all right."

"But I can't forget. I know the clothes are all right. It's me that's all wrong. I tell you I ain't used to this kind of thing. I wasn't born to it and it don't come natural to me."

"Neither was Mr. Black 'born to it,' but he has got used to it and so can you if you will try."

"Oh, I'll try. But I'm beginnin' awful late in life. I know you'll be ashamed of me, Serena. You ought to have a different husband."

"I don't want a different one. I wouldn't change you for anybody. My chance has just come; I am only just beginning and I mean to go on and improve myself and our position in life all I can. All I ask you to do is not to hold me back by complaining."

The "little dinner" was not as little as it might have been. Annette had taken pains to make it as elaborate and as costly an affair as she could. This was not solely on the Dotts' account.

She had invited Mr. and Mrs. Fenholtz and the impression was to be made upon them, if possible. But, unfortunately, the Fenholtzes did not attend. Mrs. Fenholtz wrote that she had a prior engagement and sent regrets, just as she had previously done on the occasions of Mrs. Black's other "little" functions.

However, the leading lights of Scarford Chapter attended and the display of gowns and coiffures was more varied and elaborate than at the open meeting. Serena, seated at the right hand of B. Phelps, was in her glory. She felt that at last she was in touch with the real thing. Daniel, sandwiched between Annete and Mrs. Lake, was not as happy.

After dinner there was music and bridge. Daniel was fond of music, but most of the songs, sung by a thin young lady with a great deal of hair and a decollete gown, were in a language which he did not understand, and the piano solos seemed to him to be made up of noise and gymnastics with very little melody. He watched Serena, however, who, in turn, was watching Mrs. Lake and the rest; when they applauded, she applauded and the captain followed suit.

Bridge was an unknown quantity to both of them, and they sat and looked on while Mrs. Black made it "without" and found fault with her partner when they lost. The thin young lady, who had obliged with the vocal selections, asked the captain if he played "nullos."

Daniel, who was not sure whether "nullos" was a musical instrument or a game, replied that he wasn't sure, but he didn't think he did; after which he retired into the corner to avoid further questioning.

They reached home about two o'clock, and the captain fell sound asleep in the taxi and had to be shaken into consciousness when the machine reached the Dott door.

"My soul, Serena," he said, "don't those folks ever go to bed? Time I had finished the ice cream I was ready to curl up like a cat in front of the fire; but the rest of them seemed to be just startin' in to be lively."

"But wasn't it splendid?" explained his wife. "You and I never went to anything like THAT dinner before, Daniel Dott."

The captain admitted that they never did. "Could you make anything out of that game they were playin'?" he asked. "What was it they called it?"

"Bridge. No, I couldn't, but I'm going to. I'm going to learn it just as soon as I can. Mrs. Black says everybody plays it now."

After they were in bed he said, "Serena, what was that black stuff they had on the toast at the beginnin' of that supper? Looked like tar, but it tasted kind of salty and good."

"Don't say supper, Daniel. It was a dinner. All city people have dinner at night. That was caviar on the toast."

Silence for a moment. Then Captain Dan said reflectively, "Caviar? Caviar, eh? I've heard of that somewhere before; where was it? Yes, yes, I know. 'Twas a caviar sandwich the waiter asked that young fellow I met in the Rat Cellar to have. I never found out who that young fellow was, and yet I know I've met him somewhere before. I wish I could remember where it was."

The next day there were more calls, and Serena was asked to attend a committee meeting as a guest. She attended it and returned more full of Chapter enthusiasm than ever. She announced that she might be asked to prepare a paper to be read before the Chapter, and that she intended to study and prepare for it. Study and prepare she did, and, between dodging callers, or helping to entertain them, and keeping out of his wife's way while she was busy with the encyclopedias which she had taken from the library, the captain began to feel somewhat deserted. Hapgood's company was too stately to be congenial, and Daniel sought refuge in the kitchen, where Azuba, as usual, was always ready to talk.

Azuba was brimming over with the novelty of city life. She had been to the theater once already since her arrival, and to the moving picture show three times.

"Don't talk to ME," she said. "If them pictures ain't the most wonderful things that ever was, then I don't know. I never expected to see such sights—soldiers paradin', and cowboys a-ridin', and houses a-burnin', and Indians scalpin' 'em! I was so worked up I hollered right out."

"I should think you would. An Indian scalpin' a house is enough to make anybody holler."

"They didn't scalp the house; what sort of foolishness would that be—the idea! They scalped the folks IN the house. That is, they would have scalped 'em, only along come the cowboys wavin' pistols and hurrahin'—"

"Could you hear 'em hurrah?"

"No, but I could see 'em. And the way they went for them Indians was a caution. And—Oh, say, Captain Dott, there was one set of pictures there made me think of you. 'Twas all about some people that wanted to go into society. She had a paralyzed father and they had a child, a real pretty girl, and, would you believe it, they commenced to neglect their child and go off playin' cards and dancin' and carousin' around, and the child was took down sick and the poor paralyzed grandfather—"

"Grandfather? Thought you said it was a father."

"'Twas the WOMAN'S father—the child's grandfather. Well, anyhow, the poor thing had to take care of it, and the nurse went to sleep and the father come home and found her dyin'—"

"Who, the nurse?"

"No, no, the child. The nurse wa'n't sick; but the child was terrible sick."

"What was the matter with the child; paralysis, too?"

"I don't know what was the matter with it. 'Tain't likely 'twas paralysis. Well, anyhow, what happened was that the child's mother and father neglected it on account their fashionable goin's-on, and the child up and died. 'Twas the most affectin' thing. There was the child a-dyin', and the mother and father cryin', and the old grandfather goin' all to pieces—"

"All to pieces! That's worse than paralysis. Hold on a minute, Azuba! Was all this in the picture?"

"Yes."

"And you paid to see it?"

"Course I paid to see it. They wouldn't let me in for nothin', 'tain't likely."

"Well, seems to me you've made a mistake. If cryin' and misery is what you want, I don't doubt you can find a lot of funerals to go to for nothin'. But what was there about all this mess of horrors that made you think of me?"

"Oh, I don't know, unless the way you and Mrs. Dott are goin' in for society in Scarford. Course your child is grown up, so that's different, though, ain't it?"

"Yes, and there isn't any paralysis in the family, so far as I know. That's a mercy. Don't you get paralysis, Azuba. If you do, it will take you longer to get breakfast than it does now."

"That's all right. You ought to be thankful you've got me to get breakfast. If I wa'n't here you'd have to get it yourself, I cal'late. Your wife's too busy these days, and that Hapgood man wouldn't do it. I know that."

Relations between the butler and Azuba were already somewhat strained. He considered her a rude and interfering person and she considered that he would bear watching.

"He's always recommendin' folks for us to trade with," she told Captain Dan. "What business is it to him who we trade with?—unless he gets a little somethin' for himself out of it. He won't do it more than once—not if I catch him at it."

The invitation to dine with the Fenholtzes came about a week after the dinner at the Blacks'. Daniel, who opened the letter containing the invitation, was very much pleased. But when Serena came back from the lodge meeting she received the news rather coldly.

"When is it they want us?" she said. "Next Tuesday night? Mrs. Lake said something about coming around that evening to help me read my paper and criticise it."

The captain was surprised and troubled. "She could come some other time, couldn't she? I think 'twas real kind of the Fenholtzes to ask us. Seems to me we ought to go. You and I haven't even been to pay back that call yet."

"I know it. I've meant to, but I've been so busy. Besides, I don't know whether it is worth while or not. The Fenholtzes have got a great deal of money, but all the Chapter people say they are sort of back numbers."

However, she decided to accept the invitation, and they went in state. But the state was largely on their part. The dinner was a very simple affair compared to the elaborate spread of the Blacks, and the two or three people whom they met were quite different from Mrs. Lake and her friends. Captain Dan enjoyed himself hugely. He sat next to Mrs. Fenholtz at the table, and her quiet conversation on every-day subjects he could understand. Before the dinner was over he was thoroughly at ease, and when later on, in company with the Honorable Oscar and the male guests, he sat smoking in the library, he found himself spinning yarns and joking as freely as if he had been in the back room of the Metropolitan Store in Trumet.

The shouts of laughter from the library could be heard in the parlor, and Serena grew nervous.

"Your husband must be very entertaining," said Mrs. Fenholtz. "I haven't heard Mr. Fenholtz laugh so heartily in a long time."

Mrs. Dott was fearful that Daniel might be making himself ridiculous. She didn't mention her fears. Her own remarks were delivered with a great deal of dignity, and she quoted Mrs. Black and the encyclopedia often. On the way home she took her husband to task.

"What in the world were you talking about with those men?" she demanded. "I never heard such a noise as they made. I do hope you didn't forget yourself."

The captain rubbed his chin. "I don't know but what I did forget myself, Serena," he replied. "I know I had a good time and never thought about my clothes after the first ten minutes. Could you hear 'em laughin'? I was tellin' em' about Azuba's goin' to the movin' pictures then."

His wife was shocked. "And Azuba is our cook," she said, "and they know it. I don't know what sort of servants they think we have. They must think you're pretty familiar with them."

"Good land, Serena! I've been familiar with Zuba all my life. If I was to put on airs with her she'd take me down in a hurry."

Mrs. Dott sighed. "I'm afraid you did forget yourself," she declared. "I think if you could hear what the Fenholtzes are saying about us now you'd be ashamed. I'm sure I should."

And at that very moment Mr. Fenholtz was saying: "That man Dott is all right. I have not laughed so for years. And he has common sense, too. I like him."

His wife nodded. "So do I," she said; "and I think I should like Mrs. Dott, too, if she had not been spoiled by Annette Black and the rest of those foolish women she associates with. If she could only have gone to the Woman's Club first I think she might understand, but now I'm afraid it's too late."

At the next meeting of the Chapter Serena read her paper. She mounted the platform with fear and trembling. She left it exalted and triumphant. The paper had been applauded and she had been congratulated by her fellow members. Stories of the "vast" wealth inherited by the Dotts had been circulated freely, and these, quite as much as the wonderful paper, were responsible for Serena's bound into popularity.

But the popularity was there, and the unconscious Serena believed it to be real. That meeting was the beginning of her obsession. Thereafter she talked chapter and society and opportunity and advancement, and ate them and drank them, too—at least the meals—those at home—seemed to the captain to be made up of very little else.

Then came the reception idea. Annette—she and Mrs. Dott were calling each other by their Christian names now—had dropped the hint concerning it. She had said that a good way in which to repay social obligations was by doing it all at once, by giving a dinner, or reception, or a tea, to which everyone should be invited.

Serena decided that the reception was perhaps the better, all things considered. And so preparations for the reception began. The captain found it practically impossible to talk to anybody. Hapgood was busy; Serena was busier, and Azuba was busiest of all.

Wherever he went he seemed to be in the way, and when he fled for walks up and down the streets the crowds of strange faces made him feel lonelier than ever. On the evening before that upon which the reception was to be held he returned from one of these walks to find Serena in tears.

"Why, good gracious sakes!" he exclaimed. "What's the matter?"

"Matter!" sobbed his wife. "Oh, dear me! Everything is the matter! I'm so tired I don't know what to do, and Annette and Mrs. Lake were coming here tomorrow to help me, and now they can't come. They'll be at the reception, of course, but they can't come before; and there's so much to get ready and I don't know whether I'm doing it right or not. What SHALL I do!"

Daniel shook his head. "Seems to me I'd do the best I could and let it go at that," he advised. "If they ain't satisfied I'd let 'em stay the other way. I wish I could help you, but I don't know how."

"Of course you don't. You don't have any sympathy for the whole thing, and I know it. You haven't any sympathy for ME."

The captain sighed. He had a vague feeling that he could use a little sympathy himself, but with characteristic unselfishness he put that idea from his mind.

"I guess what you need is a manager," he said. "Somebody that's used to these sort of things that could help you out. I wish I knew where there was one."

Hapgood appeared and announced that dinner was served. Serena hurriedly dried her eyes and they descended to the dining-room. Just as they were about to take their seats at the table the doorbell rang. Hapgood left the room and returned a few moments later bearing a card on a tray. Serena took the card, looked at it, and then at her husband. "Why, Daniel!" she exclaimed under her breath. "Why, Daniel! WHO do you suppose is here?"

Her husband announced that he didn't know. He took the card from her hand and looked at it. It was a very simple but very correct card, and upon it in old English script was the name "Mr. Percy Hungerford."

Daniel's face reflected the astonishment upon his wife's. "My soul!" he muttered. "Percy Hungerford! Why, that's—that's the cousin; the one Aunt Laviny cut out of her will; the one that would have had all this place and all the money if we hadn't got it. What in the world does he want?"

Mrs. Dott rose. "I don't know," she gasped. "I can't imagine. But I suppose we must see him. We've got to. Did you ask him to wait, Hapgood?"

Hapgood bowed respectfully. "Mr. Hungerford is in the drawing-room, ma'am," he said.

To the drawing-room moved Serena, followed by her husband. "Good evening, Mr. Hungerford," said the lady. "How do you do? My husband and I—"

She paused. The expression on Mr. Hungerford's face was an odd one. She turned to Daniel, and his expression was odder still. Mr. Percy Hungerford was the young man whom his friend had addressed as "Tacks," the young man with whom Captain Dan had exchanged repartee in the Rathskeller of the Palatine Hotel.

CHAPTER VII

Of the two men, Mr. Hungerford was the first to recover presence of mind. For just an instant the color rushed to his cheeks as he recognized the captain and saw that the latter recognized him. Then: "Why, how do you do, Captain Dott?" he said. "By Jove, this is extraordinary, isn't it! Strange that relatives shouldn't know each other when they meet. How do you do?"

He stepped forward with extended hand. Captain Dan, who had expected almost anything but this bland cordiality, scarcely knew what to say or do. He took the proffered hand mechanically and dropped it again.

"Well!" he stammered. "Well!—I declare I—I didn't expect to—"He paused. Mrs. Dott, who had been watching this scene in bewilderment, spoke before he could finish his sentence.

"Why, what is it?" she asked. "Have you—"

Mr. Hungerford smiled. "Your husband and I have met before," he explained. "Just a casual meeting and we weren't aware of each other's identity. I'm afraid I was not as cordial as I might have been on that occasion, Captain. I hope you'll forgive me, I'm sure."

Daniel hesitated; then he smiled. "Why, I guess I can forgive my half if you can yours," he said slowly.

Before the puzzled Serena could ask another question the visitor turned to her. "I'm sure you must be very much surprised to see me here," he said. "I'm somewhat surprised to be here myself. I've spent a greater part of the past month in New York and have only just returned—that is, to stay. I fully intended to call before, and should if I had been in town. Ah!" with a sigh, as he seated himself and looked about him, "how familiar it all seems!"

The Dotts looked at each other. Serena sank into a chair. Captain Dan remained standing. "Does it?" said the former rather feebly.

"Indeed it does. One almost expects to see Auntie coming in at the door. Dear old Auntie! I can scarcely realize that she has gone."

Again Serena looked at Daniel and he at her. This was so strange, so different from the attitude which a disappointed legatee might be expected to assume that neither of the pair knew exactly how to reply. But Mr. Hungerford did not appear to notice the look or the hesitation.

"This house seems like home to me," he said. "I've spent so many happy hours here. When old Hapgood opened the door for me I almost ordered him to take my bags to my room." He laughed languidly.

"Are—are you stopping at the hotel?" queried Mrs. Dott.

"Not yet. In fact, I'm not really stopping anywhere. I've just arrived. I must be hurrying back to dinner, I suppose, but I couldn't resist coming here first. It seemed the natural thing to do."

Voices were heard in the hall. One of the voices was Azuba's; she was informing Mr. Hapgood that if that soup didn't go back on the stove pretty soon it might just as well be on ice. The words were distinctly audible, and Serena colored. Mr. Hungerford rose.

"I'm sure I must be keeping you from your own dinner," he said. "Why—why—" faltered Serena. She looked appealingly at Daniel, and the latter's instinctive hospitality asserted itself. He had disliked the young man "Tacks" when he met him in the Rathskeller. Now that "Tacks" had become Mr. Percy Hungerford, Aunt Lavinia's cousin and his own distant relative, the dislike was only partially abated. But to turn him away from the door hungry seemed wrong somehow.

"Hadn't you better—" he began.

"Have dinner with us?" finished his wife.

Mr. Hungerford protested. "Oh, I couldn't think of it," he declared. "No doubt you have guests—"

"Oh, no, we haven't. We're all alone and it would be no trouble at all. We should like to have you stay. Shouldn't we, Daniel?"

"Sartin, no trouble at all," said Daniel heartily.

"Well, if you insist. It is a frightful imposition—I shouldn't think of it, of course, but—well, thank you so much."

So Hapgood received orders to lay another plate, and Mr. Hungerford, still murmuring protests, suffered himself to be conducted to the dining-room.

All through the meal the captain regarded him with puzzled curiosity. That he had come to the house merely for a friendly call he could scarcely believe. He had heard little or nothing of the conversation between Hungerford and his friend at the table in the Rathskeller, and yet the attitude of the former on that occasion had not indicated a temperament likely to forgive "dear Aunt Lavinia" so freely or to display such angelic cordiality toward those who had come into possession of her property. But the cordiality remained unchanged, and the visitor, so far from bearing a grudge toward his more fortunate relatives, continued to treat them as though they were near and dear friends, and do everything in his power to relieve their constraint and to make himself agreeable. The dinner ended and they adjourned to the drawing-room, with Captain Dan's mental question "What in the world is this young chap really up to?" still unanswered.

Serena had asked herself that same question when the caller first came, but now she was beginning to be ashamed of her suspicions and to think them unfounded. Mr. Hungerford was agreeable; there was no doubt of that. He led Serena into speaking of the Chapter and her work there, and he displayed a knowledge of and an interest in that Chapter and its members which was very gratifying.

The coming reception was mentioned, and the visitor's interest in that was more gratifying still. He asked Mrs. Dott who was to assist her in receiving, and when she answered the question his approval of the selections was unqualified. He suggested one or two little ideas which he said might add to making the affair a success.

"That'll be lovely," she said, "and we can do it just as well as not. And there's music; I know we really ought to have music, and I had meant to have somebody play the piano. But the woman I wanted can't come, and now I don't know what to do. What would you think about that, Mr. Hungerford?"

Mr. Hungerford suggested hiring one or two professional musicians. "A violinist, or harpist, or both, perhaps," he said. "I happen to know of a young fellow who plays exceptionally well, and his sister is really a very accomplished performer on the harp. Of course they should be engaged in merely a professional capacity. They are not persons who would mingle with our set, but they're not at all objectionable, really."

The diplomatic phrasing of this remark had its effect. It indicated that Mrs. Dott's "set" was an exclusive one and, incidentally, that the accomplished and polished Mr. Hungerford considered his host and hostess as social equals.

"There!" exclaimed Serena. "I think that will be just fine. Do you suppose you could get these—these—er—persons you speak of to come and play for us?"

"I think so. I should be glad to make the attempt if you wish it, Mrs. Dott."

"Cost somethin', won't it?" observed Captain Dan casually. Mr. Hungerford regarded him with well-bred surprise.

"Why, of course," he said, "there will be some expense. I think fifty dollars will cover the bill."

There was no doubt that the captain was surprised. "Fifty DOLLARS!" he repeated. "Why—"

His wife interrupted. "That will be all right, Mr. Hungerford," she said.

"Of course, there are many whom you can obtain for less, and, if you feel that that figure is too high, I shall be glad to try elsewhere. I have had little experience outside of the best, but—"

Serena interrupted again. "We don't want anybody but the best," she declared. "Be still, Daniel. This isn't Trumet."

Daniel drew a long breath. "There ain't much doubt of that," he observed. "But, all right, Serena, if you and Mr. Hungerford think it's all right, I guess it is."

"Music," went on Mr. Hungerford, "is almost a necessity, in these days, when everyone dances. Is this a formal reception, or had you intended clearing a floor for dancing, Mrs. Dott?"

Mrs. Dott had not intended any such thing; she had not thought of it. But she concealed the fact from her visitor with remarkable presence of mind.

"Oh, of course!" she said.

The conversation continued, a conversation limited to Mr. Hungerford and his hostess, while Captain Dan remained a silent and amazed listener. The young gentleman was invited to attend the reception, Serena making many apologies for the informality of the invitation, and the guest expressing himself as delighted.

"Of course," he said, "I wouldn't intrude for the world, but I don't feel like an intruder in this house, where I have spent so many happy hours. Feeling as I do,

I'm going to make another suggestion which, under different circumstances, might be considered an impertinence. I am at leisure to-morrow—in fact, all this week—and if there is anything that I can do to help you and Cousin Daniel, in this matter of the reception or any other, I shall be at your service. I do hope you will permit me to help and that you will not consider me presuming in offering to do so."

It was quite evident that the offer was very welcome. Mrs. Dott accepted it with enthusiasm and called upon her husband to confirm the acceptance. He did so, but with less warmth, and it was agreed that the obliging Mr. Hungerford should drop in the next morning after calling upon his protege, the violinist. A half hour later he said "Good-night," and departed.

"There!" said Serena. "If that isn't Providence, then I don't know. And it only goes to show how one person can misjudge another without knowing anything about him. I've always had a prejudice against that Mr. Hungerford simply because of what you told me of meeting him years ago, and now I don't think I ever met a kinder, nicer young man. Did you, Daniel?"

The captain hesitated. "I—I," he stammered, "well, Serena, I will give in that he seemed nice and obligin' enough to-night, but you see there's just one thing that—"

Serena turned on him. "Yes, I know," she said. "There's always 'one thing' about everybody that I like. He's a gentleman! and a different kind from any that we've ever met. That makes YOU suspicious, of course."

"Now you know it isn't that; but—but—"

"But what?"

There was more hesitation on the captain's part. He had intended to tell of the meeting at the Rathskeller; then he remembered the young man's explanation and apology and thought better of it. He finished his sentence in another way.

"But I don't see what he came here for," he said.

"He came here to see us. And, I think, considering how he was treated in Aunt Lavinia's will, it was awfully nice of him to come at all. And, as for helping me out on that reception, he's been a perfect godsend already. I should THINK you would appreciate it."

Before the next day was over, and long before the first of the evening's guests arrived, the services of the new-found friend of the family were appreciated even by the reluctant Daniel. Mr. Hungerford came early and proceeded immediately to make himself useful. He had seen the violinist, and the latter and his sister had promised to be on hand. He took Hapgood in charge and superintended the arranging of the drawing-room and the library for the reception and the dancing. When the messenger from the florist came with the flowers which Serena, acting upon the suggestion of Mrs. Lake and Mrs. Black, had ordered, he saw that they were placed in exactly the right positions for effect. Being urged to stay for lunch, he stayed. And his conversation during the meal was so fluent, so aristocratic in flavor, and yet so friendly, that Serena became more and more taken with him. With the captain he was not quite as much at his ease. But he did his best to be agreeable, and Daniel, still vaguely suspicious, found nothing tangible upon which to base distrust. There was so much to be done in the afternoon that, acting upon a hint so delicate that it could scarcely be called a hint, Mrs. Dott urged him to send to the hotel for his bag and stay at their home overnight. He accepted and was even busier than he had been during the forenoon session. He was never so busy as to perform manual labor with his own hands but he managed to convey the impression of being always ready and always helpful.

To say that Mrs. Black and Mrs. Lake were, upon their arrival, surprised to find him there would be expressing their feelings far too mildly. They knew Mr. Hungerford, but, heretofore, that gentleman had moved in circles other than their own. To find him here, an associate and friend of the people she had called "countrified," was most astonishing. She wondered, but she could not help being impressed, and her attitude toward her dear friend Serena was never so gushingly cordial. As for Mr. Hungerford, he greeted the Chapter representatives with condescending urbanity. When the reception began, somehow or other, Cousin Percy was in the receiving line.

Captain Dan, uncomfortably starched and broad-clothed, received likewise, but his remarks to those who pressed his hand and murmured compliments were rather commonplace and very much alike; this consisted principally of "How d'ye do's" and "Glad to see you's"; and it was only when the Honorable and Mrs. Fenholtz came that he appeared to remember anything else. It was evident that Mr. and Mrs. Fenholtz were as surprised as the rest to see Mr. Hungerford there. The Honorable, seizing an opportunity when the captain was for a moment alone, whispered in his ear.

"Where did he come from?" he asked, with a jerk of the head in Cousin Percy's direction.

"Him?" replied Daniel. "Oh, he came last night."

"Is that so? Is he a friend of yours?"

"Well, he ain't—isn't exactly a friend, I guess. He's a sort of relation, a nephew of Aunt Laviny's."

"Oh, oh, I see—I see."

There was something in the tone which caused Captain Dan to ask a question in return.

"Know him, do you?" he inquired.

"Yes, I know him, but—it is all right, Olga; I'm coming."

He passed on to make room for another assortment of new arrivals, lady members of the Chapter, and Daniel's curiosity remained unsatisfied.

After the reception proper, came a social and, to Daniel, very uncomfortable hour, and then Mr. Hungerford, who seemed to have taken upon himself the position of master of ceremonies, suggested dancing.

The collation followed the dancing, and Azuba and Mr. Hapgood served it, assisted by four waiters who, at Mr. Hungerford's suggestion, had been hired for the occasion. The butler's serving was done with grace and elegance, not to mention dignity. Azuba served as if the main object to be attained was to provide each guest with as much food as possible in the shortest possible time. But the food was good and the guests seemed to enjoy it. Some of them seemed to enjoy Azuba, and Mr. Fenholtz was observed by the indignant Serena to laugh heartily every time the transformed maid-of-all-work addressed him.

As they were leaving he said to Captain Dan: "Captain, that maid of yours is a wonder. I thought Mrs. Fenholtz and I had tried every variety of servant, but she is something fresh."

Daniel grinned. "She's fresh enough, if that's all you want," he admitted. "She reminds me of home."

The Honorable shook his hand. "Home is a good thing to remember," he said earnestly, "and a bedder thing not to be ashamed of. You are not ashamed of your home and you do not forget it. That is why I like you. Good night!"

Somehow this remark pleased the captain greatly, but when he repeated it to Serena, she did not seem pleased.

"I don't know what we shall do with that Azuba," she said. "She mortifies me to death, and yet you won't let me get rid of her."

Her husband did not answer. In the matter of Azuba he was as determined as ever. Amid the new life into which he had been thrown, head over heels, the housekeeper was the one familiar substantial upon which he could rely.

Next morning Serena was suffering from headache and had breakfast in her room. Mr. Hungerford, also, did not descend to the morning meal. Daniel wrote a long letter to Gertrude, describing the reception, after his own fashion, but taking care to seem as cheerful as ever. He did not feel cheerful, but there was nothing to be gained by troubling his daughter, as he reasoned.

Mr. Hungerford remained through that day and the next day and the next. At the end of that time he sent for his trunks and settled down to make the Dott house his home, for "a short season," he said. This, of course, was done only after much protest on his part and strenuous urging on the part of Serena.

"Of course he can stay," she said in conversation with her husband. "Why, Daniel, I don't know what I should do without him. His coming was a special Providence, just as I told you. Just see how he helped at that reception. There's no reason why he can't be here; we've got plenty of room. And it will only be while he's on his vacation, anyway."

Daniel rubbed his chin. "I know," he admitted; "so he says. But how long a vacation is it goin' to be?"

"How do you suppose I know that? I haven't asked him, it isn't likely."

"No, I didn't suppose you had; but it seems kind of funny he hasn't told you himself. What's it a vacation from? What's he do for a livin'? Anything but run receptions?"

"That's it—sneer! He does a great many things. He is interested in literary work, so he says. He writes for a living, I suppose that means."

"Humph! Has he got any answer?"

"Answer? Answer to what?"

"Why, to his writing. Has the livin' sent him word 'twas on the way, or anything like that? I don't want to be mean, Serena. But I can't quite make that young fellow out. Why did he come here, anyway? That's what sticks in my mind. What sort of a chap is he? You know what that lawyer man said about him. Nigh as I could make out from that, he thought he was a kind of high-toned loafer, sportin' round on his aunt's money. Why does that kind of a fellow come to live along with us?"

"He came here because he isn't that kind of a fellow at all. He explained about that. He thinks it was largely owing to those lawyers' influence that Aunt Lavinia treated him as she did in her will. But he doesn't hold any grudge. I felt so sorry for him, and that was one of the reasons why I thought we, the only relations he has, ought to be kind and show him hospitality at least. I never thought you were inhospitable, Daniel."

"I ain't, Serena. But—but—Well, I'll tell you. I haven't told you before, although I meant to, but he and I met once since we've been in Scarford. I told you about the meeting, but I didn't know then who I met. Now I—"

"I know. He told me about that, too. He was the one you met at the hotel that afternoon. He said he was ashamed of his behavior that day, that he was tired, out of sorts, and discouraged. He thought you had been listening to what he and his friend had been saying, and it made him cross. He said that he apologized when he first came to the house, and I remember that he did, and he asked me whether I thought any further apology was necessary. I said no, of course it wasn't."

"Well, I don't suppose it is. But—well, there was somethin' else. It seemed to me that afternoon at the Rathskeller that he and that chum of his had been drinkin'."

"Drinking? Do you mean that they were intoxicated?"

"No, not exactly that; but they had a couple of cocktails while I was there."

"Is that all? Oh, dear me! Daniel, you are SO old-fashioned. Your ideas don't change a single mite. In Trumet a cocktail is a dreadful thing; but here it isn't. Why, everybody drinks a cocktail before dinner. The Blacks always have them. There were cocktails at that dinner at their house."

"I know there was, but I didn't see you drinkin' yours, Serena."

His wife hesitated. "No," she admitted rather reluctantly, "I didn't. I've been temperance all my life and somehow I couldn't bring myself to do it. I hope Annette didn't think it was bad manners, but I just couldn't somehow. Perhaps I ought to have tried—"

"Tried! Don't talk that way. If I see you startin' in to drink cocktails I shall begin to think the world's comin' to an end. The first cocktail you drink will be the signal for me to clear decks for action. There's some things I WON'T stand, and that's one of 'em!"

"There, there! Don't get excited! I shan't begin at my time of life. But I shan't be narrow, either. If all you've got against Cousin Percy is that he drinks a cocktail once in a while I think you'd better get over it as soon as you can. He does help me, Daniel, in my Chapter work and all the rest of it, and I'd like to have him stay here at present. Now won't you be nice and obliging, same as you usually are, and let him stay, for my sake? You will, won't you, dear?"

Captain Dan said that he would, and yet he said it with considerable inward reluctance. There was no real reason why he should have distrusted Percy Hungerford. His distrust was based upon generalities and a knowledge of human nature acquired during his years of knocking about among men. His wife's words made an impression. If what she said was true, his conscience told him that he should be kind and generous in his attitude toward the literary person. But—well, the "but" was still there.

During the next fortnight the captain's sense of desertion and of being almost a stranger in his own house grew stronger than ever. There were more callers and more calls to return; there were more bridge parties and teas. His wife astonished him by announcing that she was going to take lessons in bridge and that Mr. Hungerford had found a teacher to perfect her in that branch of knowledge.

"Of course," she said, "it will cost quite a little, but Cousin Percy says there's no use having a teacher at all unless you have a good one, and three dollars a lesson isn't too much, because you learn so quickly from an expert. I was sure you would be willing for me to take the lessons, Daniel."

Daniel shook his head. "I'm willin' for you to do most anything that pleases you, Serena," he said, "but three dollars a lesson for learnin' how to play cards seems to me a pretty good price. If it was me I should feel as if 'twas doubtful whether I'd get as much out of it as I put in."

"Oh, no, you wouldn't after you had taken a few. You'll like it then."

"I like it! Good Heavens, you don't mean—"

"I meant that you're going to take lessons, too, of course. You must learn to play bridge—everybody plays it. And you used to like cards."

"I used to like high-low-jack, and I could manage to take a hand at euchre without raisin' too big a disturbance; but I never could learn that bridge and play it with those women friends of yours—never in this world."

And he positively refused to try in spite of his wife's pleading. However, he consented to the employment of the bridge teacher for her and, thereafter, two hours of each alternate afternoon, Sundays excepted, were spent by Mrs. Dott and two other female students in company with a thin and didactic spinster who quoted Elwell and Foster and discoursed learnedly concerning the values of no-trump hands. The lessons were given at the Dott home and Mr. Hungerford was an interested spectator. Daniel, who was not interested, and felt himself in the way, moped in his own room or went upon more of the lonely walks about town.

Chapter meetings and Chapter activities occupied more of Serena's time. There were "open" meetings occasionally and these Captain Dan seldom attended. Mr. Hungerford acted as his wife's escort and seemed to enjoy it, in his languid fashion. Chapter politics began now to have their innings. There was to be a national convention of the Ladies of Honor, a convention to be held in the neighboring city of Atterbury, and Scarford Chapter was to send delegates.

Mrs. B. Phelps Black, who aspired to national honors, was desirous of being one of these delegates, but so were many others, and Mrs. Black's candidacy was by no means unopposed. She called upon Serena for help, and into the fight in aid of her friend Serena flung herself, heart and soul.

There were meetings, and more meetings, and letter writing, and canvassing of voters. Here again, Daniel was of no use. Cousin Percy's experience—he seemed to have had all sorts of experience—helped amazingly. By this time he was as much a member of the Dott household as Serena herself—more than the captain, who began to feel that he was not a member at all. Even bridge was side-tracked for the more absorbing political game, and evening after evening Captain Dan spent alone.

One night, or rather one morning, for it was nearly two o'clock, he was awakened by a series of violent shakes, and opened his eyes to find his wife bending over him.

"Daniel, Daniel, wake up!" she cried.

The captain groaned. "Hey! what is it?" he asked sleepily. Then, with a little more interest, "Is the house afire?"

"No, no, but do wake up and listen. I've had the greatest honor done me. You will hardly believe it. The delegates to the Atterbury Convention were elected tonight."

Captain Dan sat up in bed. "Not you?" he shouted.

"Yes, I. And, more than that, I was the one selected to read a paper there. There, Daniel Dott! aren't you proud of your wife?" There was a little hesitation in her husband's manner, and yet he tried his best to be enthusiastic. "Oh, yes," he said, "but then I was proud of you before, Serena. But—but what does this mean? Have you and I got to traipse way over to Atterbury?"

"Not you. You're not going. None of the men are. This is a women's convention. Men are not invited."

"I know. But I've got to go there with you. You ain't goin' off travelin' by yourself."

"I'm going with the other Chapter delegates; we will travel together."

"How long are you goin' to be gone?"

"I'm not sure. Three or four days probably."

"And I've got to stay here alone?"

"Why, you won't be alone. Cousin Percy will be here, and there's Azuba."

"Yes, and that everlastin' Hapgood, I suppose. Say, Serena, have you GOT to go?"

"Got to? Why, I WANT to! It's an honor. Don't you want me to go?"

"Why—why, I suppose I do; but—but—"

"But, what? Oh, you DON'T want me to go! I can see—and I thought you'd be so glad!"

She was almost in tears. Daniel's sensitive conscience smote him once more. "Land sakes!" he protested. "Of course I want you to go, Serena! I—I was just kind of lonesome, that's all. I get that way sometimes, lately. Seems as if you and I don't see as much of each other as we used to. Do you think it's all worth while?"

"Worth while! Why, Daniel Dott!"

"There, there! don't take on. I suppose you know best about such things. But I get kind of blue settin' around here thinkin', without you to talk to; and Gertie isn't here."

"Yes, I suppose you do. Well, after this convention is over I shall have a little more time, I hope. And Gertie will be home pretty soon. It's almost time for her Christmas vacation."

"Yes, I know it is. My! we'll be glad to see her, won't we?"

"Of course we will. But, do you know, Daniel, I've been so busy that I almost forgot about Christmas and Gertie's vacation and everything. It was Cousin Percy that reminded me of it."

"Reminded you of what?—of Christmas?"

"No, of course not—of Gertie's vacation. He said that she was coming and that he should be glad to make her acquaintance."

"HE said so? How did he know? I never told him."

"I don't remember that I did, either. But I suppose I must have. He is very much interested in Gertie and how she was getting on at college and all that."

"Humph! He seems to know a lot. But, there! I recollect now—Gertie said she met him at college. Well, Serena, I won't complain any more. You can go to Atterbury if you want to. I'll get along all right."

And to Atterbury Mrs. Dott went. It was the first time since the old sea-going days that Captain Dan and his wife had been separated longer than twenty-four hours.

The three days passed somehow. The wanderer was to return on Thursday morning, but she did not. Instead came a telegram, reading as follows: "Meeting and paper great success. Send immediately one of my latest photographs. Serena."

The puzzled Daniel sent the photograph preceded by a telegram of his own which read: "When are you coming home? Why don't you write? Have been worried about you. Answer."

The answer was delayed still another day. When it came, it was in the shape of a very short note stating that Saturday was the date of return. Serena wrote that she was having a lovely time. She

would tell him all about it when she got back. "And," she added, "I am sending you by this mail copies of the Atterbury paper. Please show it to any of the Chapter members whom you may meet."

Captain Dan unfolded the paper and gazed at the page marked with blue pencil. Here, under black headlines, which screamed the success of the convention of the Ladies of Honor, was a horrible blotted outrage resembling a stout negress peering through a screen door and labeled, "Mrs. Serena Sarah Dott, of Scarford, whose brilliant paper scored the success of the meeting." It was only by a process of deduction that Daniel realized the thing to be a reproduction of the photograph he had sent. He glanced hurriedly over the account of the meeting, catching here and there phrases like "Mrs. Dott's forte is evidently platform speaking"—"clear thought, well expressed"—"tumultuous applause." He felt that he ought to read the account from beginning to end, but also that he could not. Azuba, however, when it was shown to her, had no such feeling.

"Well, there now, Captain Daniel!" she exclaimed. "Ain't you a lucky man to have a wife as notorious as she's gettin' to be! I swan to man, if it ain't—"

The captain interrupted her. "Azuba," he said, rather testily for him, "if you use that word again I don't know as I won't make you eat a dictionary. My wife may be famous and she may be a platform speaker, but I'm blessed if I'll have her notorious, not if I can help it."

"But she is notorious, ain't she? Look at her right there in the newspaper, with all that piece about her in print! Why, what ails you, Daniel Dott? Just look at that photograph!"

Captain Dan rose. "Yes," he said drily, "I've been lookin' at it. That's part of what ails me."

On Saturday he was at the station to meet his wife. Serena was inwardly jubilant, although, because of the presence of Mrs. Lake and Annette, she tried to appear dignified and calm. But when she and her husband were alone on their way to the house her jubilation burst forth.

"Oh, it was a wonderful success!" she declared. "I declare, I wish you might have been there. Oh, Daniel, it was splendid!"

Lunch was a mere formality on her part. She talked incessantly, while Cousin Percy and her husband listened. Mr. Hungerford's congratulations were hearty. His praise was as close to fulsome flattery as it could be and not overstep the mark.

Daniel offered congratulations, too. He was glad that his wife had succeeded, but the pleasure was solely because of her happiness. Several remarks which Serena had made seemed to prophesy that the excursion to Atterbury was but the beginning.

All that afternoon Mrs. Dott spent in her room. She was going to be very busy, she said, and she must not be interrupted. It was only just before dinner that the captain found a moment for an uninterrupted interview. He entered the room to find her seated at the writing table, her fingers ink-stained, and the table covered with closely written sheets of manuscripts. She looked up when he appeared.

Daniel regarded her gravely. "You look tired, Serena. You're doin' altogether too much of this sort of thing. You ought to stop, or you'll be sick. Now, you just rest a while. My, it does seem good to have you back again! We can have an evening together now. I'll tell you what we'll do: You tell Hungerford you're tired and then come right up here, and I'll come, too. Then we can sit and talk."

But Serena shook her head. "No, Daniel," she said. "I can't talk to-night."

"Then don't; I'll do the talkin'. Land's sakes! it'll be enough just to look at you. I don't feel as if I'd seen you for a hundred years."

Another shake of the head. "I'm sorry, Daniel, but I can't be with you at all to-night. I must present my report to the Chapter and I shall probably not be home till very late."

Daniel sprang from his chair. "Serena Dott!" he cried. "Do you mean to tell me that you're goin' out to that Chapter thing again TO-NIGHT! after bein' away from me all this time!"

"I can't help it, Daniel. I must present my report. It's my duty to do it. The Chapter expects me and I must be there."

"Expects you! I expected you, didn't I? And, by the everlastin', I think I had a right to expect you! I'm your husband, ain't I? Seems to me I am entitled to a little of your society."

"I can't help it, Daniel. The Chapter—"

Captain Dan's feelings got the better of his prudence. "Damn the Chapter!" he shouted. "I wish you and I had never heard of it, nor anybody that belongs to it."

The instant after the words left his lips he would have given a good deal to recall them, but it was too late. His wife slowly rose.

"Daniel Dott!" she gasped. "Daniel Dott! You—YOU—why—my husband talking to me like that! The man who should be proud and glad that I have found my lifework—speaking to me like that! Oh! oh! what shall I do! How CAN I bear it!"

She fell back into the chair, her head sank upon her arms over the manuscript of the precious report, and she burst into a storm of sobs.

Daniel was as much overcome as she. He hurried to her side and in an agony of remorse bent over her.

"There, there, Serena," he pleaded. "Don't do so. I didn't mean it. It kind of—"

He would have put his arms about her but she pushed them away. "And swearing at me," she sobbed.

"I didn't mean to swear, Serena. I never swore at you before in my life. I didn't mean to this time. Please forgive me, won't you? Please?"

But Serena was not ready to forgive. The sleepless nights and days of wild excitement had thrown her nerves into a state where it needed but the slightest jar to break them completely. She sobbed, and choked, and gasped, her fingers clutching at her hair. Daniel, hanging over her, tried in vain to put in a word.

"Please, Serena," he kept saying. "Please."

Suddenly the sobs ceased. Serena's hands struck the desk and she rose so abruptly that her husband had scarce time to get out of her way.

"Serena," he cried.

But Serena cut him short. "Go away," she commanded. "Go away and leave me. I don't want to speak to you again."

"But, Serena—"

"Go away. Don't come near me again to-night. Go, go, GO!" And Daniel went, slowly, reluctantly. He was scarcely past the sill, his hands still upon the knob of the door, when that door was closed from within with a slam. He made one more effort to speak, but he heard the key turn and his wife's voice commanding him to go away. He descended the stairs to the library and threw himself into a chair. Mr. Hungerford, smoking one of his host's cigars and reading the evening paper, looked at him curiously and asked what was the matter.

Daniel turned on him. "Nothin'," he roared. "Nothin', do you hear?" Then he rushed from the library to the hall, seized his hat and coat from the rack and hurried out of the house. He walked and walked, but if, upon his return, anyone had asked him where he had walked he could not have told them. This was the first serious quarrel that he and his wife had had during their married life.

It was half-past seven when he returned and found Azuba fidgeting in the dining-room. "For mercy sakes!" Azuba demanded. "Where have you been?"

"Out!" was the gloomy rejoinder. "Where's the rest of the folks?"

"Gone to Chapter meetin'."

"Both of 'em?"

"Yes. It was an open meeting and Mr. Hungerford went along, too. Where are you goin' now? Don't you want anything to eat? It's been waitin' for you for an hour."

"Let it wait; I don't want it."

He walked from the room. Captain Dan didn't talk to anybody. He sat alone in the library, miserable and downhearted. After a while Azuba came and announced that she guessed she'd get a mouthful of fresh air, if she wasn't needed. Receiving no answer, she apparently considered the request granted and the captain heard the back door shut. Still the captain sat in the library, a huddled, pathetic heap in the armchair, gazing at vacancy. Occasionally he sighed.

The doorbell rang. Aroused from his doleful reverie by the sound, Daniel jumped from his chair and, going to the hall, shouted for Azuba. Then he remembered that Azuba was not on the premises and answered the ring himself. He had forgotten to push the button of the porch light and, peering out into the dark, he could see only that the person standing upon the top step was a woman. A carriage had drawn up at the curb and the driver was unloading a trunk from the rack.

"Good evenin'!" said Daniel.

The answer was a surprise. There was a laugh, and then a pair of arms were thrown about Captain Dan's neck and a girlish voice said: "Good evening! Is THAT all you've got to say to me?"

Daniel's answer was a shout that might have been heard at the next corner.

"What!" he roared. "GERTIE! Where'd you come from?"

CHAPTER VIII

"But aren't you glad to see me, Daddy?" asked Gertrude.

The captain, who had scarcely taken his eyes off her since her arrival at the house, drew a long breath. "Glad to see you!" he repeated. "I never was more glad to see anybody in MY life. How'd you happen to come so soon?"

"I hadn't expected to come, but I changed my mind. Now tell me all about yourself. How are you, and how's Mother? Mother has gone to the Chapter meeting, you say. Did she go alone?"

"No, she didn't go alone. That—Cousin Percy went with her."

"Cousin Percy? Oh, you mean Mr. Hungerford. Do you call him Cousin Percy? How funny!"

She seemed much amused. Her father smiled, but it was a rather sheepish smile.

"'Tis kind of funny, I suppose," he admitted. "I don't know as he really is a cousin. Fact is, I guess he ain't any real relation."

"Of course he isn't. He was Aunt Lavinia's second cousin, or something like that, but she was only your aunt by marriage. I don't see why you should speak of him as 'Cousin Percy.' Did he ask you to?"

"No-o; I don't know as he did. But, you see, he always calls your mother Cousin Serena and me Cousin Daniel, and—and—well, I guess we've kind of got into the habit. Your mother began it and, now that he's been here so long, I've caught the disease, I shouldn't wonder."

"Long! Why, he hasn't been here more than a month, has he?"

"Hey? No; no; now that you mention it I don't suppose he has. But it seems a lot longer than that to me."

He sighed. Gertrude regarded him keenly. Unconscious of the regard he sat there, lost in thought, apparently forgetful of her presence. She reminded him by saying: "Why does it seem longer?"

He started and looked up. "Hey? Why?" he repeated. "Oh, I don't know. So many things have happened, I guess."

"What kind of things?"

"All kinds. But there—tell me about yourself. How's college? And how's John? Land sakes! I ain't said a word about John, and he's about as important as anything on earth just now, or he ought to be. How is he?"

"John is well and very busy. He sent his love to you and Mother, and he hopes to run down here before very long and spend a few days with us."

"That's good. I suppose YOU don't hope he'll come. Ha! ha! no, of course not. He's doin' all the hopin'."

"Well, perhaps not all. But there, Daddy, don't waste time talking of John or me. I want to hear about you and about Mother, and how you like living in Scarford."

"Why, I wrote you all about that."

"Yes, I know you did, but I want to hear more, lots more. And I want to see the house. Now, Daddy, you must show me all the rooms right away. We can talk as we go."

She led the way and Daniel followed. The house was shown from top to bottom. Gertrude asked many questions, the majority of which seemed to have little to do with the new establishment and more with the life which her parents had spent in it. Captain Dan answered these questions in the intervals between rooms, and his answers were less guarded than they might have been under different circumstances.

When they returned to the library, the captain, who had been waiting for some expression of approval from his daughter, suddenly blurted out: "Well, why don't you say somethin', Gertie? Don't you like it?"

Gertrude, seated in the easy chair, her elbow resting on the chair arm and her chin supported by her hand, answered promptly.

"No," she said, "I don't like it at all."

"What! Don't LIKE it? Don't like this house? Well, for mercy sakes!"

"Oh, not the house; I like that well enough. I liked our old one quite as well—but never mind that now. The house is all right. It is the rest of it that is all wrong. I don't like that."

"The rest of it? What do you mean?"

Gertrude did not answer. Instead she raised her head and looked at him. It was a long look and a steady one, and the captain found it hard to bear. He fidgeted for a moment and then blurted out: "Well, what is it? Why are you starin' at me like that?"

The stare continued.

"What is it?" demanded Daniel. "What does ail you, Gertie? Or is it me?"

His daughter nodded. "Yes," she said, "it is you. Why don't you tell me all about it, Daddy? I have a right to know. Why don't you tell me?"

"Tell you? Tell you what?"

"You know. Why don't you tell me? You have told me so much already that you may as well make a clean breast of it. Why, you silly old Dad, what do you suppose brought me here a week ahead of my vacation? Why do you think I came?"

"Why do I think—? Why—why, you came because you wanted to see your mother and me, I suppose. I thought you was as anxious to see us as we was to see you."

"So I was; but that wasn't reason sufficient to make me leave my work at college before the term was over, leave it for good, very likely. I came because I was sure you needed me. And your letters made me sure."

Daniel gasped. His letters had been triumphs of diplomatic evasion, so he considered. He had been so careful to write nothing of his troubles, to leave out everything which should hint at his disturbed state of mind.

"My letters!" he exclaimed. "My letters made you think—made you sure—"

"Yes; your letters and mother's. Hers were full of all sorts of things, the very things that you never mentioned. She didn't say she was having a good time here, but it was plain enough that she was. You said it in every letter but it was perfectly plain that you weren't. And her last letter was so short—she was so busy with the Atterbury preparations that she could not write more, she said—and yours was so very, very long, and SO full of lonesomeness—"

Her father interrupted. Lonesomeness was the very thing he had tried to keep out of that letter.

"Gertrude Atwell Dott!" he shouted. "How you talk! I never wrote a word—"

"Yes, you did. It was all there, between the lines. I could read it, for you and I have been acquainted a good many years. As soon as I received that letter I made up my mind to come at once. Since I have been here I have asked a good many questions, and you have answered them. But I didn't need the answers. Just to look at you was enough. You are miserable, Daddy dear, and, because you are you, you won't admit it. But you've got to; you've got to tell me the whole story. I want to know all about everything."

The wind was taken completely out of Daniel's sails. He could only sit there, guilt written plainly upon his face, and stammer frantic protestations.

"No, no," he declared. "It ain't so. You're all wrong, Gertie. The idea of you sayin' your mother was neglectin' me."

"I didn't say it. You have said it a dozen times, but I haven't."

"I said it? I never. Your mother is a fine woman, Gertie; as good a woman as ever was."

"I know that. And she would not neglect you wilfully for the world. But she has not had experience. She takes people and things at their face value. She doesn't understand—Why are you smiling? Is it so funny?"

Captain Dan rubbed the smile from his lips. In spite of his perturbation he had been amused for the moment.

"Why," he observed, "I don't know as 'tis, but—but—well, I couldn't help wonderin' how old you'd got to be in the last couple of months, Gertie. About how much experience have YOU had, young lady? now that we're speakin' of it."

Gertrude's earnestness was too real to be shaken by this pertinent inquiry.

"I have had a good deal," she declared. "One can get a lot of experience in college. There are as many kinds of character there, on a small scale, as anywhere I know. You ARE neglected, Daddy; you are lonely and miserable. Now, I want you to tell me all about it."

But her father had, in a measure, recovered his composure, and he declined to tell. He had been longing for a confidant, and here was the one he had longed for most; but his sense of loyalty to Serena kept him silent.

"There's nothin' to tell," he vowed stoutly. "I'm all right."

"Nonsense! I shall lose patience with you pretty soon, and I don't want to. Judging by what I have seen and learned so far, I am likely to need a great deal of patience in this house, and I can't waste any. Mother has gone head over heels into this precious Ladies of Honor work of hers, hasn't she?"

"We-ll, she's terrible interested in it, of course; but she's so smart anyhow, and here in Scarford she's got the chance she's been lookin' for."

"And she is very much in society here, isn't she?"

"Yes."

"What kind of society is it?"

"Hey? What kind? Why, it's the genuine gilt-edged kind, I should say. I never saw such clothes, nor such dinners, nor dances. It—"

"Hush! Yes, I can believe all that. You wouldn't be likely to see them—in Trumet. And I can believe in the gilt; the genuine part is what I am most doubtful of. Mrs. Black is as influential with Mother as ever, isn't she?"

"Yes. She and Serena bein' such close friends, it—"

"I know. Tell me, Daddy, are the rest of Mother's friends like the Blacks?"

"Pretty much. They're all the same tribe—that is, I mean they're all brilliant, fashionable folks."

"I see. What sort of friends have YOU made?"

This was straight from the shoulder and the captain was somewhat staggered.

"Well," he admitted, after a slight pause, "I—I ain't made so dreadful many friends, Gertie. Most of the men here are—are kind of different from me, seems so. They belong to clubs and such, and they're out a lot nights. I don't care for goin' out much; I've always been a great home body—you know that, Gertie. I don't doubt, if I joined the club and went to 'stag' dinners and so on, I'd have more friends. It ain't their fault, you know, it's me."

"Yes, it always is you, isn't it, Daddy? No one else is to blame, of course. Well, I'm very glad I came when I did. How many evenings have you spent alone, as you were spending this one?"

"Not a great many. I just—"

"Why didn't you go to the Chapter to-night? It must have been an open meeting, otherwise Mr. Hungerford couldn't have gone. Why didn't you go with Mother?"

Here was the one question Daniel had dreaded most. To answer it truthfully meant telling of the quarrel between Serena and himself. He could not tell that, not even to his daughter.

"I—I didn't feel like goin', somehow," he faltered.

"That's strange. I knew that you were not particularly interested in the Chapter—at least you never were in Trumet—but I never knew you to stay at home when Mother asked you to go with her. Did she ask you?"

"Now—now, Gertie, 'tain't likely I—I—"

"Never mind; you needn't answer. Tell me more about this new relative of ours, 'Cousin Percy.' Do you like him, now that you really know him?"

"Why—why, yes, I like him all right enough, I guess. Course he and I are different, in some ways; but, then, he's younger by a good many years."

Gertrude nodded slowly. "I see," she said. "You've made up your mind not to tell me anything, haven't you, Daddy? You wouldn't hurt anyone's feelings for the world, and you are afraid I may blame Mother. Well, I am not going to blame anyone yet. And I am not going to quiz you any longer. But I came home to find out things, and I am going to find out. If you won't help me, I must help myself."

Her father leaned forward and patted her hand. "Now—now, Gertie," he pleaded nervously, "don't be foolish. Everything's all right, I tell you. Don't go stirrin' up any trouble. I am so tickled to have you here I don't know what to do. Let's be contented with that. Don't—Hello! here comes the Chapter folks now, I guess. Maybe your mother won't be glad to see you! Oh, Serena, who do you think is here? I'll bet you'll be some surprised!"

There was no doubt of the surprise; neither was there any doubt as to Serena's joy at seeing her daughter. An outburst of greetings and questions and explanations followed. Gertrude explained that she had had an opportunity to leave college a week earlier than the end of the term and had availed herself of it.

"I just had to see you and father," she declared. "I couldn't wait any longer. I've been telling father so; haven't I, Daddy?"

She accompanied this question with a glance which Captain Dan recognized as a warning. He nodded. "Yes," he said.

Serena suddenly remembered that the family was not alone. "Oh!" she exclaimed. "What have I been thinking of? Your coming home like this, Gertie, has made me forget everything else. Cousin Percy—Why, where is Cousin Percy?"

Mr. Hungerford, who, from motives of delicacy or other reasons, had stepped back into the hall, where he could see and hear without being too conspicuous, now made his appearance.

"Gertrude," said Mrs. Dott, "this is our cousin, Mr. Percy Hungerford. Oh, yes—why, you and he have met."

Mr. Hungerford bowed. "I had the pleasure of meeting Miss Dott one evening a year or two ago," he observed politely. "No doubt she has forgotten me, however, by this time."

Gertrude shook her head. "Oh, no," she said. "I remember you very well, indeed. How do you do, Mr. Hungerford?"

The young gentleman announced that he was quite well. He made a move as if to shake hands, but as there was no corresponding move on Miss Dott's part, he put his hand in his pocket instead.

"That evening—the evening of the college dance—is one of my pleasantest recollections," he observed. "I am ashamed to say that I have forgotten the names of the young ladies, but forgetfulness is one of my failings."

"He meets so many people," cut in Serena.

Gertrude smiled. There was a mischievous twinkle in her eye. "I'm sure he hasn't forgotten us all," she declared.

"He didn't forget you, anyway," declared Daniel.

"Oh, thank you, Daddy. You've saved my self-respect. But I was not referring to myself. There are others whom I am sure Mr. Hungerford has not forgotten. Isn't that true, Mr. Hungerford?"

Cousin Percy appeared somewhat disconcerted.

"Why," he stammered, "I can't recollect—"

"Can't you! Oh, that is dreadful! Do you correspond with so many young ladies that you can't remember their identity? Oh! oh! And Margaret was SO proud of those letters! Really, Mr. Hungerford!" She shook her head. Her eyes were brimming over with fun. Cousin Percy's cheeks had lost something of their aristocratic pallor.

Margaret Babcock, the daughter of a well known glass manufacturer, had been one of the list of feminine acquaintances whom he had honored with long distance familiarity. She was an impressionable young person and her papa was very wealthy. The correspondence had broken off when her mother discovered one of the letters. The latter had forgotten, for the moment, that he met Miss Babcock at the college dance; therefore he was confused.

But the confusion was short-lived. He recovered quickly. "I BEG your pardon, Miss Dott," he said with a laugh. "I had forgotten Miss Babcock. Poor Margaret! She was of an age when letters, especially masculine letters, are delightfully wicked. She asked me to write, and I was foolish enough to do so. I presume my humble epistles furnished harmless amusement for the class. Very glad to have contributed, I'm sure."

"You did contribute. We all enjoyed them so much—especially Margaret. She is a year older than I, Mr. Hungerford."

Serena, who, like the captain, did not understand a great deal of all this, decided to change the subject. She began to describe the Chapter's meeting and to tell of her great success at Atterbury, and the enthusiastic reception by the Scarford members of her report. Mr. Hungerford seized the opportunity to deprive the family of his society. He was rather tired, he explained, had a bit of writing to do before retiring, and, if they would excuse him, would go to his room.

"And now, Mother," said Gertrude, "tell me more about yourself, and about the Chapter, and the friends you have made, and everything."

Serena did not need to be asked twice. She told a great deal, warming to her subject as she proceeded. She told of their arrival in Scarford, of the kindness shown by the Blacks and Mrs. Lake and the rest. She told of their adventures in society, of the Blacks' dinner, of the reception, of her bridge lessons. Gertrude listened, saying nothing, but watching both her parents intently as the narrative proceeded.

Daniel, fidgeting in his chair, waited, nervously expectant, for the protest which he felt sure his daughter might make at any moment. But no protest came. Only once did the young lady interrupt, and then it was to ask a question.

"I suppose Daddy enjoys all this as much as you do, Mother?" she said.

Mrs. Dott's expression changed. The radiant joy, which had illumined her face as she described her progress at bridge, faded, and she seemed on the verge of tears.

"Don't, Gertie," she begged. "Don't ask me about your father, please. No, he doesn't enjoy it at all. He has no sympathy for my aims and ambitions. He takes no pride in my advancement. To-night—only this very night, he said to me—Oh, I can't tell you what he said! Don't ask me, please."

Captain Dan almost slipped from his chair in the agony of justification. "I never meant it, Gertie," he declared. "It just happened, I don't know how. I'll leave it to you; I'll leave it to anybody, if—"

For the first time his wife noticed his presence. "Leave it to anybody!" she repeated wildly. "I wish you would! I wish you could hear what people think of it. Why, Cousin Percy said—"

For the second time since lunch the captain forgot to be prudent. "Cousin Percy said!" he shouted. "He said! Do you mean to say you told him—THAT? What business was it of his, I'd like to know? What did he say? If he says it to me, I'll—I'll—"

Gertrude motioned him to stop. "There! there!" she commanded. "Daddy, be quiet. Mother, you're tired out. You must go to bed. I'll go up with you, and we can talk while you are getting ready. Daddy will wait here."

She led the sobbing Serena from the room. Captain Dan, his feelings divided between deep contrition at his own behavior and anger at Mr. Hungerford's interference in the affairs of himself and wife, obeyed orders and remained where he was.

It was a long wait. He smoked a cigar half through, lighting it three times in the process. When it went out for the fourth time he dashed the stump into the fireplace and took to pacing up and down the room. This reminded him of other days, days when he had paced the deck of his three-master, counting the hours which separated him from his wife and his home. He thought of the welcome he had always received when he reached that home. Oh, why—WHY had he ever retired from the sea? That was where he belonged; he was of some use in the world there.

Twelve o'clock struck before Gertrude re-entered the library. She entered quietly and, walking over to her father's chair, laid a hand on his shoulder. He looked up at her in mute appeal.

"It's all right, Daddy," she said. "You can go up now."

"But—but she—is she—"

"She has forgiven you, I think. You must be very kind to her."

"Kind to her? Kind! Why, Gertie, I never meant to be anything else. I wouldn't have—"

"Of course you wouldn't. Why didn't you write me the truth long, long ago? If I had only come sooner! If I had only known! Oh, WHY did you let things reach this state? Why didn't you stop it?"

"Stop it? Stop what?"

"Oh, everything. Don't you remember that I told you to send for me if you needed me? And don't you remember that I wrote you if you felt this moving to Scarford was wrong to say no and stick to it? Why didn't you do that?"

"Why, I—I—Serena, she was so set on comin' and all that, that—"

"I know. You needn't tell me. And yet, in a way, it seems strange. I remember some things Laban Ginn, Azuba's husband, told me about you and your ways aboard ship; he said your crews obeyed every order you gave as if it was what he called 'Gospel.' You, and no one else, was master there. However, that is not pertinent just now. Run along to bed, there's a dear."

Daniel obediently rose. "But what are you goin' to do, Gertie?" he asked.

"I don't know what I am going to do. First of all I am going to see and find out for myself. Then I shall decide. One thing seems certain: I shall not go back to college."

"Not go back! Not go back to college? Why, it's your last term! What'll your mother say? What'll John say?"

Gertrude's lips closed tightly and she gave a determined toss of her head.

"John will say what I say, I think," she declared. "As for Mother—well, what she says won't make any difference, not at present. Good-night, Daddy. Now don't worry, and," she repressed a smile, "be very careful and, if you must express your opinion of the Chapter, do it in the back yard or somewhere out of hearing."

She kissed him and he went slowly and fearfully upstairs. Serena's attitude of reproachful and self-sacrificing forgiveness he met with meek repentance and promises not to offend again. He got into bed, worn out and troubled, but with a ray of hope in his bosom, nevertheless. Gertie had come home; Gertie was going to do something or other, he did not know and could not guess what. At any rate she was with him, and he could see her every day. Perhaps—perhaps—still wondering perhapses he fell asleep.

Next morning at breakfast the young lady seemed to be in good spirits and, except for Serena's absence—Serena had breakfast in her room, a proceeding which was apparently developing into a habit—the meal was to Daniel quite like one of the happy breakfasts of Trumet days. Mr. Hungerford marred the captain's pleasure somewhat by joining the pair before they left the table, and to him Gertrude was surprisingly cordial and communicative.

Gertrude and he found a kindred taste for pictures and art in general, and before the captain's second cup of coffee was disposed of Mr. Hungerford had invited Miss Dott to accompany him to a water-color exhibition at a neighboring studio.

"Is the artist a friend of yours?" she asked casually.

"Oh, no," was the languid answer. "He's a queer old gink—old chap, I mean—whose work is quite the go about here recently. I've seen only two or three of his paintings, but they're really not bad. I think you'd enjoy the exhibition, Miss Dott."

"I'm sure I should. I should like to see the pictures and the—er—gink as well. Thank you very much, Cousin Percy."

When they were alone, Captain Dan turned to his daughter in puzzled amazement. "What did you call him 'Cousin Percy' for?" he demanded. "Thought you thought your mother and I callin' him that was funny; you said you did."

Gertrude laughed. "Did I?" she replied. "Well, perhaps I think so still."

Whatever she may have thought, it did not prevent her continuing to be very cordial to the newly discovered relative. He and she were together a good deal during the day. The remainder of the time she spent with her mother. Captain Dan scarcely saw her except at luncheon and dinner. Once he found her in the kitchen talking with Azuba, and on another occasion she and Mr. Hapgood were in conversation, but for her father she could spare only odd moments. The captain did not know what to make of it. When, taking advantage of a fleeting opportunity, he asked her she only laughed.

"I am very busy, Daddy," she said. "You mustn't bother."

"Bother! How long since my company was a bother to you, Gertie? It never used to be."

"It isn't now, and you know it. But, as I say, I am very busy. Business first, pleasure afterwards."

"Humph! I'm glad I'm a pleasure, even if it's the kind that comes after everything else. What have you and your ma been talkin' about upstairs for the last hour?"

"A great many things—society and the Chapter and—oh, all sorts."

"Want to know! What were you and Azuba talkin' about?"

"About household matters and the people IN the house."

"People in the house! What people?"

"You and mother and Mr. Hun—that is, Cousin Percy—and Hapgood."

"That's all there is, except yourself. What was you and Hapgood havin' a confab on; more household matters?"

"Yes, in a way. Daddy, have Mr. Hungerford and Hapgood known each other long?"

"I guess so. He was Aunt Laviny's butler for a good many years, and Percy was a regular visitor there."

"Has our cousin many friends here in Scarford?"

"Why, he seems to know 'most everybody; everybody that's in what he and your mother call society, that is."

"But has he any intimate friends? Have you met any of them?"

"I met one once."

He told of the meeting in the Rathskeller. Gertrude evinced much interest.

"What was this friend's name?" she asked.

"'Monty,' that's all I heard. Queer name, ain't it—isn't it, I mean. But it ain't any queerer than 'Tacks'; that's what he called Hungerford."

"Has this 'Monty' called here? Has he been here at the house?"

"No-o, no, he hasn't. I caught a glimpse of him at the club, that time when I went there with Barney—Godfreys! it's a good thing Serena didn't hear me say that—with Phelps Black, I mean."

"Daddy, sometime when you have an opportunity, ask Mr. Black about this Monty, will you?"

"Sartin, if you want me to. But what do you care about Percy Hungerford's friends?"

"I don't—about his friends."

With which enigmatical remark she moved away to join Cousin Percy, who had just entered the room.

During the next three days, Daniel's feeling that his daughter was neglecting him grew stronger than ever. Her "business," whatever it might be, occupied practically all her time, and the captain and she were scarcely ever alone. He had regarded her coming as the life preserver which was to help him through the troubled waters to dry land, and so far he was as helplessly adrift as before. Serena had forgiven his profane expression concerning her beloved Chapter, that was true, but Serena also was "busy" during the days and evenings, and at bedtime she was too tired to talk. Gertrude was with her mother a great deal, and with Cousin Percy almost as much. Daniel did not like Mr. Hungerford. He had grown to tolerate him because Serena liked him so much, and declared him such a help in her literary and political labors, but the captain had found secret comfort in the belief that his daughter did not like him any better than he did. Now it looked as if she was beginning to like him, after all. And there was no doubt whatever that Cousin Percy liked her.

Gertrude's apparent interest in her mother's social and Chapter affairs was another disquieting feature of the situation, as Daniel viewed it. Mrs. Black and Mrs. Lake called one afternoon and to them the young lady was cordiality itself. They talked "Chapter," of course, and to her father's horror Gertrude talked it, too.

Being invited to attend the next meeting she announced that she should be delighted to go.

"You didn't mean it, did you, Gertie?" pleaded the captain. "You didn't mean you was figgerin' to go to that devilish—to that Chapter?"

"Hush! Yes, of course I meant it."

"But—but YOU!"

"Hush! Daddy, don't interfere. I know what I'm about."

Daniel was doubtful. If she had known she surely would not think of going. The meeting was a protracted one, and, on their return, Serena, finding the lower rooms apparently deserted, went upstairs. Gertrude was about to follow, but a figure stepped from the shadows of the library and detained her.

"Why, Daddy!" she exclaimed. "What are you doing up at this hour?"

"Sh-sh!" in an agitated whisper. "I—I've been waitin' for you, Gertie. I just had to talk to you. Come in here."

He led the way into the library. "Don't say anything," he whispered; "that is, don't say very much. Serena'll be wantin' to know where I am in a minute. Gertie, what are you up to? WHY did you go to that Chapter?"

"Hush, Daddy, hush! It is all right."

"All right! Yes, I know it's all right so far. That's what your mother used to say, back in Trumet, when she first started in. You begin by sayin' it's all right and pretty soon it IS all right. It ain't all right for me—it's all wrong. Why did you go to that meetin'?"

"I went because I wanted to see for myself. And I saw."

"Yes, you saw. And you heard, too, I'll bet you. Well, did you like it?"

"LIKE it! Daddy, tell me: There is another Woman's Club in Scarford, isn't there? This can't be the only one."

"No, it ain't. I believe there's another. A different one—a sensible one, so I've heard tell. Mrs. Fenholtz she belonged to the other one. She wanted Serena to join, but Annette Black had her innin's first, and after that 'twas all off."

"I see, I see."

"You see; but what are you goin' to do? Are you goin' to any more of them blessed meetin's?"

"I probably shall. Daddy, dear, you must trust me. It is all right, I tell you."

Ordinarily this would have been enough. But to-night it was not. Captain Dan had spent some troubled hours since dinner and his nerves were on the ragged edge.

"All right!" he repeated impatiently. "Don't say that again. Is it all right for you to be gettin' into the same mess your mother is in? Is it all right for you to be talkin' about society and Chapters and—and I don't know what all? I did trust you, Gertie.

I said so. I told Serena so this very afternoon. She was talkin' about Cousin Percy, she's always praisin' him up, and she said you liked him just as much as she did. He was a cultivated, superior young man, she said, and you recognized it. I laughed at her. I says, 'That's all right,' I says, 'but I wouldn't take too much stock in that. Gertie knows what she's up to. She's got some plan in her head, she told me so. She may pretend—'"

His daughter interrupted him. “Father!” she exclaimed indignantly. “Why, Daddy! did you tell Mother THAT?”

“Course I did! Why not? It’s so, ain’t it? What is the plan, Gertie? You are pretendin’, aren’t you? Don’t tell me you ain’t! Don’t tell me—”

“I shan’t tell you anything. You’ll spoil—But there! good-night.”

“Gertie! Gertie! hold on. Don’t—”

Serena’s voice sounded at the head of the stairs. “Gertie!” she called. “Who is it you’re talking with? Is your father there? Why doesn’t he come to bed?”

“He’s coming, Mother, right away. So am I. Good-night, Daddy.”

The next forenoon, as Azuba was blacking the stove, Gertrude entered the kitchen. “Good-morning, Azuba,” she said. “Are you alone?”

“Yes, yes, I’m alone.”

“Where is Hapgood?”

“Land knows! Upstairs, lookin’ out for that Hungerford man’s clothes, I guess likely. Well, you went Chapterin’ and advancin’ last night, I understand. What did you think of it?”

“Think? I thought—Oh, Azuba!”

“Yup. It’s ‘oh, Azuba,’ I guess. That’s what I’ve been sayin’ to myself for quite a spell. I’d have said it to your pa, too, if it would have done any good.”

“It wouldn’t. We mustn’t say a word to him, or anyone else.”

“I know. And yet, when I think of the way things are goin’ at loose ends I have the shakes. Do you know what it’s costin’ to run this place the way it’s run? I know. And I know, too, that nobody else seems to know or care. Your pa trusts everything to his wife, and she trusts everything to that Hapgood. And there’s Serena’s health. She’s gettin’ more nervous all the time, and just wearin’ herself out with her papers and conventions and politics and bridge and society. Don’t talk to me! And it ain’t no use to talk to her. There’s got to be somethin’ more’n talk.”

Gertrude nodded. “So I think,” she affirmed. “Azuba, I have a scheme. It may be the best idea in the world and it may be the worst, but I am going to risk it. And you must help me. Will you?”

“Sartin sure I will!”

“And you won’t tell a soul, not a living soul?”

“Not one, livin’ or dead. You needn’t look at me like that. I swan to mercy, I won’t tell anybody.”

“Good! Then listen.”

Azuba listened, listened in silence. When her young mistress ceased speaking she shook her head slowly.

“Well,” she observed, “it looks some like hoppin’ out of the fryin’ pan into the fire, but, even if it turns out that way, perhaps it’s just as well to be roasted as fried. Humph! no, ‘twon’t do to tell anybody. I shan’t, and you mustn’t.”

“I don’t intend to.”

“Um! Not even John Doane?”

“Well,” doubtfully, “I may tell John later on. He’ll have to trust me, too.”

“So he will. Fur’s that goes, it’s a good thing for men folks to learn to trust us women. All right, Gertie, I’m with you till the last plank sinks. But,” with a chuckle, “I’m kind of sorry for your pa. The medicine may cure us all in the end, but it’ll be a hard dose for him to take, won’t it?”

CHAPTER IX

Captain Dan's foundations were slipping from beneath him. His daughter's return had seemed to him like the first ray of sunshine breaking through the clouds and presaging the end of the storm. Now, it began to look as if the real storm was but beginning. Gertrude was apparently contracting the society and Chapter disease. So far from influencing her mother to give up the "crazy notions" which were, Daniel firmly believed, wrecking their home and happiness, she was actually encouraging and abetting these notions.

The young lady was certainly spending a great deal of time with her mother and her mother's friends. When Mrs. Black and Mrs. Lake called for consultations concerning Chapter affairs, Gertrude took part in these consultations. Daniel, peeping into the library, saw the four heads together over the table, and heard his daughter's voice suggesting this and that. Invitations to various social functions came, and it was Gertrude who urged acceptance of these invitations. Captain Dan's pleas for quiet evenings together at home went for nought.

"You needn't go, Daddy," said Gertrude. "Mother and I know you don't care for such things. She and I can go without you."

"Go without me? Look pretty, wouldn't it, to have you two chasin' around nights all by yourself, without a man to look after you!"

"Oh, Cousin Percy will go with us. He is always obliging that way. Cousin Percy will go, I am sure."

The captain was equally sure. Cousin Percy was altogether too willing to go anywhere, at any time, provided Miss Dott went also. This very obvious fact did not add to Daniel's peace of mind.

Rather than have his family escorted by its newest member, he resolved to sacrifice his own inclinations and go himself.

Miss Canby—the blonde young woman who played the piano at the Black home on the night of the dinner—issued invitations for an "At Home" in her apartments. All the Dott household—Mr. Hungerford included—were invited. Mrs. Black, who came to call, was enthusiastic. She was again the dear friend and counselor, with all the old cordiality and a good deal of the old condescension.

This condescension, however, was confined to Serena and Captain Dan. Toward Cousin Percy she was extremely polite, but never patronizing, perhaps because that gentleman was so languidly at ease in her presence. She seemed to be a bit afraid of Cousin Percy, afraid and somewhat suspicious.

To Gertrude she was gushingly friendly, overwhelmingly so, and the friendship was, to all outward seeming, returned. Daniel, who had gathered from his daughter's previous remarks that she disliked the great Annette, was surprised and dismayed.

"For goodness sakes, Gertie," he demanded, "what did you kiss her for? Do you love her so much you have to hug her every time you see her?"

Gertrude laughed. "Do you think I do?" she asked.

"I don't know what to think. It's a mighty sudden love, that's all I've got to say. Do you want her here ALL the time?"

"Well, when she is here I know where she is."

"So does anybody within hearin'. I never saw such a change in a person as there is in you. You used to go out of the room when that Black woman came into it. Now you kiss her when she comes."

"No, Daddy; I kiss her when she goes."

With which puzzling statement the interview ended.

B. Phelps accompanied his wife when the latter called to discuss the Canby invitation. Daniel was glad he came. Black and he were not altogether congenial; the captain would not have chosen him as an intimate; but at least there would be someone present with whom he could exchange a word.

Mr. Hungerford was, for a wonder, not in when the callers came. He went out very little nowadays, except when Miss Dott and her mother went; then he was always ready to go.

Annette declared that the Canby "At Home" was certain to be a most unusual affair. "So—er—well, so different," she explained. "Miss Canby is a very unusual woman, a unique woman, and her affairs are always as unique as she is. So truly Bohemian. I adore Bohemians, don't you, Gertrude?"

Gertrude said she did. "I don't know that I've met a great many," she added, "but I'm sure they must be very enjoyable."

"Oh, they are! And Miss Canby is one. The very first time I attended a gathering at her home I said to myself: 'THIS is true Bohemianism.'"

Captain Dan was astonished. "Why!" he exclaimed, "Miss Canby's folks came from Down-East somewheres—Bangor, Maine, I think 'twas. She told me so, herself."

The remark was received in various ways, by various individuals. Serena frowned; Gertrude bit her lip; B. Phelps Black burst into a roar of laughter.

"I did not mean my statement literally, Captain Dott," explained Annette in gracious toleration. "But when people are independent and free from the usual conventionalities, as Miss Canby is, we speak of them as Bohemians."

Daniel understood little or nothing of this. He understood perfectly well, however, that he had blundered somehow, a glance at his wife's face told him that. Gertrude smiled at him kindly and observed: "Father is like myself, his acquaintance in Bohemia has been limited."

Captain Dan muttered that he guessed likely that was so, adding that he had an Armenian steward once who was a pretty good fellow.

Then he subsided. Serena took up the conversation, changing the subject to the ever fruitful one of her beloved Chapter. Gertrude joined in the discussion, a proceeding which her father noticed with apprehension.

Mr. Black accepted an invitation to smoke, and he and Captain Dan went into the library. After the cigars were lighted, B. Phelps, lowering his voice so as not to be heard in the adjoining room, said suddenly: "Dan, is that daughter of yours going off her head like the rest of the females?"

Daniel was indignant. "Off her head!" he repeated. "She's as smart and sensible a girl as ever lived. What are you talkin' about?"

Mr. Black waved his hand. "Keep your hair on, Dan," he counseled pleasantly. "I always thought she was as sensible as she is pretty, and that's saying something. But what has got into her since she got here in Scarford? You used to tell me she didn't care anything for society and all the rest of it; now she seems to be as daffy as her—well, as my wife, if you like that better."

"Daffy! See here, Barney Black, I—"

"Hush! Don't begin to yell or we'll have that hen convention in the parlor down on us. I'm not finding any fault with your daughter. I'm only talking for her good and yours. What does she care about this confounded Chapter foolishness?"

"She don't care nothin' about it."

"She seems to be mighty interested in that talk they're having in there now. And she was as joyful as the rest of 'em over this Canby woman's 'At Home.'"

The captain was quite aware of the apparent joy; and Gertrude's growing interest in her mother's Chapter and its members was too obvious to be denied. Nevertheless, he tried to deny it.

"Oh, that's nothin'," he declared. "She and Serena have always been plannin' together over things, and this Chapter's like the rest, that's all. As for the 'At Home,' why—why—well, Gertie's young, and young folks generally like a good time."

"A good time! Great Scott! Have you ever been to that Canby apartment and seen the crowd that—No, of course you haven't. Dan, if my wife heard me she'd take my head off, but you're an old friend of mine and I like your daughter. Listen to me: Don't let Gertrude go to that 'At Home' if you can help it."

"Don't let her! How am I goin' to help it?"

"I don't know. Keep her in the house. Lock the door and hide the key."

Captain Dan's indignation was rapidly changing to alarm. "See here, Barney," he demanded, "what are you tryin' to say, anyhow? What's wrong with this Miss Canby?"

"Nothing's wrong with her, so far as I know. And yet there isn't anything right. She's good enough, I guess, and she can play the piano like a streak, but she's a fool. She and the gang she is with are bleached-haired, frowzy-headed idiots, who hope they are Bohemians—whatever that is. They like to do what they call unusual things; they like to shock people—think it's smart. Don't let your wife or Gertrude—Gertie, especially—get in with that crowd. They don't belong there. And there's something else."

He hesitated. Daniel, trembling with anxiety, urged him to continue. "What is it?" he begged. "What is the somethin' else?"

"Oh, nothing. It isn't my business anyhow. I ought to keep still."

"Keep still! After sayin' as much as you have? You go ahead or I'll shake it out of you one word at a time."

"Well, then, don't get mad. Remember I'm saying it merely as a friend. Is Gertie engaged to be married?"

"Sartin she is. To a fine fellow, too. What of it?"

"Why, this: If she is engaged why is she trotting about with this precious cousin of yours—this Percy Hungerford?"

Captain Dan started violently. He had asked himself that very question many times during the week which had just passed. To have someone else ask it, however, was too much.

"By Godfreys!" he sputtered, "what do you mean? Do you mean to hint—"

"I'm not hinting anything. Be quiet, or I'll stop right here. What do you know about Hungerford, anyway? Why is he here at your house?"

"Here! Why—why, he's here 'cause we asked him to stay. He's on his vacation and he's just makin' us a visit. As to knowin' anything about him, what do you mean by that? Do YOU know anything about him?"

"Not much. Neither does anyone else; that's the queer part of it. While old lady Dott—your Aunt Lavinia—occupied this house, he was here a good deal. He didn't do anything then, except to be a general high-flyer around town with a few chums like Monty Holway, who is another gay young bird with money. After Mrs. Dott went abroad to live, he left Scarford and went to Providence a while; after that to Boston and New York, and various places. Now, all at once, he comes back here and settles down on—with you and your wife. What did he do that for?"

"I—I don't know. He didn't intend to settle. Says he didn't, anyway. As for bein' a sport—well, he's told us about that, told

Serena the whole yarn. He owned up that he never took life very seriously while Aunt Laviny lived; had plenty of money and didn't have to. But now it's different. He's realized that he must work, same as other folks, and he's doin' it. He works for some magazine or other, doin' what he calls literary work."

"Humph! What magazine is it?"

"I don't know. I never asked."

"Well, all right. I tell you, honestly, Dan, there's a feeling that he is working you and the family for easy marks."

Daniel hesitated now. He had had faint but uneasy suspicions along this very line, although these, like other suspicions and misgivings, he had kept to himself. He shook his head.

"No, no," he said, "you're wrong there, Barney, sure you are. Why, Percy has done a lot of writin' and such since he's been here. He goes to his room 'most every afternoon to write, and he's helped Serena with her Chapter papers and speeches more than you could imagine. As for Gertie's trottin' around with him, that's just foolishness. She's gone to picture shows and such when he asked her to, but that's only because she likes such things and wanted company her own age. It's all foolishness, I tell you. If anybody says 'tain't, you tell 'em I say they're lyin'. By Godfreys! If they say it to me I'll—"

"There! there! Keep your hair on, I tell you."

"'Tis on, what there is left of it. But, Barney, what sort of talk have you been givin' me? If Hungerford ain't all right, how is it that he knows so many folks in this town? How is it that he's invited everywhere, to all sorts of places, into everybody's houses? Invitations! Why, he gets more'n we do, and," with a sigh, "land knows that's enough, nowadays."

B. Phelps grunted contemptuously. "It is easy enough to get invitations," he observed. "When you've been in this town as long as I have you'll know that any young fellow, who is as good looking and entertaining as he is, will be invited to all sorts of things. The girls like him, so do their mothers—some of them. But there! I may be all wrong. Gertrude's a bully girl; I always liked her—wished a good many times I had a daughter like her. I should hate to see her get in wrong like—well, like some people you and I know. You keep her at home as much as you can."

This conversation remained in Captain Dan's head for days. It disturbed him greatly. Several times he made up his mind to speak to Serena concerning it, but each time he changed his mind. He even thought of writing a note to John Doane, urging the latter to run down to Scarford for a few days, but he was fearful that to do this might be a mistake. So Daniel did nothing further than to remonstrate mildly concerning the acceptance of Miss Canby's invitation. He need not go unless he wished, said Serena, she and Gertrude and Cousin Percy could go and he could stay at home and rest. Gertrude said the same. When the evening came, the whole family went, the captain included.

Annette had characterized the gifted Miss Canby as unusual, and the social affairs given by her as unique. After the first half hour in the "Bohemian" apartments, Daniel would have agreed with her, although his opinion might have been more emphatically expressed.

Gertrude, strolling about in the company of a young gentleman found her father seated in a corner, sheltered by a Japanese screen and an imitation palm, and peering out at the assembled company with a bewildered expression on his face.

"Well, Daddy," she asked, "are you having a good time?"

Daniel, who had not noticed her approach, started and looked up. "Hey?" he asked. "A good time! Yes, I'm havin' a good time. I haven't had a better one since I went to the sideshow at the circus. Who's that long-legged critter with the lay-down collar and the ribbon necktie? What ails him?"

Gertrude looked and laughed. "That is Mr. Abercrombe, the poet," she said. "Nothing ails him; he is a genius that's all."

"That must be enough, then. "What—"

He stopped. His daughter's escort had caught his attention. The young man's face was familiar.

"Why!" he faltered, "isn't this—"

"This is Mr. Holway, Daddy. I wanted you to meet him."

Her tone was quite serious, but there was an odd expression in her eye. Mr. Holway, blond, immaculate and blase, bowed. Then he, too, started.

"Eh!" he exclaimed. "Why, by Jove!"

Captain Dan nodded. "Yes," he observed, quietly. "Well, I'm much obliged to you, Gertie, but Mr. Holway and I have met before."

Gertrude's surprise, real or assumed, was great. "Have you?" she cried. "Why, how odd! When?"

Mr. Holway, himself, answered. He seemed confused and his explanation was hurriedly given.

"Your father and I met one afternoon at—at the Palatine," he stammered. "I—I should have known. I'm ashamed of my part in that, Mr. Dott. I really am. I owe you an apology. I hope you—I hope—"

Captain Dan nodded. "All right," he said briefly. "Don't say any more about it."

"But—but I hope you and Miss Dott won't—won't think—"

"We won't. I won't, anyway. Well, Gertie, what have you been doin'? 'Most time to go home, is it?"

"Time to go home? Why, Daddy, we've just got here. We haven't been here an hour yet."

"Haven't we? Seemed a good deal longer than that to me. All right, don't you worry about me. I can stand it, I guess. Where's your mother and—and Cousin Percy?"

"Mother is in the next room with Mrs. Lake and some more of the Chapter members. Cousin Percy is—Oh, here he comes now."

Hungerford appeared, strolling in their direction. He seemed surprised when he saw his relatives in company with Mr. Holway.

"Hello, Monty!" he said. "You here? How are you?"

The two young men shook hands. Gertrude smiled upon them both. "Father and Mr. Holway were renewing acquaintanceship," she observed, cheerfully. "It seems that they have met before."

Cousin Percy's acknowledgment of this statement was a brief "Oh, indeed!" He and his friend exchanged glances.

"The—er—performance is about to begin, I believe," announced Mr. Hungerford. "Shall you and I adjourn to the next room, Cousin?"

Gertrude shook her head. "Oh, thank you," she said, "but Mr. Holway has been telling me the most interesting stories about Scarford and the people in it, and I want to hear the rest. He is dreadfully sarcastic; I should not listen, I know, but I want to. Come, Mr. Holway."

She moved away, the flattered "Monty" in her wake. Mr. Hungerford gazed after them. He appeared not altogether pleased.

"Very sociable, chatty chap, that friend of yours, I should judge," observed Captain Dan drily.

"Um-hm!" grunted Cousin Percy. "Been chatting to you, has he?"

"No-o, not much this time. But you remember I've had the pleasure before."

Mr. Hungerford doubtless remembered; he looked as if he did. Then he, too, strolled away.

Miss Canby's rendition on the piano, of what she was pleased to call "A sweet little thing of Tschaikovsky's—one of my favorites," was enthusiastically applauded, and she obliged with another, and still another. Then Mr. Abercrombie was prevailed upon to read one of his own outpourings of genius, a poem called "The Tigress," in which someone, presumably the author, described the torments involved in his adoration of a feminine person with "jetty brows and lambent eyes," whose kiss was like "a viper's sting" and who had, so to speak, raised the very dickens with his feelings.

Daniel was not enthusiastic over the poems. He could not understand a great deal of them, but he understood quite enough.

When B. Phelps Black winked at him from his seat at the other side of the room, he did not return the wink, although he knew perfectly well what it meant.

The poems were bad enough, according to his figuring, but when Miss Beatrice Dusante tripped into the circle to slip and twist and slide and gyrate in "one of her delightful Grecian dances," he found himself looking about for a convenient exit. Discovering none he remained where he was and blushed for the company.

The Bohemians, however, did not blush; neither, to his amazement, did Serena, who looked on and applauded with the rest. He found some comfort in the absence of his daughter, who was not among the seated guests, but, at last, even this comfort was dispelled. He caught a glimpse of Gertrude, still accompanied by the attentive Mr. Holway, standing in the back row. Gertrude looked as if she did not care for Miss Dusante's dancing any more than he did. Mr. Hungerford, also, did not appear interested. He was looking at Miss Dott and "Monty," and there was a frown on his face.

Upon their return, after they were together in the library at home, Daniel's shocked indignation burst forth.

"Well!" he declared, "that's enough. That's the limit, that is! What kind of a gang IS that, anyway?"

His wife regarded him with astonishment. "Gang!" repeated Serena. "Why, what are you talking about, Daniel?"

"I'm talkin' about that gang at that Canby woman's place to-night. Haven't they got ANY respectability? How'd they come to let that dancin' thing in there? Couldn't they stop her? Why—"

Serena interrupted. "Stop her!" she repeated. "How could they stop her? She was an invited guest."

"Who invited her? That's what I want to know."

"Miss Canby, I suppose. She is a friend of hers."

"A friend! A FRIEND!"

"Yes. Now, Daniel, don't be silly. I know what you mean, and I must say I sympathize with you just a little. Annette explained to me afterwards though, so I suppose it is all right. Annette says that this Miss Dusante's dancing is all the rage now. She has made a study of the ancient Grecian dances and she does them everywhere. She is paid high prices for it, too."

"I don't doubt it. I should think she'd want to be. Did you see the way she was dressed? I never—"

"Hush, Daniel! That was the old Greek costume. Miss Canby told me all about it; the old Greeks used to dress like that."

"They did! Then it didn't take 'em long. Why!" with a sudden turn upon his daughter, "You were there; I saw you lookin' on. YOU didn't like that Greek dancin', did you?"

Gertrude hesitated. Her cheeks were red and, for a moment, she seemed to find it difficult to speak. Then, after a quick look at her mother, she answered, calmly: "Like it! Why not, Daddy? It is all the rage, just as Mother says, and it is certainly graceful. I rather think I should like to learn it myself. I understand Miss Dusante gives lessons."

Daniel's mouth opened and remained open. Cousin Percy stared at the speaker. Even Serena, defender of the dances of the ancient Greeks, looked shocked.

"Why, Gertie!" she cried. "Gertie! You! the idea!"

"Why not, Mother?"

"Why not! I never heard you speak like that before."

"I never saw any dances like those before. I have heard about them, of course, but I never saw them. We never did a great many things that we are doing now. We are learning all the time; that's what you told me, Mother. I never went to a Bohemian 'At Home' before."

Serena's eyes snapped. "Well, you'll never go to another one," she declared, "if it's going to have this effect on you."

The young lady smiled. "Why, of course I shall," she cried. "I want to learn, just as you do, Mother. And I mean to. Good-night!"

She left the room and they heard her ascending the stairs. Daniel and Serena looked at each other.

Captain and Mrs. Dott had a long talk before retiring. The captain derived some satisfaction from the talk; it seemed to him that their daughter's declaration of independence had startled Serena somewhat. She even went so far as to admit that, in spite of Mrs. Black's explanations and gracious commendations, she, herself, had not been impressed by Miss Canby's guests. She and Gertrude would have an interview in the morning, she declared.

Captain Dan waited hopefully for the result of that interview. The hope was crushed when Serena reported to him.

"It is all right, Daniel," said Mrs. Dott. "I guess Gertie didn't really mean what she said about taking lessons of the Dusante woman. She thought the dances graceful, and they were, of course. But Gertie is older now and she expects to have her own way more than she has had it. She said a lot of things to me, things that she hasn't said before. It seems that when she first came home she was inclined to think I had exaggerated when I wrote her about the lovely people here in Scarford, and the Chapter, and the brilliant women in it. Now, she sees I was right. She has helped me a good deal already with my Chapter work, and she means to do more. She is going to join the Chapter herself. She—why, what's the matter?"

Daniel had made a choking noise in his throat; he appeared to be strangling. "Noth—nothin'," he gasped. "I'm all right. But—but you said—why, how can Gertie join the Chapter? She's goin' back to college soon as her vacation's over."

Serena shook her head. There was just a shade of doubt, almost of trouble, in her voice as she answered.

"No-o," she said, "no, Daniel, she isn't. She isn't going back any more. She thinks it isn't necessary."

"Not necessary! Why, how you talk, Serena! Not necessary to finish out her last term! One of the things that troubled me most, back there in Trumet before we was rich, was that I might not afford for her to finish out at that college, and now, when I can, she ain't goin'. I say she is. I say she's got to."

"I don't believe that will make any difference, Daniel. She seems to have made up her mind. I'm kind of sorry, I must say, but she is obstinate. You can talk to her, if you want to, but I don't think it will do any good."

Serena was right; although Captain Dan did talk to his daughter his arguments and persuasions were quite useless.

"No, Daddy," said Gertrude, "I am going to stay right here. I told you that if I were needed I should come home. I shall not go back. It is only the last half term, anyway."

"Yes, but then's when the girls have all their best times, all the dances and—and entertainments and society times. You said so. Do you want to miss all those?"

Gertrude smiled. "Oh," she observed, "I expect to have a great many 'society times,' as you call them, right here in Scarford. It's no use, Daddy; my mind is made up. Don't you worry, it is all right."

"Well—well, I—I must say—See here, are you really going to join that Chapter thing?"

"Yes."

"You are! After all you said—"

"Yes, no matter what I may have said."

"By—by time! I don't know what to do with you. I—I set a lot of store by you, Gertie. I kind of banked on you. And now—"

Gertrude's expression changed. She patted his cheek. "Keep on banking on me, Daddy dear," she whispered, "perhaps I'm not altogether hopeless, even yet."

But her father, for once, refused to believe her. "I don't like it," he declared. "And other folks don't like it, either. Why, Barney Black got after me only the other day about you. He wanted to know why you—you, an engaged girl—was cruisin' around so much with this Cousin Percy of ours. He thought 'twas queer. I said—"

Gertrude rose to her feet. Her arm was snatched from the captain's shoulder so quickly that he jumped. "Daddy!" she cried, her cheeks blazing, "do you mean to say that you have been discussing me with—with Mr. Black?"

"I didn't start it, he did. He said—"

"I don't care what he said. Oh, the impertinence of it! And you listened! listened and believed—"

"I didn't say I believed it."

"You did believe it, though. I can see you did. I shan't try to comfort you any more. You deserve all that is coming to you. And," with a deliberate nod, "it is coming."

"Comin'! It's HERE! What do you think John would say if he knew you weren't goin' back to college?"

Gertrude looked at him. Her lips twitched. "Oh," she said, mischievously, "as to that—well, Daddy, you see, he DOESN'T know it."

That afternoon Daniel wrote a letter. He said nothing to anyone, not even Serena, about the letter, but wrote it in the solitude of the library and posted it with his own hands. Just before sealing the envelope he added this postscript: "Whether you come or not, don't tell a soul that I wrote you this. And, if you do come, just let them think it was all on your own hook. THIS IS IMPORTANT."

On Saturday evening there was to be a meeting of the Chapter, and on Tuesday Serena returned from committee with the joyful news that Gertrude was to be admitted to membership at that meeting. The young lady expressed herself as delighted. Captain Dan said nothing. Later, he visited Azuba in the kitchen, and there he received another shock.

Azuba was not, as usual, busy with her cooking or scrubbing. She was seated in a chair by the window, reading a paper. She looked up as he entered, but immediately resumed her reading. The captain waited for her to speak. As a general thing he did not have to wait.

"Hello, Zuba," he hailed.

Azuba turned a page of the paper. She did not answer.

"Hello!" he hailed again. "What's the matter, Zuba? Gone into a trance, have you?"

"Hey?" Azuba did look up then, but at once looked down again. "Hey?" she repeated. "No, I ain't in no trance. I'm readin', that's all."

"I should think that was enough, if it fixes you so you can't speak to anybody. Must be mighty interestin' readin'."

"Hey? Interestin'? I guess 'tis interestin'! It's more'n that, it's upliftin', too. I'm just beginnin' to realize what I am."

"That so? Well, what are you?"

"I'm a woman, that's what I am."

She made the declaration with the air of one imparting news of a startling discovery. Daniel laughed. "Is that so!" he exclaimed. "Well, well! I always suspected it, Zuba, but I'm glad you told me, just the same. Does it say so in that paper?"

Azuba rose from her chair. She did not laugh; she was intensely serious. "It says a lot of things," she announced, "a lot of things I never thought of afore. I don't mean that exactly. I've thought of 'em, but I never knew how to make anything out of my thoughts. Now, I'm beginnin' to realize. I'm a woman, I am, a free woman. That paper is for free women. Have you read it, Cap'n Daniel?"

Captain Dan took the paper which she extended to him at arm's length. He recognized it immediately. It was "The Woman's Voice," official organ of the National Guild of Ladies of Honor.

He glanced at the paper and tossed it on the table. "Yes," he said shortly, "I've read some of it."

Azuba seized the discarded journal as if it were a precious treasure, a thing to be treated tenderly and with reverence. "Some of it!" she repeated. "Humph! I'd read all of it, if I was you. 'Twould do the men good if they was made to read every number ten times over. It's a wonderful paper. It's opened MY eyes, I can tell you that."

She went on to preach the glories of the "Voice," and concluded by reading an editorial which, like Mrs. Lake's addresses at Chapter meetings, contained a great many words and, to the captain's mind, little understanding.

He listened, fidgeting impatiently, to perhaps two-thirds of the editorial, and then he interrupted.

"Hold on! Heave to!" he ordered. "For the land sakes, Zuba, what's set you goin' like this? Are YOU goin' to—to—"

"To what? Am I goin' to what?"

"Are you goin' to 'advance' or whatever you call it? What ails all you women, anyway?"

"What ails us? Hain't I been readin' you what ails us?"

"You've been readin' a whole lot, but I've heard it all before. You want to be 'free'! Confound it, you ARE free, ain't you? What is it you want? Want to vote? Go ahead and vote. I'M willin'."

But Azuba laughed scornfully. "Vote!" she repeated. "I don't care whether I vote or not."

"Then what do you want?"

"We want—" Azuba hesitated, "we want—what this paper says we want. And," with determination, "we're goin' to have it."

"All right, have it, then! Meantime, let's have dinner. It's pretty nigh half-past five, and the table ain't set. And," with a sniff, "there's somethin' burnin' somewheres, I smell it."

This statement had an effect. Azuba dropped the precious paper and sprang to open the oven door.

"Well!" she declared, "it's all right. 'Twas that cranberry pie, and 'twas only beginnin' to scorch. It's all right."

"Glad to hear it. Now, say, Zuba, you take my advice; you're a practical, sensible woman, I always said so. Don't you get to be silly, at your age."

Azuba bristled. "At my age!" she repeated. "Humph! I ain't so much older than some folks in this kitchen, nor in the rest of the house, either. What do you mean by silly?"

"I mean—I mean—well, I mean don't you get to joinin' lodges and readin' papers and racin' out every night in the week to somethin' or other. It's silly—just silly."

"Oh, is it! Well, other women do it. Your wife's been doin' it ever since we got here. _I_ ain't got money; nobody's left ME a cart load of dollars and a swell front house. But I've got rights and feelin's. I'm a woman, a free woman, and if it ain't silly for Mrs. Dott and Gertie to want to advance and—and so on, I cal'late 'tain't silly for me either. Perhaps you'd like to have me tell Serena that you said she was silly. Shall I?"

Daniel did not answer, but his look was answer sufficient. Azuba smiled triumphantly. "Practical," she sneered. "No, Cap'n Daniel, I ain't been practical so far, but I'm goin' to be. I'm a-goin' to be. You watch me."

Her employer's guns were spiked. He marched out of the kitchen, slamming the door viciously. The library was tenanted by Cousin Percy, who was taking a nap on the lounge. Upstairs, Gertrude was helping her mother with a "report" of some kind. Hapgood, the butler, was in the hall, and he bowed respectfully.

"Yes, sir," he said. "Did you wish anything, sir?"

"No," snarled Captain Dan, and went out for a walk. This was the last straw. If Azuba was going crazy the situation was hopeless indeed. Hapgood, left alone in the hall, grinned, strolled into the library and, regardless of Mr. Hungerford's presence, filled his pockets with cigars from his employer's box. Downstairs, in the kitchen, Azuba was busy getting dinner. At intervals she burst out laughing.

That evening Mr. "Monty" Holway called.

CHAPTER X

Mr. Holway's call was, ostensibly, a call upon the Dott family in general, but it was to Gertrude that he addressed most of his conversation. In the presence of Captain Dan he appeared a trifle ill at ease, a fact which the captain attributed to circumstances attending their first meeting. Serena seemed somewhat surprised at the call. She regarded her daughter and Mr. Holway with an odd expression, and, so it seemed to her husband, was apparently dissatisfied or disturbed.

Mr. Hungerford was the most surprised of all. Mr. Holway also seemed embarrassed, and a bit on his guard. "Hello, Tacks!" he said.

"Hello," he said, gruffly.

"How goes it?" inquired Monty.

"All right enough. Oh—er—Gertrude, I've found out about that recital affair. It is next Wednesday afternoon. I have arranged for us to go."

Gertrude smilingly declared that she was much obliged. "I don't know, of course," she added, "what Mother's plans for that day may be, but if she is not busy I'm sure we shall be pleased to go."

Mr. Hungerford hesitated. "Well," he said, "to tell you the truth, I had supposed that Mrs. Dott might be rather busy. It is your committee meeting afternoon, isn't it, Mrs. Dott? and so I arranged for only two."

"Oh, that will be all right. You and Mother can go, then. I don't mind at all. Really, I don't. It is all right, Mother," turning to Serena, who had been about to speak, "you can go just as well as not. You must. Never mind the committee meeting; I'll act as your substitute there."

Cousin Percy was not overcome with joy; at least, he managed to restrain his ecstasy. Mr. Holway volunteered a word.

"Is it the Wainwright Recital you are talking about?" he inquired, eagerly. "I can get cards for that. I'll see that you go, Miss Dott. By George! I'll—I'll go myself. Yes, I will, really. We'll all go."

This prompt suggestion should have cleared the air. Somehow it did not. Mr. Hungerford merely grunted. Gertrude shook her head. "No," she said, "I think, perhaps, I had better not go, after all. But it is ever so nice of you to offer, Mr. Holway. You and Cousin Percy can take Father and Mother. That will be splendid."

"Don't bother about me," put in Daniel, hastily. Recitals were almost as distasteful as Chapter meetings or "At Homes" to his mind.

"It won't be any bother, I'm sure," declared Gertrude. "Will it, Cousin Percy? Will it, Mr. Holway?"

Both the young gentlemen murmured their pleasure at the prospect of acting as escorts to the elder members of the Dott family. Serena said she would "see about it," she couldn't say for certain whether or not she would be able to attend the recital. Captain Dan said nothing.

The conversation dragged somewhat after this. "Monty" and Mr. Hungerford addressed the greater portion of their remarks to Gertrude, only occasionally favoring Serena and Daniel with a word or question. At last, however, after Mr. Holway had given a very full account of a "dinner dance" which he had recently attended, "a very exclusive affair, only the best people, you know," Percy, who had been listening impatiently, turned toward him and drawled: "I remember that dance. I heard you enjoyed yourself, old chap. Said I imagined so, considering your company. By the way, that must be getting quite serious, that affair of yours. When may we expect the announcement?"

Holway colored. His usual facility of speech seemed to have deserted him. "Announcement!" he stammered. "Announcement! What—what—"

His friend laughed. "Oh, it's all right, old man," he observed. "Don't get excited. She's a charming girl. No one blames you."

"Monty" continued to sputter. Gertrude was all excitement. "Oh, how interesting!" she said. "Do tell us about her, Mr. Holway. Do I know her?"

"Know her!" Mr. Holway's indignation was intense. "I—I don't know her myself. He's just guying, Miss Dott. He—he thinks because he—he is so confoundedly fascinating, and has so many—so many—"Oh, that reminds me, Tacks," turning upon the smiling Hungerford, "I saw a friend of yours yesterday. She looked quite desolate, quite broken-hearted, my word she did. You were a little cruel there, weren't you, my boy? Everyone expected—"

He did not finish the sentence, but his expression indicated that much was expected. It was Cousin Percy's turn to color. "Don't be an idiot, Monty," he snapped. "Don't mind him, Gertrude; he has an amazing idea of repartee, that's all."

Serena volunteered a remark concerning the weather just then. She observed that it might be raining, it had looked that way before dinner. Mr. Holway possibly considered that a hint was involved; at any rate, he rose and announced that he must be going. Gertrude begged him not to hurry, they had all enjoyed his call so much, she said. Cousin Percy suddenly declared that he would accompany his friend on his way, a walk would do him good.

After they had gone, Daniel turned to his wife. "Humph!" he observed, "what sort of talk do you call that? I thought those two were chums; and yet I didn't know but they was goin' to fight one spell. It's a good thing you hove in that about the rain when you did, Serena."

Serena was grave. "Gertie," she inquired, "did you ask that young man to call here?"

Gertrude was the picture of surprised innocence. "Ask him to call?" she repeated. "Mr. Holway, do you mean? I don't know. I think not. Why?"

"WHY?" Captain Dan almost shouted it. His wife motioned him to be quiet.

"Hush, Daniel," she said. "You know why, Gertie, as well as I do. You are engaged to be married."

Gertrude smiled. "Of course I am," she answered. "What of it?"

"What OF IT?"

"Hush, Daniel, hush! Engaged girls, Gertie, are not supposed to have young men calling upon them."

"Oh," with a shrug. "I don't know that he was calling on me. He did not ask for me when he came. Besides, merely because I am engaged isn't any reason why I should retire from the world altogether, is it? Mrs. Lake says—"

Daniel struck the table with his fist. "Mrs. Lake!" he shouted. "Mrs. Lake don't live with her husband. She's a grass widow, that's what she is."

"She is one of Mother's dearest friends, and any friend of Mother's should be good enough for me."

The captain choked. "You—you talk to her, Serena," he stammered; "I can't."

Serena looked more troubled than ever. "Gertie," she faltered, "if Mrs. Lake has been advising you—to—to—"

"She hasn't advised me at all. If I have learned anything from you and your Chapter friends it is to be broad-minded and independent. If Mrs. Lake is not a living example of independence, who is?"

Serena could not seem to find an answer at the moment. Her husband tried again.

"Gertie Dott," he declared, "I—I don't know what to make of you, all at once. And John Doane wouldn't either. If John knew—"

Gertrude interrupted. "That's enough, Daddy," she said, firmly. "I am quite willing John shall know; when I am ready I shall tell him. He is a dear, good fellow, in his way, but—"

She hesitated. Her parents asked a question in concert. "But what?" they demanded.

"Why—why, nothing of importance. But I am learning here in Scarford. My opportunity has come, just as yours did, Mother. I am a free woman and I shall not be a slave—a SLAVE to any man."

With which remark she walked from the room. Her astonished parents looked at each other. Daniel was the first to speak.

"My soul and body!" he gasped. "What—what—Serena, did you hear what she said? That about John? That he was a good fellow—in his way?"

Serena shook her head. "I—I don't believe she meant it, Daniel," she said. "She's just a little carried away, that's all. All this society—this altered social position of ours—has turned her head the least bit. I'll have another talk with her pretty soon."

"I should say you'd better. Serena, do you know what I've done? I've written—"

He paused. The disclosure which, on the impulse of the moment, he had been about to make was, for him, a serious one. He had written the letter "on his own hook," without telling his wife of his action. What would she say if he told her now, so long afterward?

"You've done? What have you done?" asked Serena sharply.

The captain still hesitated. Before his mind was made up the front door opened and Cousin Percy made his appearance. He did not speak to the Dotts either, but tramped savagely up the stairs. His face, as seen by the electric light, was flushed and frowning.

Serena turned to her husband. "How cross he looked," she said, wonderingly. "What do you suppose has happened?"

Speculation concerning Cousin Percy's evident perturbation caused her to forget the disclosure Captain Dan had been about to make.

By the time she remembered to ask about it the captain had decided not to tell. None of the Dott household attended the Wainwright recital. Mr. Holway called on Wednesday, just after luncheon, to say that he had obtained the necessary cards, but his kindness went for nought. He stayed, so it seemed to Daniel, a good deal longer than was necessary, and Mr. Hungerford, who remained in the room every moment of the time, evidently thought so, too. So did Serena. Gertrude, however, was very cordial, and again begged the visitor not to hurry.

Saturday evening was that of the Chapter meeting, the meeting at which Gertrude was to be made a member. That forenoon Azuba electrified her mistress by expressing an ardent desire to become a member also.

"Why, what do you want to do that for, Azuba?" asked Serena in amazement.

"Why shouldn't I want to? You're a member, ain't you? Gertie's goin' to be a member to-night, ain't she?"

"Yes. But—but—"

"Well, but what?"

"I didn't know you were interested in such things. You never were when we lived in Trumet."

Azuba dismissed the past with a scornful sniff and a wave of the hand.

"Trumet!" she repeated. "We're in Scarford now, and Scarford's a progressive, up-to-date place. We've all changed since we've been here, and I'm changin' much as anybody. I've been hearin' your papers, when you read 'em to Gertie and the cap'n, and I've been readin' 'The Voice,' too. I'm goin' to be as up-to-date as the next one, even if I do have to wash dishes for a livin'. Serena—Mrs. Dott, I mean—I'd like first rate to join that Chapter of yours. You put my name in tonight and maybe it can be voted on next meetin'."

"But—but, Azuba, are you sure you know what it means? Do you think your husband would want you to—"

"My husband! What's he got to do with it? If we free women have got to be slaves to our husbands it's a pretty state of things, I must say. You don't ask your husband every time you go to meetin' whether he likes it or not. Husbands! Don't talk to me about husbands! THEY don't count."

Serena said that she would see what could be done and hurried away to discuss the new development with the family. "Of course she can't join," she declared. "It is ridiculous. The idea! I supposed she had more sense."

Daniel chuckled. "So did I," he observed, "until she got shoutin' independence to me the other day. All right, Serena, if Zuba Jane Ginn is goin' to make speeches at your Chapter meetin's, I'll go any time. You won't have to ask me but once."

He laughed aloud. His wife was vexed. "Of course you think it's a great joke," she said. "What do you suppose Annette and Mrs. Lake and the rest would say if I proposed my servant girl as a member? What are you grinning at now?"

Captain Dan, repressing his grin with difficulty, explained that he was thinking of what they would say. Serena, giving him up in disgust, turned to her daughter.

"Gertie," she begged, "why don't you say something? Azuba can't join that Chapter and you know it."

Gertrude shook her head.

"I suppose, she can't," she replied. "And yet, I'm afraid, Mother, that you will find that fact rather hard to explain to her. Azuba doesn't consider herself a servant, in the ordinary sense, at all. She feels, I think, that she is a friend of the family. And she has a right, of course, to improve and advance in every way. I am very much pleased to know she is so ambitious."

"Ambitious! Azuba Ginn! What does she know about progress or advancement? Who put such ridiculous ideas in her head?"

"Perhaps I did. She and I have had some long talks on the subject. I am very hopeful of Azuba. I shall help her all I can."

"Help her! Help her to what? To be too high and mighty for her place? Help her to be dissatisfied with her station in life?"

"Yes; why not? None of us should be satisfied, short of the very highest. Why, Mother, if you had been satisfied we might all be stagnating in Trumet."

Serena abandoned the argument.

After dinner that evening Gertrude and Serena hastened upstairs to dress for the Chapter meeting. Mr. Hungerford, after expressing his regret that the gathering was not to be an "open" one and he, therefore, would not be permitted to see Miss Dott become one of the elect, went out.

Just as the ladies descended the stairs the doorbell rang. Hapgood answered the ring, and the voice which replied to his polite query concerning the caller's name was a familiar one.

"Why!" exclaimed Serena, "it is—isn't that—"

"It's John!" cried Gertrude. "Why, JOHN!"

Mr. Doane pushed past the butler and entered the hall. His glance took in the group at the foot of the stairs, but it lingered upon only one member of it.

"Gertie!" he said, and stepped forward. Captain and Mrs. Dott looked the other way; Hapgood gave his attention to the closing of the door.

A moment later the young man was ready to shake hands with the less important inhabitants of the mansion. He did so heartily. "My!" he exclaimed, "but I'm glad to see you all. How are you?"

Serena answered. Captain Dan, his first surprise over, seemed nervous. "We're real well," declared Serena. "And it seems awfully good to have you here. Gertrude and I—"

Gertrude interrupted. "But, John," she said, "how did you happen to come so unexpectedly? I didn't know—you didn't write me a word about it."

"I didn't know it, myself. You know our junior partner, Mr. Griffin, has been very ill. He is very ill even yet, but he is a little better, and so I grabbed the opportunity. I should have come before, just as soon as—"

He paused. Daniel, in the background, was grimacing and shaking his head.

"As soon as what, John?" asked Gertrude.

"As soon as—as soon as I could. You're glad I came, aren't you; even if it was rather sudden?"

"Of course I am. You know it."

Her tone was hearty enough, and yet Mr. Doane seemed to find something lacking in it. Serena, too, looked quickly at her daughter.

"Of course she's glad," she declared. "So are we all. But what are we thinking of? Take off your things. Where's your trunk? Have the man bring it right in."

Captain Dan ushered the newcomer into the drawing-room. John exclaimed at the grandeur of the apartment.

"Whew!" he whistled. "You're fine, aren't you? Gertie wrote me how grand you were and I have been anxious to see the new house. Gertie—why, Gertie! what is it?"

Gertrude was standing in the doorway. She looked perplexed and troubled. John noticed, for the first time, that she was wearing her coat and hat.

"Were you going out?" he asked.

Gertrude hesitated. Serena answered for her. "Gertie and I were going out," she said. "It is Chapter night and she was going to be made a member. But you won't go now, of course, Gertie. I'll go—John will excuse me, I know—and you can join at the next meeting. It will be all right, I think."

But Gertrude still hesitated. Her father was surprised. "Why, Gertie!" he cried. "What are you standin' there for? 'Tain't likely you'll go to that meetin' now that John's come all the way from Boston to see you. Tell him you ain't goin'."

The young lady was plainly much disturbed. She looked at Mr. Doane and it was evident that she wanted to say something very much indeed. What she did say, however, was a surprise to everyone. "I—I ought to go, John," she faltered. "It is a very important meeting. I can't tell you—now—how important it is."

John's disappointment showed in his look, but his answer was prompt. "Then go, by all means," he said. "I'll go with you, if I won't be in the way."

But this self-sacrificing proposal was dubiously received by both the ladies. Serena shook her head. "I'm afraid you couldn't do that, John," she said.

"It isn't an open meeting, and men are not admitted. But Gertie doesn't need to go."

"Yes, I do, Mother."

"No, you don't. Of course you won't go and leave John here alone."

"Daddy will be with him and I shall hurry home as soon as I can. I must go, John; I really must. I will explain why later. If I had only known that you were coming! If you had only written me! WHY did you come without writing?"

Captain Dan, fearful of the answer, and indignant at his daughter's conduct, burst into protest. "You ought to be glad he's come, anyhow," he declared. "I cal'late he thought he'd surprise you, Gertie. And now you're goin' to clear out and leave him, just on account of that—that Chapter of yours. You never used to be crazy about Chapters. But since you've got here to Scarford—I can't help it, Serena; I'm mad clean through. Can't YOU tell that girl to stay to home where she belongs?"

"Gertie," began Serena, again; but her daughter would not listen.

"Don't, Mother!" she cried, "you are wasting time. We shall be late, as it is. John knows that my going is necessary, or I should not do it. He trusts me to that extent, I hope."

"Of course," said Mr. Doane heartily. "Run along and don't say any more about it. Come back as soon as you can, that's all. Shan't I come after you? I can wait outside until the thing is over."

"No; I don't intend to wait until it is over. Mother and I can take a cab. Come, Mother."

Serena reluctantly led the way to the hall.

"One moment, Mother," said Gertrude. She left Serena on the step and hurried back to the drawing-room. Captain Dan and John were standing there in silence.

"Daddy," said the young lady, "I think I left my pocketbook upstairs in my room. Will you get it for me?"

The captain ran to the stairs. Gertrude stepped quickly over to her lover. "John," she whispered, "you will forgive me, won't you, dear? I MUST go. It will spoil everything if I don't. You see—why, Daddy! you haven't found that pocketbook so soon!"

Daniel had reappeared in the doorway. "I sent Hapgood for it," he announced. "It's a good thing to make him work once in a while. He'll be down in a minute."

Gertrude did not seem pleased. "Oh!" she exclaimed. "Well, never mind. Why! here is the pocketbook in my bag, after all. Good-by, John. You and Daddy will have a lot to talk about, I know. Good-by."

The door closed behind her. Captain Dan stepped to the foot of the stairs.

"Found it yet?" he shouted.

Hapgood answered from above.

"No, sir, not yet."

"Then keep on lookin' till you do. It's a good excuse to keep him out of the way," he explained, turning to Mr. Doane. "Come on into the sittin'-room—library, I mean. The furniture ain't so everlastin' straight up and down there and there's somethin' to smoke."

In the library, with lighted cigars and in comfortable easy chairs, the two men looked at each other.

"Well, John," began the captain, "you—you come, didn't you?"

"Yes, of course. I should have come as soon as I got your letter, but I couldn't get away. I was going to tell you that."

"Yes," drily, "I know you was. If I hadn't cut across your bows, you would. Didn't I write you not to mention that letter to a livin' soul?"

"You did. But I couldn't understand why. What is all this secrecy, anyhow? And what is troubling you about Gertie?"

"Well, now, I don't know as there's anything."

"Humph! I judged there was a little of everything. What is the matter? Out with it.

"Well—we-ell—you see—you see—"

"I don't see anything, Captain Dott."

"You saw how she was set on goin' to that Chapter meetin', didn't you?"

"Yes, but what of it?"

"What OF it? Did she ever use to want to go to such things? And she's goin' to join the thing—join it, herself! As if one loon—I mean as if one Chapter member in the family wasn't enough. I thought when Gertie come home she'd probably keep her ma from goin' off the course altogether. But she didn't—she didn't. John, Gertie's got the Chapter disease worse than her ma ever had it, I do believe. You've got to talk to her, John."

John laughed. He did not take the situation very seriously. If Gertrude wished to become interested in the Chapter, he was willing she should. She probably had a good reason for it. Her insisting upon attending a meeting on the very evening of his arrival was odd—it did not seem like her—but she doubtless had a good reason for that, too.

"Why don't you talk to her yourself, Captain?" he asked.

"Me! Me talk to her! I have, and what good has it done? She won't listen to me any more. I don't mean she ain't kind to me and lovin' and all that—she wouldn't be Gertie if she wasn't that—but when it comes to Chapter business she's all on her ma's side."

"Why not talk to her mother, then?"

Daniel straightened in his chair. "To Serena!" he repeated. "Talk against Chapter to Serena! One time—just one—I did talk that way. I biled over and I damned that Chapter and the gang in it, cussed 'em in good plain United States. Once was enough."

He was so very serious that his companion fore-bore to laugh. "Why?" he asked.

"Why! John, you ain't married or you wouldn't ask that. I'm a peaceable body and I like peace in the house. That one damn made me miserable for two days. I never swore to Serena afore and I never will again. No, swearin' aboard ship is one thing but ashore in your own house, to the women folks you care for, it don't go. I can't talk to Serena about that Chapter—not even if I'm left alone ALL the time, same as I'm left to-night."

John nodded. He thought that, at last, he had reached the milk in the cocoa-nut. Captain Dan, with his love for home and his hatred of lodges and societies, had refused to be interested in his wife's pet hobby, and felt himself neglected and forsaken. He had brooded upon it, and this outburst and the letter he had written were the consequences.

"Oh, well," he said. "I shouldn't worry. The Chapter here is a large one and Mrs. Dott is interested in it. The interest will wear off when it gets to be an old story."

"Wear off! With Gertie goin' it harder than her mother ever thought of?"

"Oh, Gertie doesn't mean it."

"She DON'T! Perhaps you don't think she means it when she goes to every 'tea' and 'recital' and 'at home' and crazy dido from here to Beersheba and back. Is THAT goin' to wear off? Chasin' around with Cousin Percy and that Holway and land knows who?"

"What? Captain Dott, you're making mountains out of mole hills."

"That's what I said. That's what I used to think. It's this Scarford that's doin' it. It's this Scarford and the society crowd we've got in with. Annette Black—Barney Phelps's wife—is in society, and so's the Lake woman and that Canby piano pounder and that Dusante—my Godfreys! you ought to have seen her, John! She was the brazen thing. Dancin' around! And Gertie up and says she might like to dance that way. She! And Cousin Percy laughin' because she said it."

"Hold on! Wait a minute, Captain. What about this Cousin Percy of yours? He's living here with you, I know that; but what sort of a chap is he? And Holway—who is Holway?"

Daniel went on to explain who Holway was. Also he spoke of Mr. Hungerford and his ways and his intimacy with the family, particularly Gertrude. He gave his opinion of Hungerford and of Holway, the latter's friend. When John asked questions which implied a belief that the situation was not really as bad as the narrator thought it, Captain Dan, growing warmer and more anxious to justify himself, proceeded to make his statements stronger. Serena was crazy on the subjects of Chapter and Chapter politics and fashion and money and society, and Gertrude was getting to be even worse. It wasn't any use to talk to her. He had tried. He had told her she was engaged and ought to be more careful. He wasn't the only one who thought so. Barney Black had said the same thing.

John Doane listened, at first with the smile of the disbeliever, then with more and more uneasiness. He trusted Gertrude, he believed in her, but if these stories were true he could not understand. Captain Dan, with the best intentions in the world, and with the happiness of his daughter and John uppermost in his mind, succeeded in laying a mine which might wreck that happiness altogether.

At last something—perhaps the expression on his visitor's face—caused him to feel that he might have said too much. He hastened to rectify the mistake.

"Of course you mustn't think Gertie ain't all right, far's you're concerned, John," he said. "She is—I—I'm dead sure she is. But, you see—you see—You do see, don't you, John?"

Mr. Doane did not answer. He seemed to be thinking hard. "Yes, I suppose I do."

"And you know Gertie's all right—at heart, I mean? You mustn't be jealous, nor anything of that kind."

John laughed. "Don't talk nonsense," he said curtly.

"No, I won't. But—er—what are you thinkin' about?"

"Nothing. Humph! I can't understand—"

"Neither could I. That's why I wrote you. You see why I wrote you, don't you, John?"

"Yes—yes, I see why you wrote me; but—but I can't see why she didn't. She hasn't written me a word of all this."

And then the captain, in his anxiety to explain, made another indiscreet remark.

"Well," he observed, "I suppose likely she was afraid you might think that, now she had money—more money than she ever had before, I mean—and was in a different, a higher-toned crowd than she had ever been, that—that—well, that she was likin' that crowd better than the old one. She might have thought that, you know, mightn't she?"

Mr. Doane did not answer. Daniel had made a pretty thorough mess of it.

"Of course," went on the captain, "as far as Cousin Percy is concerned—"

John stirred uneasily. "Cousin Percy be hanged!" he snapped. "That's enough of this foolishness. Let's change the subject. How is Nate Bangs getting on with the store at home?"

At half-past ten the doorbell rang. Daniel sprang to his feet. "Here they are!" he declared. "Gertie come home early, just as she said she would. That's 'cause she wanted to see you, John. Hi!" shouting at Mr. Hapgood, who had long since given up the search for the missing pocketbook and had been dozing upstairs, "Hi! You needn't mind. Go aloft again! Go below! Go somewhere! We don't need you. I'll let 'em in, myself."

The butler, looking surprised, obeyed orders and went—somewhere. The captain flung open the door.

"Well!" he hailed. "Here you are! And pretty early for Chapter night, too. We're waitin' for you, John and I. Shall I pay the cab man?"

Serena, the first to enter, answered. "No," she said, "he is already paid."

"That so? Did you pay him, Serena? Thought that was my job usually. I—" Then, in a tone go entirely different that John Doane, in the drawing-room, noticed the change, he added, "Oh! oh! I, see."

"Come in," went on Serena. "Come right in, Cousin Percy."

She entered the drawing-room, followed by Gertrude and—Mr. Percy Hungerford.

"John," said Serena proudly, "we want you to meet our cousin, Mr. Hungerford. Percy, this is John."

John and Hungerford exchanged looks. The latter gentleman extended a gloved hand. "Charmed," he observed.

John expressed pleasure at the meeting. "So—so Cousin Percy came home with you, did he?" inquired Daniel.

"That was kind of unexpected, wasn't it?"

Mr. Hungerford himself answered. "Why," he declared, "not altogether, on my part I hoped for the pleasure. It seemed rather rough for Miss Dott and her mother to come alone, and so I hung about until the affair was over."

"He had a carriage all ready for us," declared Serena. "It was so thoughtful of him."

"Not at all. Great pleasure, really."

Gertrude made the next remark. "We did not need a carriage," she said. "Cousin Percy need not have troubled."

"John offered to come for you," said Daniel. "So did I. We'd have both come, but you wouldn't have us. Wouldn't accept our invitation, would they, John? Gave us to understand they didn't like our company."

"Cousin Percy did not wait for an invitation," explained Serena. "He just came. He is so thoughtful."

Gertrude looked annoyed. She had been regarding Mr. Doane. "Mother," she said sharply, "don't be silly. We did not ask for an escort and we didn't need one. The whole thing was quite unnecessary and unexpected. Come, Mother, do take off your things. Oh, I'm so glad to get home."

The ladies retired to remove their wraps. John made a move to go to their assistance, but Mr. Hungerford, attentive as usual, got ahead of him.

"Well, Daddy dear," said Gertrude, as they re-entered, "what have you and John been doing while we were away? I suppose you've had a long talk?"

Daniel colored. He looked at Mr. Doane, who, in spite of himself, colored also, and was tremendously annoyed because he did so. "Yes," said the captain hastily. "Yes, we talked. We talked, didn't we, John?"

"We did," affirmed John.

"I'm sure you did. And what about?"

"Oh—oh, about everything. How did the Chapter doin's go off? You're a member now, I suppose, Gertie?"

"Yes," was the brief reply.

"Um-hm! Well, I hope you're satisfied—I mean I hope you'll like it. Didn't make a speech, did you?"

Gertrude did not answer. Serena, to her husband's surprise, appeared vexed.

"But she did though, by Jove!" exclaimed Cousin Percy. "She did, and I'm told it created a great sensation. Miss Canby told me about it as I was waiting for you to come out, Gertrude. She said you gave them a brand-new idea. Something about the privileges of the Chapter being extended to the hoi polloi, wasn't it?"

The new member of Scarford Chapter looked more annoyed than ever. "I spoke of the Chapter's advantages being extended," she said, "that's all."

"And enough, too," cried her mother, impatiently. "Quite enough, I should think. If I had known you were going to do that, I should have stayed at home. It was that foolish Azuba who put the notion in your head. You'll be proposing her name next, I suppose."

Daniel burst into a roar of laughter. "What do you think of that, John?" he cried. "Zuby Jane makin' speeches! There's advancement for you, ain't it?"

John smiled, but rather faintly. He had scarcely taken his eyes from Cousin Percy's aristocratic presence. The latter gentleman turned to him.

"Well—er—Mr.—Mr. Doane," he observed carelessly, "how do you like Scarford, as far as you've seen it?"

John replied that he had seen very little of it.

"You'll find it a bit different from Trumet, I imagine."

"No doubt. I can see that already."

"But John doesn't come from Trumet," explained Serena; "that is, not now. He is in business in Boston."

Cousin Percy seemed surprised. "Indeed!" he drawled. He did not add "He doesn't look it," in words, but his manner expressed just that. Daniel caught his wife's eye. "Well, Serena," he observed, with a meaning wink, "I guess likely you're tired, ain't you? Time to go aloft and turn in, I should say."

Serena nodded. "Yes," she answered. "Gertrude, you and John will excuse us, won't you? Good-night! Good-night, Cousin Percy."

"Good-night!" said Mr. Hungerford.

"You'll excuse us, John, I'm sure," went on Serena. "Of course you and Gertie will want to talk, and," with a slight pause and a glance at Percy, "we will only be in the way. Come, Daniel."

Captain Dan paused in the doorway. "Ain't you tired, too, Cousin Percy?" he inquired.

It was a fairly broad hint, but Mr. Hungerford did not take it. "Oh, no," he replied; "not at all. Good-night, Captain."

He seated himself on the sofa. Daniel, frowning, followed his wife upstairs.

The conversation which ensued was confined almost altogether to Hungerford and Gertrude. John Doane had little to say, and less opportunity to say it. Each remark made by the young lady was answered by Percy, and that gentleman talked almost incessantly.

John began to feel himself an outsider. After a time he ceased trying to talk and relapsed into silence.

Gertrude noticed the silence and, seizing a moment when her entertaining cousin had paused, perhaps for breath, said, almost sharply: "John, why don't you say something? You haven't spoken for five minutes."

John said very little, even in reply to this accusation. "Haven't I?" he observed. "Well, what shall I say?"

"You might say something, considering that you and I haven't seen each other for so long."

Mr. Hungerford rose. "I hope I haven't interfered," he announced. "Didn't mean to intrude, I assure you. Beg pardon—er—Doane."

John did not answer. Gertrude also rose. "Good-night, Cousin Percy," she said, with a gracious smile. "Thank you so much for the carriage and your escort."

"Quite welcome. Pleasure was mine. Goodnight, Gertrude. Oh, by the way, I believe you and I are to go over that paper of your mother's tomorrow. She asked my advice and said you would assist, I think. I shall look forward to that assistance. Good-night, Doane. Glad to have met you, I'm sure."

He strolled out. Upon reaching his room he discovered that his cigar case was empty. Hapgood not being on hand and, feeling the need of a bedtime smoke, he tiptoed down the stairs and through the back hall into the library. The room was dark, but sufficient light shone between the closed curtains of the drawing-room to enable him to locate Captain Dan's box. Silently and very slowly he refilled the case.

John Doane and Gertrude, alone at last, looked at each other. The former was very solemn. Gertrude, quite aware of the solemnity, but not aware of its principal cause was nervous and a bit impatient.

"Well, John," she asked, after a moment's wait, "aren't you going to say anything to me even now?"

John tried his best to smile. It was a poor attempt. "Why, yes," he said slowly, "I came all the way from Boston to see you and talk to you, Gertie. There is no reason why I shouldn't say—whatever there is to say, I suppose."

Gertrude looked at him. The tone in which this speech was delivered, and the speech itself amazed and hurt her. Incidentally, her temper having been sorely tried already that evening by Mr. Hungerford, it made her angry.

"All the way from Boston," she repeated. "Well, I never knew you to complain in that way before. I'm sorry to have caused you so much trouble."

"It wasn't a trouble, Gertie. You know I would go around the world for you."

"Then why speak of coming all the way from Boston? Whose fault was it, pray? Did I ask you to come?"

And now, John, who had been fighting his own temper for some time, grew angry.

"You did not," he declared. "But I judge it was time I did."

"Indeed! Indeed! Why?"

"Well—well, for various reasons. Of course, had I known my coming would interfere with your—your precious Chapter affairs and—"

"John, I had to go to that meeting. If you had written you were coming I shouldn't have gone. I should have made other arrangements. But you didn't write."

"I wrote every day."

"Yes, but you did not write you were coming here."

"I didn't think it was necessary. You wrote every day, too, but you didn't write—you didn't write—"

"What?"

"A good many things that—that I have learned since I came here."

"Indeed! What things? How did you learn them?"

"I—" John hesitated. To bring Captain Dan's name into the conversation would be, he felt, disloyal. And it would surely mean trouble for the captain. "I—I learned them with my own eyes," he declared. "Gertie, I can't understand you."

"And I don't understand you. I told you, at the only moment we have had together, I told you then that I would explain about the Chapter. I said that I must go or everything would be spoiled. You very nearly spoiled it by coming as you did."

Mr. Doane's expression changed. It had softened when she reminded him of the whispered word in the drawing-room. The last sentence, however, brought his frown back again.

"Well!" he exclaimed. "Well—humph! that's easily remedied. I came in a hurry and I can go the same way."

"John! John, what do you mean? How can you speak so to me! Would you go away now that—that—"

"You wouldn't miss me so much, I should imagine. Cousin Percy will be here, and you and he seem to be very confidential and friendly, to say the least."

Gertrude gasped. She was beginning to understand, or imagined that she was.

"Why, John!" she cried. "You're not jealous!"

John looked rather foolish. "No-o," he admitted doubtfully, "I'm not jealous. Of course I'm not, but—"

"But what? Don't you trust me, John? Don't you?"

"Of course I do. You know I do, but—See here, Gertie, you said you were going to explain—to explain something or other. Do it, then. I think I am entitled to an explanation."

But Gertrude's merriment had vanished. Her eyes flashed. "I shall not explain," she said. "You don't trust me. I can see you don't."

"I do. I do, Gertie, really; but—but—"

"But you don't. You think—you think—oh, I don't know WHAT you think! No, I shall not explain, not now, at all events. Good-night!"

She hastened from the room. John ran after her. "Gertie," he cried, "you're not going? You're not going to leave me in this way, without a word? I do trust you. I only said—"

"It wasn't what you said; it was the way you said it. I am shocked—yes, and hurt, John. I shall not speak to you again to-night. To-morrow perhaps, if you beg my pardon and I am really sure you do trust me, I may tell you—what I was going to tell. But not now. I—I didn't think you would treat me so."

She put her handkerchief to her eyes and hurried up the stairs. John, standing irresolute on the lower step, hesitated, fighting down his own pride and sense of injury. That moment of hesitation was freighted with consequence. Then: "Gertie," he cried, hastening after her, "Gertie, wait! I do beg your pardon. I didn't mean—"

But it was too late. Gertie's chamber door closed. John went slowly up to his own room, the room to which the butler had carried his bag. A few minutes after he had gone the curtains between the library and drawing-room parted and Mr. Hungerford appeared. He was very cautious as he, too, ascended the stairs. But his expression was a pleasant one; there was no doubt that Cousin Percy was pleased about something.

CHAPTER XI

Captain Dan stirred uneasily. In his dream he had navigated the *Bluebird*, his old schooner, to a point somewhere between Hatteras and Race Point light. It was night all at once, although it had been day only a few minutes before, and Azuba, who, it seemed, was cook aboard the *Bluebird*, was washing breakfast dishes in the skipper's stateroom. She was making a good deal of noise about it, jingling pans and thumping the foot of the berth with a stick of stove wood. The captain was about to remonstrate with her when Serena suddenly appeared to ask him if he had not heard the bell, and why didn't he come into the house, because dinner was ready. Then Azuba stopped pounding the foot of the berth and began to thump him instead.

"Don't you hear the bell?" repeated Serena. "Wake up! Daniel! Daniel!"

Daniel stirred and opened his eyes. The *Bluebird* had vanished, so had Azuba, but the thumps and jingles were real enough.

"Hey?" he mumbled, drowsily. "Stop poundin' me, won't you?"

"Pounding you! I've been pounding and shaking you for goodness knows how long. Don't you hear the bell?"

Daniel, still but two-thirds awake, rolled over, raised himself on his elbow and grunted, "Bell! What bell?"

"The door bell. Someone's at the door."

Captain Dan slid out of bed. His bare feet struck the cold floor beneath the open window and he was wide awake at last. The room was pitch dark, so morning had not come, and yet someone WAS at the door, the front door.

"For mercy sakes!" he grumbled, glancing at his watch hanging beside the head of the bed, "it's quarter past one. Who in time is turnin' us out this time of night?"

Serena, nervous and frightened answered sharply. "I don't know," she snapped. "It's something important though, or they wouldn't do it. Hurry up and find out, can't you?"

Her husband hastened to the closet, found his slippers and bathrobe and shuffled out into the hall. The bell had awakened other members of the household. A light shone under the door of John Doane's room, and from Gertrude's apartment his daughter's voice demanded to know what was the matter.

Daniel announced that he didn't know, but cal'lated to find out, and shuffled down the stairs. Captain Dan unlocked the front door and flung it open. A uniformed messenger boy was standing on the steps.

"Telegram for John Doane," announced the boy. "Any answer?"

Daniel seized the proffered envelope. "How in time do I know whether there's any answer or not?" he demanded pettishly. "I ain't read it yet, have I? Why in the nation didn't you ring up on the telephone, instead of comin' here and routin' out the neighborhood?"

The boy grinned. "Against the rules," he said. "Can't send telegrams by 'phone unless we have special orders."

"Well, I give you orders then. Next time you telephone. Hold on a minute now. John! oh, John!"

Mr. Doane, partially dressed, his coat collar turned up to hide the absence of linen, was already at the head of the stairs, and descending.

"Coming, Captain Dott," he said. "For me, is it?"

"Yes. A telegram for you. What—good land, Gertie! you up, too?"

Gertrude, in kimono and cap, was leaning over the rail. "What is it?" she asked quickly.

John announced, "A wire for me," he said. "I'm afraid—" He tore open the envelope. "Yes, I thought so. Mr. Griffin is worse and they want me at once. I must go—now. When is the next train for Boston, Captain?"

Daniel was very much flustered. "I don't know," he stammered. "There's a time-table around on deck somewheres, but—you ain't goin' now, John? To-night?"

"Yes, I must."

Gertrude hastened to find the time-table. John turned to the messenger.

"Know anything about Boston trains?" he asked.

"Yup. Two-twenty express through from New York. That's the next."

John stepped to the drawing-room and looked at the clock. "I can get it, I think," he announced. "I must. If I can get a cab—"

"I'll 'phone for one. But—but, John, you hadn't ought to—"

"Any answer?" demanded the messenger boy, intent on business.

"Yes. Say that I am leaving on the two-twenty. On the two-twenty. Got that, have you?"

"Sure, Mike! Prepay or collect?"

"I'll—I'll pay it, John." Captain Dan reached under his bathrobe. "Hey!" he exclaimed. "I declare I forgot I didn't have on—All right, John, I'll pay it. You go get ready."

Mr. Doane was on his way to his room. The captain paid the messenger and hastened to telephone for the cab. When the vehicle arrived, John was ready. His farewells to Daniel and Serena were hurried ones.

"I'm awfully sorry I can't stop longer," he declared. "I really shouldn't have come at all, under the circumstances. I—"

He paused. Gertrude was standing by the door. She was very grave and her eyes looked as if she had not slept. John went over to her; he, too, was grave.

"Gertie," he faltered, "Gertie—"

Serena interrupted. "Daniel!" she said, "Daniel!"

The captain looked at her. She frowned and motioned with her head. The light of understanding dawned in her husband's eyes.

"Hey? Oh, yes!" he cried hastily. "Come into the front room, Serena, just a minute. I want to speak to you."

They entered the drawing-room together. Gertrude and John were alone. For a moment neither spoke. Then the young man, bending forward, whispered: "Gertie," he asked anxiously, "aren't you—haven't you anything to say to me?"

"I thought, perhaps, you had something to say to me, John."

"I have. Gertie, I—"

There was a sound from above. Cousin Percy Hungerford, fully dressed and debonnair as always, was descending the stairs. "What's the row?" he drawled. "I heard the racket and decided the house must be on fire. What's up?"

Whatever else was "up" it was quite plain John was sorry that Mr. Hungerford was up because of it. His tone was decidedly chilly as he answered. "A wire for me," he said shortly. "I'm called to Boston at once."

"Really! Sorry to have you go, Doane, I'm sure."

He spoke as if he were the host whose gracious pleasure it had been to entertain the guest during the latter's stay. John resented the tone.

"Thanks," he said crisply. "Gertie, I—I hope—"

He hesitated. It was not easy to speak in the presence of a third person, particularly this person. Cousin Percy did not hesitate.

"Gertie," he observed, "your—er—friend is leaving us at the wrong time, isn't he? There's so much going on this coming week.

Really, Doane, you're fortunate, in a sense. Miss Dott and I are finding the social whirl a bit tiresome; you will escape that, at least."

Captain Dan appeared at the entrance to the drawing-room. "I say, Hungerford! Percy!" he hailed impatiently.

Mr. Hungerford did not seem to hear him. He was regarding Miss Dott with anxious concern. "Really, Gertrude," he said, "I shouldn't stand by that open door, if I were you. You have a slight cold and you must be careful. Step inside, I beg of you."

His begging was so tender, so solicitous, so intimate. John Doane's fists clenched.

"Hi!" It was the cabman calling from the street. "Hi! we've only got twelve minutes to catch that train."

John turned, involuntarily, toward the door. Gertrude, startled by the cabman's voice and aware of the need of haste, stepped to one side. Cousin Percy chose to put his own interpretation upon her movement.

"Thank you, Gertrude," he said feelingly. "That's better; you will be out of the draft there. Thank you."

John Doane, who was still hesitating, hesitated no longer. He seized his bag. "Good-by, all," he said, in a choked voice.

He strode through the doorway. Gertrude, for a moment, remained where she was. Then she followed him.

"John!" she cried, "John!"

John, half way down the steps, halted, turned, and looked up at her.

"Good-by, Gertie," he said.

"But, John, are you—aren't you—"

She stretched out her hands. Mr. Hungerford, pushing by the Captain and Serena, stepped in front of her.

"Here, you!" he shouted, addressing the cabman; "what are you thinking about? Why don't you take the gentleman's bag?"

The driver sprang to get the bag, incidentally he seized his prospective passenger by the arm. "Come on!" he shouted. "Come on! We'll miss the train. Ten to one we've missed it, anyhow."

"Oh, DO hurry, John!" cried Serena, anxiously. "You WILL miss it. You MUST go!"

And Mr. Doane went. Daniel drew a long breath. "Well!" he said slowly, "he's gone. Yes, sir, he's gone, ain't he."

Serena turned on him. "Yes, he's gone," she observed sarcastically, "but he isn't going very fast. Why in the world didn't you order an electric cab instead of that Noah's Ark? Half the neighbors have been waked up and they'll see it. How many times must I tell you?"

"Well, now, Serena—"

"Don't talk to me! Don't! My nerves are all of a twitter. I—I—oh, do let me go to bed! Gertie—why, Gertie, where are you going?"

Gertrude was on her way to the stairs. She did not appear to hear her mother's question.

"Gertie!" cried Serena again.

There was no answer. The young lady hurried up the stairs and they heard her chamber door close. Cousin Percy shrugged his shoulders. "Too bad our friend was called away so suddenly," he observed.

No one replied, not even Serena, who was not wont to ignore the comments of her aristocratic relative. Her next remark was in the nature of an order and was addressed to her husband.

"Come!" she said fretfully. "Do come to bed!"

Daniel, pausing only to extinguish the lights, obeyed. Mr. Hungerford, with another shrug and a covert smile, preceded him up the stairs.

There were some inmates of the Dott mansion who, probably, slept peacefully the remainder of that night, or morning. But neither Captain Dan or Serena slept. Mrs. Dott's nerves kept her awake, and the combination prevented Daniel from napping. She was fretful and impatient of trifles, and the least contradiction or upset of her plans was likely to bring on fits of hysterical weeping. It was so in this case. Daniel, trotting for smelling salts and extra pillows and the hot water bottle, was not too calm himself. His plans, the plans founded upon John Doane's remaining in Scarford for a time, had been decidedly upset. He pleaded with his wife.

"But I don't see what ails you, Serena," he declared. "John's gone, that's true enough, but you didn't know he was comin'. He was here, a little while, and that's some gain, ain't it? I don't see—"

"See! You wouldn't see if your eyes were spyglasses. I thought when John came that Gertie—"

"Yes. That Gertie what?"

"Oh, nothing, nothing! Oh, my poor head! It aches so and the back of it feels so queer. Can't you get me another pillow?"

"Sure I can! You've got three already, but I can fetch another. It's all this society business that's breakin' you down, Serena. That everlastin' Chapter—"

He was sorry as soon as he said it, but said it had been. He spent the next hour in explaining that he did not mean it.

Serena was not on hand at breakfast time. Neither was Gertrude. That young lady came into the library at ten o'clock, looking pale and worn and with dark circles under her eyes. She had a thick envelope in her hand.

"Daddy," she said, "will you post this for me?"

Her father looked up from the pile of papers on the writing table before him. He, too, appeared somewhat worried.

"Sartin," he announced promptly. "I've got a stack of stuff for the postman, myself. Bills and checks they are, mostly. Say, Gertie," gravely, "it costs a sight to run this place, did you know it?"

"I suppose it does."

"You bet it does! Why, I never realized—But there, I suppose likely these bills are heavier than usual. But, of course they are. I'll ask Serena about 'em by and by, when she's better. Give me your letter, Gertie, I'll mail it."

"You won't forget?"

"Not a mite. I'll put it right here with the others and give 'em to the postman when he comes. Humph! it's to John, isn't it? You're pretty prompt in your writin', ain't you? But that's natural; I remember when I used to write your mother twice a day. It's a wonder she stood it and kept her health, ain't it. Ha! ha!"

He chuckled and turned back to his bills and the checkbook. Gertrude left the room. Captain Dan wrote and enclosed and affixed stamps. The pile of envelopes on the table grew steadily larger. Mr. Hungerford entered, seeking the cigar box.

"Good-morning," he observed, cheerfully.

Daniel looked up, grunted, and went on with his work. Cousin Percy smiled. A querulous voice called from the second floor. "Daniel!" called Serena. "Daniel, where are you? Why don't you come up? I am all alone."

The captain sprang to his feet, "Comin'! Serena!" he shouted. "Comin'!"

He hurried out. Mr. Hungerford, left alone, helped himself to a cigar and strolled about the room. The pile of letters on the table caught his attention. Idly he turned the envelopes over, examining the addresses. All at once his interest became less casual; one of the written names had caught his attention.

Five minutes later the postman rang the doorbell. Captain Dan ran downstairs, entered the library, seized the letters from the table and hastened to hand them to the carrier.

"Daddy!" called Gertrude from above, "did you post my letter?"

"Sure!" was the prompt answer. "Just gave it to the mail man. It's on the road now."

Serena's "nerves" were in much better condition the following day, and her spirits likewise. Gertrude, however, was still grave and absent-minded and non-communicative. Toward Mr. Hungerford in particular she was cool and distant, answering his chatty remarks and solicitous inquiries concerning her health with monosyllables, and, on several occasions, leaving the room when he entered it.

She seemed nervously expectant when the postman brought the mail, and depressed when each consignment contained no letter for her. This depression was so marked that her father asked the cause.

"What ails you, Gertie?" he inquired.

Gertrude, who was standing by the window, looking out, answered without turning her head.

"Nothing," she said shortly.

"Well, I'm glad of that. Ain't frettin' about John, are you?"

His daughter looked at him now, and the look was a searching one. "About—Why should I fret about him, pray?" she asked slowly.

"I don't know. I thought maybe his goin' away so sudden was a sort of disappointment to you. 'Twas to the rest of us. Hey? Did you say somethin'?"

"No."

"Oh, I thought you did. Well, you mustn't be disappointed, Gertie. You see, business is business. John did what he thought was right and—"

"Daddy, do be still. I do not intend to trouble myself about—him. Don't talk to me, please. I don't feel like talking."

Daniel talked no more, at that time, but he wondered, and determined to ask Serena her opinion when the opportunity came.

It did not come immediately. A new development in Chapter politics was occupying Mrs. Dott's mind, a development so wonderful and so glorious in its promise that that lady could think or speak of little else. Mrs. Lake's term as president of Scarford Chapter was nearing its end. Annette Black, the vice-president, would have been, in the regular course of events, Mrs. Lake's successor to the high office. But Mrs. Lake and Annette, bosom friends for years, had had a falling out. Annette announced her candidacy in meeting, and the very next day Mrs. Lake came to Serena with an amazing proposition.

The proposition was this: Mrs. Lake, it seemed, wished to become secretary of the National Legion. In order to do this—or to become even a prominent candidate—it was necessary for her to have the support of the officers of her own Chapter. If Mrs. Black was elected president she most decidedly would not have this support.

"That woman is a cat," she declared, "a spiteful underhanded cat. She shan't be president. Now, my dear Mrs. Dott, I am counting on you—and your daughter, of course. We must select some woman for the presidency who will command the respect and get the votes of all disinterested members. YOU shall be our candidate. YOU shall be president of Scarford Chapter."

Serena gasped. "Me?" she cried. "Me? President?"

"Yes, you. You are liked and respected by every member. You are known to be rich—I mean cultured and progressive and broad-minded. We can elect you and we will."

There was one strong qualification possessed by Mrs. Dott which the bearer of good news omitted to mention. Serena was supposed to be Annette Black's most devoted friend. Announcement of her candidacy would have the effect of splitting the Black party in twain. Mrs. Lake and her followers were very much aware of this, although their spokeswoman said nothing about it.

"You'll accept, of course," gushed Mrs. Lake. "I shall be so proud to vote and work for you."

Serena hesitated. The honor of being president of her beloved Chapter was a dazzling prospect. And yet—and yet—"You will, won't you?" begged the caller.

"No," said Serena. "No, Mrs. Lake, I can't. I could not run against Annette Black. She is my best and dearest friend. No, Mrs. Lake, I am not that kind of a friend. No."

"But—"

"Please don't speak of it again. Let's talk of something else."

But Mrs. Lake did not want to talk of anything else. She urged and argued and pleaded in vain. Then she began to lose her temper. The parting was not cordial.

And then came Mrs. Black, herself. She, somehow or other, had learned of the offer to be made Serena. When she found that the latter had refused that offer because of loyalty to her, she fairly bubbled over.

"You dear!" she cried, embracing her hostess. "It was what I expected; I knew you'd do it; but I'm SO happy and SO grateful. I never shall forget it—never. And whenever I can prove my loyalty and devotion to you, be sure I shall do it."

Serena was touched and gratified, but there was just a shade of disappointment in her tone as she answered. "I know you will," she said. "Of course, I had rather be president of Scarford Chapter than anything else in the world, but—"

And then Annette had an idea. She clasped her hands. “You shall be,” she cried. “You shall be. Not this term, but the next—the very next. This term I shall be president, and you—YOU shall be vice-president.”

And on that basis it was settled. The opposing tickets were Black and Dott against Canby and a lady by the name of Saunderson, another of Mrs. Lake’s “dear friends.” The Chapter was racked from end to end. Politics became the daily food of its members.

For Serena it was almost the only food. She was too busy to eat, except at odd times and hurriedly, and she slept less than ever. Her nervousness increased and she lost weight. Daniel was worried concerning her health and would have mentioned his worriment to Gertrude had not that young lady’s mental state and behavior worried him almost as much.

Gertrude, for the first week after John Doane’s departure, was depressed and silent and solemn. Once, her father found her in her room, crying and when he anxiously asked the reason she bade him go away and leave her, so sharply and in a tone so unlike her, that he went without further protestation. He did, however, go to Serena for advice.

“Oh, I don’t know,” said Serena impatiently. “She misses John, I suppose. She thought he was going to stay and he didn’t, and she was disappointed. Don’t bother me! I’m so tired and headachy and nervous I think I shall die. Go away.”

“But, Serena, there’s—there’s somethin’ queer about Gertie and John. I don’t believe she’s heard from him since he left.”

“Then, why doesn’t she write and find out what is the matter? Perhaps he’s sick.”

“Maybe so, but perhaps she don’t want to write. Perhaps she’s waitin’ for him to do it.”

“He can’t write if he’s sick, can he? Why don’t she telegraph him?”

“That would be just the same, the way she may look at it.”

“Then wire him yourself, why don’t you? I’ll speak to her, Daniel, when I get time; I was going to. But just now I—oh, my POOR head!”

Daniel made up his mind to telegraph Doane that very afternoon, but he did not. A happening in the household prevented him. Mr. Hapgood was summarily discharged.

Azuba was responsible for the affair. Captain Dan, in the library, dolefully musing in an arm chair, heard a violent altercation in the kitchen. As it did not cease, but became more violent, he hastened to the scene.

Azuba was standing in the middle of the kitchen, her back against the table, facing the butler. Mr. Hapgood’s face was red, his fists were clenched, and he was shaking one of them under the housekeeper’s nose.

“Give it to me!” he ordered. “‘And it over now, or I’ll bash you good and ‘ard.”

Azuba merely smiled. “You’ll bash nobody,” she declared. “You’re a thief, that’s what you are—a low-down thief. Don’t you dare shake your fist at me. If my husband was here he’d—”

Hapgood interrupted, savagely consigning the Ginns, both male and female, to a much hotter place than the kitchen. Captain Dan strode into the room.

“Here!” he said sharply. “What’s all this? You,” addressing Hapgood, “what, do you mean by shakin’ your fist at a woman?”

Mr. Hapgood’s bluster collapsed, like a punctured toy balloon. He cringed instead. “W’y, sir,” he pleaded, “it wasn’t anything. I lost my temper a bit, sir, that’s all. She”—with a malignant snarl at Azuba—"she’s got a letter of mine. She stole it and won't give it up. I was angry, sir, same as any man would 'ave been, and I forgot myself. Make 'er 'and over my letter, sir."

The captain turned to the defiant Mrs. Ginn. "Have you got a letter of his, Zuba?" he demanded.

Azuba laughed. "I have," she declared, "and I'm glad of it. I've been waiting to get somethin' like it for a long spell. Stealin'! HE accuse anybody of stealin'! Here, Daniel Dott, you read that letter. Read it and see who's been doin' the stealin' around here."

She extended the letter at arm's length. It bore the printed name and address of one of Scarford's newer and more recently established grocers and provision dealers, and read as follows:

EDWARD H. HAPGOOD,

SIR:—Our order clerk informs us that you expect a higher percentage of commission on goods ordered by your household. We do not feel that we should pay this. While we, being a new house, were willing, in order to obtain your business, to allow a fair rate of commission to you for putting it in our way, and while, during the past three months, we have paid such commission, we do not feel—

Daniel tossed the note on the floor. He marched to the door leading to the back yard and threw it open. Then he turned to the butler.

"See that door?" he inquired, pointing toward it. "Use it."

Hapgood did not seem to comprehend. "Wh-what, sir?" he faltered.

"Use that door. Get out! Out of this house, and don't you dare show your nose inside it again. Here!" stepping to the rack behind the open door. "These are your—duds—aren't they? Take 'em and get out."

He threw an overcoat and hat at the astonished man-servant, who caught them mechanically.

"Get!" repeated the captain.

Hapgood apparently understood at last. His usual expression of polite humility vanished and he glowered malevolently. "So I'm fired, am I?" he demanded. "Fired, without no notice or nothin'. 'Ow about my two weeks' wages? 'Ow about my things upstairs? I've got rights, I 'ave, and you'll find it out. Blame your eyes, I—"

He darted through the doorway just in time. Captain Dan was on the threshold. "You can send for your things upstairs," said the captain. "They'll be ready—either up there or on the sidewalk. Now, my—hum—thief," with deliberate and dangerous calmness, "I'm comin' out into that yard. If I was you I'd be somewhere else when I get there. That's my advice."

The advice was taken. Mr. Hapgood was in the street by the time his employer reached the gate. Bolting that gate, Daniel walked back to the kitchen.

"Thank you, Zuba," he said quietly.

Azuba was regarding him with a surprise in which respect was strongly mingled. "You're welcome," she said drily. "But," her surprise getting the better of her judgment, "I must say I ain't seen you behave—I mean—"

She stopped, the judgment returning. But Captain Dan read her thoughts and answered them. "He's a man," he said shortly, "or an apology for one. I know how to deal with a MAN—his kind, anyway."

Azuba nodded. "I should say you did," she observed. "Well, if you'd like to hear the whole yarn, how I come to suspect him and all, I can tell you. You see—"

But Daniel would not listen. "I don't want to hear it," he said. "Tell Serena, if you want to, when she comes home. I've got too much else on my mind to bother with swabs like him. If he should try to come back again you can call me, otherwise not. I ain't interested."

And yet, if he could have seen and heard his ex-butler just at that moment, he might have been interested. Hapgood, on the next corner, out of sight from the Dott home, had met and waylaid Mr. Percy Hungerford. Cousin Percy seemed disturbed and angry.

"It's your own fault," he declared. "You ought to have been more careful."

"Careful! 'Ow should I know the fools was going to write a letter? And 'ow did I know the old woman—blast 'er—was watchin' me all the time? And now I've lost my job, and a good soft job, too. You've got to get it back for me, Mr. 'Ungerford; you've got to 'elp me, sir."

"I'll help you all I can, of course, but I doubt if it will do any good. I can't stand talking with you here. Drop me a line at the club, telling me where you are, and I'll let you know what turns up. Oh, say, have any more letters come for—you know who?"

"No, that was the only one, sir. But a telegram came this morning."

Mr. Hungerford started. "A telegram?" he repeated. "For her?"

"Yes, sir. And from 'im, it was, too."

"Did she get it?"

Mr. Hapgood winked. "It was 'phoned up from the telegraph office, sir," he said, "and I answered the 'phone. 'Ere's the copy I made, sir."

He extracted a slip of paper from his pocket. Cousin Percy snatched the slip and read the penciled words. Hapgood smiled. "Looks good, don't it, sir," he observed. "'Frisco's a long way off."

Hungerford did not answer. He tore the paper into small pieces and tossed them away. "Well," he said, after a moment, "good by and good luck. Let me know where you are and meanwhile I'll see what can be done for you. Good by."

He was moving off, but his companion stepped after him. "Just a minute, sir," he said. "Could you 'elp me out a bit, in the money way? I'm flat broke; the old 'ayseed chucked me without a penny; 'e did, so 'elp me."

Cousin Percy looked distinctly annoyed. "I'm pretty nearly broke myself," he declared, impatiently.

"Is that so, sir, I'm sorry, but I think you'll 'ave to 'elp me a bit. I think—I think you'd better, Mr. 'Ungerford, sir."

Hungerford looked at him. The look was returned. Then the young gentleman extracted a somewhat attenuated roll of bills from his pocket, peeled off two and handed them to his companion.

"There you are," he replied. "That's all and more than I can spare, just now. Good by."

"Good by, sir—for now. And thank you kindly."

Captain Dan, for all his prompt handling of the thieving butler and his professed ability to deal with men awaited the return of his wife and daughter with considerable uneasiness. Hapgood, in his capacity as trained, capable, aristocratic servant, had been a favorite of Serena's. The captain dreaded telling his wife what he had done. But his dread was needless. Serena's mind was too much occupied with politics and political ambition to dwell upon less important matters.

"I suppose it is all right," she said. "If he was a thief he should be discharged, of course. No doubt you did right, Daniel, but we shall miss him dreadfully. I don't know where we can get another butler like him."

Daniel gasped. "Good land of love!" he cried; "we don't WANT another like him, do we!"

"I don't mean another thief. Why do you pick me up in that way? One would think you took a delight in worrying me all you could. Get me a cup of tea. My nerves are all unstrung. Gertie—"

But Gertie had gone to her room; she spent the greater part of her time there now. Her mother sighed.

"She's gone," she declared. "I can't see what has got into her for the last few days. She was so interested in the Chapter. And yet, at the committee meeting this afternoon—the most important meeting we've had; when we were counting the votes which we can be sure of and those that are doubtful, she scarcely said a word. I don't know what is the matter with her."

Daniel nodded. "I think I do," he said. "It's John. Somethin's the matter between her and John. If he had only stayed here! If he would only come back!"

"Then for mercy sakes get him back! Telegraph him. You said you were going to."

Captain Dan rose. "I will," he declared. "I'll do it right now, this minute. Not till I see you to your tea, Serena," he added, hastily. "I'll tell Zuba about that first, of course."

He sent the telegram within the hour. It was an inquiry concerning Mr. Doane's whereabouts, his employer's health, how he was getting on, and when he—John—was to return to Scarford. The answer arrived, via telephone, about eight that evening.

"Doane gone to San Francisco on business of the firm," it said. "Left at midnight yesterday."

It was signed by the senior partner. Serena had gone out, of course; she was scarcely ever in now, but Gertrude, having finished dinner, was in her room as usual. Her father hurried up the stairs.

"Gertie," he cried, entering without knocking, "Gertie, what do you suppose I've just found out? It's the most astonishing news. John is—he has—Why, you'd never guess!"

Gertrude, who was sitting in the rocking chair by the window, showed her first sign of interest. At the mention of the name she turned quickly.

"What?" she cried, in a startled voice. "What? Is it—is it bad news? He isn't—isn't—"

"No, no! He's all right. But he—Here! read it yourself."

Gertrude took the paper upon which he had written the message. She read the latter through; read it and reread it. Then she turned to her father.

"But I can't understand," she faltered. "I can't—I can't understand. He didn't send this himself. He has gone to San Francisco; but—but this is signed by someone else. What does it mean?"

Daniel was frightened. It was time to explain, and yet, considering his daughter's look and manner, he was afraid to explain.

"You see," he stammered, "well, you see, Gertie, that's an answer, that is. John didn't send it, he'd gone. But, I presume likely they thought my telegram ought to be answered, so—"

Gertrude interrupted. "Your telegram?" she repeated. "YOUR telegram? What telegram?"

"Why, the telegram I sent to John. I knew you hadn't heard from him, and I thought probably—"

"Wait—wait a minute. Did YOU send a telegram to—to him?"

"Yes; sure I did. I—"

"What did you say?"

"I said—why, I said that you—we, I mean—was wonderin' about him and—and missin' him and when was he comin' back here. That's about what I said. Why, what's the matter?"

Gertrude had risen.

"You said that!" she cried. "You—without a word to me—said—you begged him to come back! Begged him! on your knees! to—to—"

"No, no! I never got on my knees. What would I do a fool thing like that for, when I was sendin' a telegram? I just asked—"

"You just asked! You said that I—I—And this was your answer! THIS!"

She dashed the message to the floor, covered her face with her hands and threw herself upon the bed. Daniel, aghast and alarmed, would have raised her but she pushed him away.

"Oh!" she cried. "The shame of it!"

"But, Gertie—what on earth?"

"Just go away, Daddy. Go and leave me. I mustn't talk to you now. If I do, I shall say—Please go. I want to be alone."

Daniel went. That he had made another blunder was plain enough, but just now he was too hurt and indignant to care a great deal.

"All right," he said shortly; "I'm goin'. That's about all the orders I get nowadays—to go away. I ought to be used to it, by this time. I'm a fool, that's what I am, an old worn-out, useless fool."

He slammed the door and descended the stairs. He had been in his accustomed refuge, the library, for perhaps twenty minutes, when the bell rang. He waited for Hapgood to answer the ring and then, suddenly remembering that the butler had departed, answered it himself.

Mr. Monty Holway smiled greeting from the steps. "Good evening, Captain Dott," he said. "Is Miss Dott in?"

Daniel hesitated. "Yes," he said, "she's in, but—"

"May I see her? Will you be good enough to give her my card?"

The captain took the card. "Ye-es," he said, "I'll give it to her, but—but—Well, you see, she ain't feelin' very well this evenin' and I don't know as she'll want to see anybody."

Gertrude herself called from the head of the stairs. "Who is it, Daddy?" she asked.

"It's—er—Mr. Holway."

"Oh, is it!" The tone was one of delighted surprise. "Ask him to come in, Daddy. I'll be right down."

She came almost immediately. She greeted the caller with outstretched hand.

"I'm so glad to see you, Mr. Holway," she said. "It was nice of you to come."

She was pale, and the dark circles under her eyes were more apparent than ever, but the eyes themselves were shining brightly. She was gay and, for her, extremely vivacious. Mr. Holway looked gratified and happy. Captain Dan looked astonished and bewildered.

CHAPTER XII

The bewilderment and astonishment remained with the captain for some time, just as his daughter's apparent light heartedness remained with her. Holway's call was longer than usual, lasting until Serena, escorted by Mr. Hungerford, returned from Mrs. Black's, where they had been discussing the all-important election.

Serena was too tired to talk, but Gertrude talked enough for all. She chatted and laughed with almost feverish gaiety until the caller, after many false starts and with evident reluctance, finally tore himself away. Then her manner changed, she was silent and thoughtful and, soon afterward, said goodnight and went up to her room.

Captain Dan forebore to trouble his wife with the news of the telegram announcing John Doane's departure for the West, and the reception of that news by Gertrude. After hearing Serena's complaints of her "nerves" and weariness, he decided that there was trouble sufficient for that night. But the next morning he spoke of it. Serena was surprised, of course, and worried likewise.

"You're right, Daniel," she said, "I am afraid you're right. She and John must have had some disagreement. I suppose it is only a lover's quarrel and they always get over them and make up again. But, oh, dear! why did they quarrel just now? Haven't I got enough on my mind without fretting about them? Well, I'll talk to Gertie this very forenoon."

She did, but the talk was unsatisfactory. When Daniel questioned her she shook her head. "I can't make Gertie out," she declared pettishly. "She acts so queer. Doesn't want to talk about John at all. She was willing enough to discuss my chances for the vice-presidency. She asked twenty questions about that and declares she is going to help me. And yesterday, when I wanted her to help, she didn't take any interest. I never saw such a change. And she is so—so fidgety and—and nervous and high-spirited and silly."

Gertrude's conduct was certainly surprising. Her determination to help her mother in the campaign she put into immediate practice. She called Cousin Percy into council, borrowed Serena's list of Chapter members, and the pair spent hours checking that list together. Then Gertrude announced that she was going to make some calls. She made them and returned, exultant.

"I think I have made two converts this afternoon," she said. "I am almost sure they will vote for you, Mother. You and I must go to Mrs. Black's to-night and talk it over with her. We MUST; it is very important."

Serena, who had hoped for an early bedtime, expressed weariness, and protested, but her protests were overruled. They went to the Blacks' and Captain Dan and Mr. Hungerford went, also. Annette was delighted to see them. Mr. Black succeeded in repressing his joy.

"For the Lord's sake, Dan!" he exclaimed, when, he and the captain were alone, "isn't there EVER going to be any let-up to this tom-foolery? Are these women of ours going stark crazy?"

Daniel gloomily replied that he didn't know.

"You're worse off than I am," continued B. Phelps. "There's two lunatics in your family and only one in mine. Your daughter's just as bad as her mother, every bit—worse, if anything. Humph! your pet cousin there is badly gone, or I'm no judge. Well, you remember what I told you about him."

Daniel nodded. He was too depressed for words.

"All right, it's your funeral, not mine. But, say! there's one ray of hope. The whole crowd may be licked to death in this election. If they are, my wife says she'll resign from the Chapter and never speak to one of the bunch again. It sounds too good to be true, but it may be."

The political work continued, mornings and afternoons, evenings and far into the nights. Serena was in it, Gertrude was in it, and Cousin Percy and Mr. Holway were in it because she was. Mr. Hungerford and his erstwhile chum did not speak to each other at all now. But at receptions and teas and dances and musicals and committee meetings one or the other was on hand at Miss Dott's elbow. And Gertrude was very gracious to them both; not more to one than the other, but exceptionally kind and agreeable to each.

The social affairs were of almost as frequent occurrence as the political meetings. Gertrude accepted all invitations and urged her mother to accept. "You must, Mother," she declared. "Now is the time when you can't afford to offend or neglect anyone. You may need their votes and influence."

"But, Gertie," pleaded poor, tired Serena, "I can't go everywhere."

"You must. If this vice-presidency is worth all the world to you, as you say it is, you must sacrifice everything else to get it."

"But, I can't! I'm almost worn out. I—I—oh, sometimes I feel almost willing to give it all up and go back to—to—almost anywhere, even Trumet, if I could rest there."

"You don't mean that, Mother."

"No; no, of course I don't."

"Because if you do, why—well, that is different. If you WANT to go back to dead and alive old Trumet—"

"I don't. I—I wouldn't for anything. You! When I have climbed so high already; when our social position has become what it is. You! talking of going back to Trumet."

"I'm not. You mentioned it; I didn't. I'm having a beautiful time. I just love our social position. And you enjoy it so, Mother. You look so happy."

Was there a trace of sarcasm in this outburst? Serena was, for the moment, suspicious. She tried her hardest to look very happy indeed.

"I am happy, of course," she declared.

"I know it. And we want to keep on being happy, don't we. So we must not decline anyone's invitation. We must go, go, go, all the time."

"But some of the invitations are from people I scarcely know at all. And some I don't like."

"That makes no difference. They may be of value to you in your campaign, or socially, or somehow. In politics or society one wishes to advance, to climb higher all the time. And to do that one must use one's acquaintances as rounds in the ladder. Use them; get something from them; pretend to love them, no matter whether you really hate them or not. That's part of the game, Mother."

This was worldly advice to be given by a young lady scarcely out of college. And it sounded so unlike Gertrude. But, then, Gertrude had changed, was changing more and more daily.

"We don't entertain enough," went on the adviser. "We should be giving some affair or other at least once a week. Invite everybody you know—everyone but the Lake crowd, of course. I'll make out a list of eligibles to-day and we'll give an 'At Home' next week."

"But, Gertie—the expense. It costs so dreadfully. We're not rich; that is, not very rich."

"No matter. Everyone thinks we are. If they didn't, most of them would cut us dead to-morrow. We must pretend to be very rich. I'll make out the list. Mr. Holway will help me. He is coming to call this evening."

Serena looked more troubled than ever. "Gertie," she said earnestly, "I think I ought—yes, I am going to warn you against that Mr. Holway. I don't like your having him call or being seen in his company."

"You don't! I am surprised. I'm sure he is very polite and agreeable. He belongs to the best club and he dresses well, and as to society—why, he is in the very heart of it; our kind of society, I mean."

"I know, I know. But—well, Cousin Percy doesn't speak well of him. He says he is a very fast young man."

Gertrude bit her lip. "Did Percy say that!" she exclaimed. "How odd! Why, Monty—I mean Mr. Holway—said almost the same thing about him. And I KNOW you like Cousin Percy, Mother."

Mrs. Dott scarcely knew how to answer. As a matter of fact she did not like their aristocratic relative quite as well as she had at first. There were certain things about him, little mannerisms and condescensions, which jarred upon her. He was so very, very much at home in the family now; in fact, he seemed to take his permanent membership in that family for granted. He had ceased to refer to himself as being on a vacation, and, as for his "literary work," he appeared to have forgotten that altogether.

But these were not the real reasons for Serena's growing dislike and uneasiness. She hinted at the real reason in her next remark. "I don't think," she said, "I don't think, Gertie, that you and he should be so much together. You are engaged to be married, you know, and John—"

Gertrude interrupted. She ignored the mention of Mr. Doane's name. "Oh, Cousin Percy is all right," she said lightly. "Of course he may be something of a sport, but that is to be expected. The trouble with you and me, Mother, is that we are too old-fashioned; we are not sporty enough."

"GERTIE!" Serena's horror was beyond words.

Gertrude laughed. "But that can be mended," she went on. "Mother, you should learn to drink cocktails and tango. I think I shall. Everybody's doing it!"

Humming this spirited ditty, which the street pianos had rendered popular, and smiling over her shoulder at her mother, she "one-stepped" from the room. Serena put both hands to her head. Her "nerves" were more troublesome than ever the remainder of that day.

There were enough troubles to rack even a healthy set of nerves. The domestic situation was decidedly complicated. No successor to the departed Hapgood had, as yet, been selected. Mr. Hungerford was partially responsible for this. At first, when told of the butler's misbehavior and its consequences, he had expressed sorrow, but had advised forgiveness and the reinstallation of the discharged one. Captain Dan, to whom these statements were made, was stubbornly indignant.

So Cousin Percy, finding Daniel obdurate, tried his influence upon Serena, whom he regarded, and justly, as the real head of the house. But Serena, too, refused to consider Mr. Hapgood's re-employment. She had talked with Azuba, and Azuba had declared that she should leave in "just about two-thirds of a jiffy" if the butler came back.

Mr. Hapgood was not re-engaged nor forgiven, and Hungerford kindly volunteered to find a competent successor. He would make some inquiries among his friends, the right sort of people, he said, and his manner indicated that the said people were accustomed to employing butlers in droves.

Azuba, therefore, was left with all the domestic cares upon her hands. These hands were quite competent, had they been disengaged, but just now they were full. Azuba was "advancing," just as she had proclaimed to Captain Dan that she intended to do. Denied admittance to the Chapter, in spite of Gertrude's efforts in her behalf she had made search on her own hook and suddenly announced that she had found what she was looking for. This, so she affirmed, was an organization called "The Free Laborers' Band," and it met in a hall somewhere or other, though no one but its members seemed to know just where that hall was. Serena made inquiries, but neither servants nor mistresses had ever heard of the "Band." Gertrude, when she heard of it, at first seemed to be much amused, and laughed heartily. Then she became very grave and declared it a splendid thing and that she was delighted because Azuba had found her opportunity.

So Azuba "advanced" and preached and went out at night and occasionally during the day. Gertrude and Serena went out all the time, when they were not entertaining themselves. Life became a never-ending round of politics and society functions, followed by, on Mrs. Dott's part, sleepless nights and "nerves" and fretful worriment concerning Gertrude. Gertrude did not appear to worry.

She grew gayer and more gay, more careless in her manner and more slangy in her speech. Mr. Holway continued to call and Cousin Percy to dance solicitous attendance. John Doane's name was never mentioned in his fiancee's presence. She would not speak, or permit others to speak, of him.

And then Mr. Holway ceased to call. His final call was a lengthy one, and he and Gertrude were alone during the latter part of it. The following day Daniel met him on the street and was barely recognized. When he mentioned the meeting to his daughter the young lady smiled, but offered no explanation. Her father did not press the point. As Holway came no more and it became apparent that he was not coming, the captain was satisfied.

Gertrude's strange behavior alarmed and troubled him, but his wife's ill health and her worn, weary expression alarmed him more. "Oh, Serena," he begged, "what makes you do it? It isn't worth it. Let's give it up and go somewhere and rest. The Queen of Sheba's job ain't worth it, let alone just bein' vice-president of Scarford Chapter."

But Serena shook her head. "I can't give it up, Daniel," she declared hysterically." I—I think I would if I could. I really do. Sometimes I feel as if I would give up everything just to be at peace and happy and contented again."

"You bet!" with enthusiasm. "So would I. And we were contented at Trumet, wasn't we? That is, I was; and you was enough sight better contented than you are now."

"I know, I know. But I can't give it up, Daniel. Don't you see? I can't! I mustn't think of myself at all. See how loyally Annette and the rest have stood by me. Their splendid loyalty is the one thing that makes it worth while. I must keep up and fight on for their sakes. I am going to be elected. I know it. After that, after the election is over, I may—I might, perhaps—"

"You might go somewhere with me and have a good, comfortable time. All right, we will. And Gertie can go, too."

The mention of her daughter's name seemed to be more disturbing than all the rest. Serena burst into tears. "She wouldn't go, Daniel!" she cried. "She—she is going crazy, I do believe. She is wild about society and bridge—she told me only yesterday she wasn't sure that playing for money was wrong. All my friends and her friends did it and why shouldn't we? And she dances all these dreadful new dances and uses slang and—and—oh, she is—I don't know WHAT she will be if this keeps on. Why does she do it? WHO is responsible?"

Daniel did not answer. He had a feeling that he could, without moving from his chair, lay a hand upon the person chiefly responsible, but he kept that feeling to himself.

"She'd go, if we wanted her to," he affirmed stoutly.

"No, she wouldn't."

"By time! she would. You and I would make her. I couldn't do it alone, I know that, but if you'll say the word and stand by me she'll go, if I have to—to give her ether and take her while she's asleep. Say the word, that's all I want you to do."

Serena did not say the word, not then. "She's all wrong, Daniel!" she cried. "She does wrong things. She is with—with Cousin Percy too much. He and she are getting to be altogether too friendly. She has dropped John for good, I'm afraid. Oh, suppose she should—"

The captain's anger burst forth at this expression of his own secret dread. "Suppose she should marry that Hungerford, you mean!" he cried.

"She's too sensible, anyway; but, if she should, I—I'd rather see her dead."

"So had I. But Cousin Percy—"

"Damn Cousin Percy!"

For once his profanity met with no rebuke. Serena did not appear to notice it.

"He is not the right sort of man for her," she declared. "He is polite and aristocratic and he has helped us in society; but he is dissipated and fast, I'm sure of it. He has been out a great deal lately and comes home late, and I have heard him come up the stairs as if—as if—Oh, WHY did you insist on his staying here, living here with us?"

"Why did I—Humph! That's all right, Serena. You back me up in that, too, and he'll go out a sight quicker than he came in. I can handle MEN even yet—though I don't seem to be good for much else."

But Mrs. Dott wouldn't hear of it. They couldn't PUT him out, she declared; think of the scandal! No, no, no! The interview ended by the captain's dismissal and Serena's getting ready for that evening's committee meeting.

It developed that Azuba's "Band" met on that same evening. Gertrude and her mother had gone—they were to dine with the committee at Annette's—and when Daniel, at seven o'clock, shouted for his dinner, no dinner was ready.

"I can't stop to fuss with dinner," said Azuba firmly. "I've got to get ready for my Band meetin'. All the afternoon I've been fussin' with my speech—I'm goin' to speak to-night—and now it's time for me to change my clothes. I'm sorry, Cap'n Dott; I never neglected you afore; but this time I've got to. There's plenty to eat in the ice-chest and you must wait on yourself. No use to talk! I ain't got time to listen."

Captain Dan was furious. This was a trifle too much. "You get that dinner!" he roared. "Get it, or you'll never get another meal in this house!"

"Won't I? Why not? Mrs. Dott said I might go to this meetin'. She'll understand."

"By time, Zuba Ginn, I'll discharge you! I don't care if you have been with us since Methusalem's time. You old foolhead! At your age—"

"I'm no older than your wife, Dan'l Dott. And you can't discharge me, neither. I wouldn't go. I'm no Hapgood. I've got rights and I'll stand up for 'em. You ain't the boss, I guess. If Serena discharges me, all right; but she won't. There! don't talk to ME. I've got other fish to fry."

She marched up the back stairs. Daniel sprang after her, but she closed the door in his face. For a moment he hesitated. Then he turned back and, re-entering the kitchen, began to pace up and down, his hands in his pockets.

He strode from the sink to the back door, wheeled and strode back again. There was an odd expression on his face. If one of his former shipmates, a foremast hand on the schooner *Bluebird*, could have seen him then, that foremast hand would have interpreted his behavior as a forerunner of trouble. He would have known that the "old man" was making up his mind to a definite course of action and that, having made it up, he would keep to that course so long as he could see or breathe. And that interpretation would have been correct. Captain Dan was desperate. He had made up his mind to fight, to "put his foot down" at last. Serena's ill health, Gertrude's conduct, the aggravating insolence of Cousin Percy, all these had helped to spur him to this pitch. And now came Azuba's open rebellion and her declaration that his command amounted to nothing, that he was not the "boss." It was true, that was the humiliating fact which stung. To be openly told so, and by his cook, was a little too much. The worm will turn—at least we are told that it will—and Daniel Dott was turning.

He jerked his hands from his pockets and opened his mouth. "Azuba!" he roared. "You, Zuba, come here!"

Azuba did not answer. She was in her room at the top of the house and, of course, did not hear the shout. Before the captain could repeat it someone knocked at the back door.

The knock was no hesitating, irresolute tap. It was an emphatic, solid thump. Daniel heard it, but, in his present state of mind, was in no mood to heed.

"Zuba!" he repeated. "Zuba Ginn, are you comin' here or shall I come after you? ZUBA!"

The back door was merely latched, not locked. Now it was thrown open, a heavy step sounded in the entry and a voice, a man's voice, said, in a shout almost as loud as the captain's, "Yes, Zuba; that's what I was cal'latin' to say, myself. Who—why, hello, Cap'n Dan! How are you?"

Daniel turned. A man had entered the kitchen, a big man, wearing a cloth cap, and carrying in one hand a lumpy oilcloth valise. He tossed the valise to the floor, grinned, and extended a hand.

"Well, Cap'n Dan," he observed, "you look as natural as life. I must have changed, I cal'late. Don't you know me?"

The captain's eyes were opening wider and wider. "Labe!" he exclaimed; "Laban Ginn! Where in the world did you come from?"

The person who had so unceremoniously entered the kitchen was Azuba's husband, mate of the tramp steamer.

CHAPTER XIII

"For the land sakes! Laban Ginn!" repeated Daniel.

Mr. Ginn grinned cheerfully. He seized the captain's hand in one of his, crushed it to a pulp, and returned the remains to the chief mourner.

"Well, say," he cried, his grin widening, "that feels natural, don't it? Last time you and me shook hands was over three years ago. How are you? Blessed if it ain't good to see you again."

Captain Dan was slowly regaining his equilibrium. "Same to you, Labe," he returned heartily. "But—but, by Godfreys, you're the last person I expected to see just now."

"Yep, I shouldn't wonder."

"Sit down, sit down. Humph! Does Azuba know you're comin'?"

"No, not yet."

"Well, sit down and I'll call her. She's here with us, of course."

"Sartin she is. Where else would she be? I knew she was here; heard you hailin' her just as I made port at the back door." He threw himself into a chair, which groaned under the pressure. "Feels kind of good to drop anchor when you've been cruisin's long as I have. No, Zuby don't know I'm comin'. Last time I wrote her was from Mauritius. I've been to clink and gone since. She WILL be surprised, won't she? Ho! ho! Did I leave the hatch open? Here, let me shut it."

But Daniel himself shut the "hatch," that is to say, the back door. He was on his way to the stairs, but Mr. Ginn detained him.

"Hold on a shake, Cap'n," he said. "I ain't hardly seen you yet. Let's have a look at you." Crossing his legs, he added, "How are you, anyway?"

Daniel replied that he was fair to middling. "Sit still and make yourself comfortable, Labe," he went on. "I'll tell Zuba you're here."

"What's your hurry? Give me a chance to catch my breath. I landed in Philadelphy a week ago," he continued. "Quit the old steamer for good, I have. Me and the skipper had some words and I told him where he could go. Ho! ho! I don't know whether he went or not; anyhow, I started for Trumet. Got there and found you'd come into money and had moved to Scarford and was livin' with the big-bugs. Some house you've got here, ain't it! Soon's I see it I headed for the back door. 'A first cabin companion like that's no place for me,' I says. Besides, I cal'lated to find Zuby Jane out in the fo'castle here. Didn't expect to locate you, though, in this end of the ship. How's it seem to be rich? Ain't got fat on it, have you."

Daniel, amused in spite of his recent ill temper, shook his head. "Not yet," he answered. "So you've been ashore a week and your wife doesn't know it? Why didn't you write to her from Philadelphia?"

"Oh, I don't know. Zuby and me's got an understandin' about that, and other things. We write letters, of course, but we don't write very often. I say to Zuby, 'Long's you don't hear from me you'll know I'm all right, and long's I don't hear from you I'll know the same. We'll write when we feel like it. I'll come home as often as I can, and when I come I'll fetch you my share of the wages.' That's our understandin' and it's a good one. We ain't had a fight since we was spliced; or, if we have, I always stop it right off—stop her part, I mean. Where IS the old gal, anyhow?"

"She's up in her room, I presume likely."

"Oh, is she? Well, she'll be down in a jiffy."

"I'll call her, if you give me a chance."

"No, no, you needn't. No 'special hurry. Had your supper yet?"

Daniel smiled grimly. "Not yet," he replied.

"Then she'll be down to get it, of course. I shan't stop her; I'm empty as a rum bottle four days out of port. You folks eat late, don't you?"

"Sometimes."

"I should think so. What's Zuby doin' up in her room this time of night?"

"She said she was goin' to change her clothes."

"Oh, yes, yes; I see. Well, 'twon't take her long. If I went up I'd only hold her back, and I want my supper. Let's have a smoke, Dan, while we're waitin'."

He patted one pocket after the other and finally located a chunky, battered pipe, which he proceeded to fill with shavings from a black plug. Daniel watched him. A new idea was dawning in his mind, an idea which seemed to afford him some pleasurable anticipation. Mr. Ginn looked up from his tobacco shaving.

"Now, tell me about all this money of yours," he commanded. "I didn't hear nothin' else at Trumet; that and your wife's gettin' to be commodore of some woman's lodge or other was all they talked about. Hey? Why, where's your pipe? Ain't you goin' to smoke?"

Daniel looked dubious. "I guess not, Labe," he said. "Zuba—well, the fact is, Zuba doesn't like people to smoke in her kitchen."

Laban's face expressed astonishment. "She don't!" he cried. "She don't? How long since?"

"Oh, almost ever since she came here. It is one of her new ways."

"'Tis, hey? Well, I like the old ones better, myself. Never you mind her ways; trot out your pipe and light up. I—"

He was interrupted by his companion, who made a flying jump toward the stove. The teakettle was boiling over.

"Let it bile," commented Mr. Ginn. "You ain't supposed to boss the galley. That's the cook's business, not the skipper's."

But Daniel carefully removed the kettle to a place of safety. "It's my business to-night," he said. "I'm gettin' my own supper."

Mr. Ginn straightened in his chair. "You be?" he exclaimed. "You BE? What for? Ain't there no women folks in the house? Ain't Zuby—why, you said—"

"I know I said, but what I say don't seem to amount to much. You see, Labe, your wife has got some of what MY wife calls advanced ideas. She belongs to some kind of a lodge herself, and this is their meetin' night. Just before you came Zuba made proclamations that I could cook my own supper. She said she couldn't stop to do it; she'd be late to the meetin' if she did."

Laban's mouth opened. The pipe fell from it, scattering sparks like a Roman candle, and bounced upon the spotless floor of the kitchen.

"For thunder sakes, Dan Dott!" he cried. "For thunder sakes, tell me what you're talkin' about? Zuby—Zuby Jane Ginn racin' to lodges and tellin' you—YOU—to cook your own meals! Go on! You're loony."

"Maybe I am, Labe, but it's so."

"It's so? And you let it be so? I don't believe it. What do you mean? How long has it been so?"

Captain Dan proceeded to tell of his housekeeper's conversion to progress and advancement. "She's a free woman, so she says, Labe," he said, in conclusion. "And a free woman has a right to be free."

"Is that so! That's what she says, hey? And you let her say it? Why, you—you—" He hesitated, hovering between candid expression and the respect due an ex-skipper of a three-master. "Wh-what do you have such goin's on in your house for?" he demanded. "Why don't you—who's that upstairs; your wife?"

"No, my wife is out. I shouldn't wonder if that was Zuba. She's on her way to the door, probably."

"She is, hey? Call her down here. Sing out to her to come down. Hi!" as the captain stepped to the stairs, "don't say nothin' about me."

Daniel, suppressing a grin, shouted up the stairs. "Zuba!" he called. "Zuba, come down here a minute."

Azuba answered, but in no complacent tone. "Don't bother me, Cap'n Dott," she protested. "I'm late as 'tis."

"Just a minute, Zuba, that's all. One minute, please."

They heard the housekeeper descending. At the bottom step she sniffed loudly. "I do believe it's tobacco smoke!" she exclaimed. "Cap'n Dott, have you been smokin' in my kitchen?"

She entered the room, waving an indignant arm. She was dressed in her Sunday best, bonnet and all.

"What!" she began, and then, suddenly aware that her employer was not alone, turned to stare at his companion. "Why!" she exclaimed; "who—oh, my soul! LABAN!"

"Hello, Zuby!" roared her husband. "How be you, old gal?"

Before she could speak or move he seized her in his arms, squeezed her to him, and pressed a kiss like the report of a fire-cracker upon her cheek. "How be you, Zuby?" he repeated.

"Oh, Labe!" gasped Azuba. "Labe!"

"I'm Labe, all right. No doubt about that. . . . Well, why don't you say somethin'? Ain't you glad to see me?"

Azuba looked as if she did not know whether she was glad or not; in fact, as if she knew or realized any little of anything.

"Labe!" she said again. "Laban Ginn! When—WHERE did you come from?"

"Oh, from all 'round. Trumet was my last port and I made that by way of Malagy and Philadelphy. But I'm here, anyhow, and that's somethin'. My! it's good to see you."

The housekeeper sat down; she appeared glad of the opportunity. Her husband faced her, grinning broadly. "Just as handsome as ever; hey, old lady," he observed. "And look at the duds! A body would think she knew I was comin', wouldn't they, Cap'n Dan?"

Daniel did not answer, although he seemed much interested in the situation.

Azuba drew a hand across her forehead. "I DIDN'T know it," she declared emphatically. "Indeed, I didn't! Why didn't you write me, Laban Ginn?"

"Write! Write nothin'! I wanted to surprise you. But there, there! Don't set around in that rig any longer. Take off your coat and bonnet and let's be sociable. And while we're talkin' you turn to and get supper. I'm pretty nigh starved to death. So's the cap'n; he said so."

Mrs. Ginn looked at Captain Dan. There was a twinkle in his eye. Azuba noticed that twinkle. "Laban," she stammered, "I—I—I CAN'T stay here and get supper to-night. I can't."

Laban was tremendously surprised—at least he pretended to be. "Can't!" he repeated. "Can't stay here, when I've just got home?"

"No, I can't. If I had known you was comin' 'twould have been different. But I didn't know it."

"What difference does that make? Zuby, don't make me laugh; I'm too hungry for jokin'. Take off your bonnet, now; take it off."

"I mustn't, really, Labe. It's lodge night and they expect me. I—"

"Take off your bonnet!"

"I can't! . . . Well, I will, for just a minute." She placed the bonnet on the table and fidgeted in her chair, glancing first at her employer and then at the clock. Captain Dan was smiling broadly.

"That's fine!" exclaimed Mr. Ginn. "Now you look like home folks. Now she'll get us some supper, won't she, Cap'n?"

Again Daniel did not answer, but his smile, as Azuba interpreted it, was provokingly triumphant.

"I can't get any supper to-night, Laban," she declared firmly. "I'm awful sorry, bein' as you've just got home, but you'll have to forgive me. I'll explain when you and me are alone."

"Explain? Explain what?"

"Why—why—" with another look, almost vindictive, at the grinning captain, "what my reason is. But I can't tell you now—I can't."

"That's all right. You can explain any old time; just now, me and the cap'n want our supper."

"I shan't get your supper. I told Cap'n Dott I couldn't before I went upstairs. I'm goin' out."

"No, no, you ain't. Quit your foolin', old lady. I'm gettin' emptier every minute. So are you, ain't you, Cap'n?"

Daniel hesitated, looked at his housekeeper's face, and burst into a roar of laughter. That laugh decided the question. Azuba rose.

"Don't talk to me," she snapped. "I'm sorry, but it serves you right, Laban, for comin' home without sendin' me word; and just at the wrong time, too. Give me that bonnet."

She reached for the bonnet, but her husband reached it first. "'Tain't much of a bonnet, anyhow, Zuby," he said. "Now I look at it closer I don't think it's becomin' to your style of complexion. Some day I'll buy you another."

"Give me that bonnet, Laban Ginn!"

"I don't like to see that bonnet around, Zuby. Let's get it out of sight quick."

His wife sprang at the bonnet, but he barred her off with an arm like a fence-rail, removed a lid from the stove, put the unbecoming article in on the red-hot coals, and replaced the lid. "There!" he said, "that helps the scenery, don't it? Now let's have supper."

Captain Dan laughed again. For an instant Azuba stared, white-faced, at the cremation of the bonnet. Then she darted to the door. "I'll go now," she cried, "if I have to go bareheaded! I'll show you! Let go of me!"

Mr. Ginn had thrown an arm about her waist. She pulled his hair and gave him some vigorous slaps on the cheek, but he smiled on.

"You want to get supper, Zuby," he coaxed. "I know you do. You just think it over now. It's too noisy out here to do much thinkin'. Where's a nice quiet place? Oh! this'll be first rate."

He bore her, kicking like a jumping-jack, across the kitchen to the closet where the pans and cooking utensils were kept. "Think it over in there, Zuby," he said calmly, shutting the door and planting himself in a chair against it. "That's a fine place to think. Now, Cap'n, you and me can have our smoke, while she's thinkin' what to give us to eat; hey?"

Judging by the thumps and kicks and screams inside the closet the housekeeper's thoughts were otherwise engaged. "You let me out, Labe Ginn!" she screamed. "Cap'n Dott, you make him let me out!"

Daniel, weary from laughing, could only gasp. "I can't, Zuba!" he answered, choking. "I couldn't interfere between husband and wife. You're a free woman, Zuba, you know. You ought to be advanced enough by this time to fight your own battles."

"That's right, Zuba," counseled Mr. Ginn. "Fight 'em out in there. You can be just as free in there as you want to. Have some of my terbacker, Cap'n?"

Captain Dan declined. The prisoner continued to thump and kick and threaten. Her jailer refilled and lighted his pipe.

"Thought over that bill of fare, Zuby?" he shouted, after a time. More thumps and threats; tears as well. Daniel began to feel pity instead of triumph.

"Hadn't you better, Labe," he began. Mr. Ginn waved him to silence.

"How about supper, Zuby?" he called. "Oh, all right, all right. I don't know as I'm as hungry as I was, anyway. You stay in there and think till mornin', and we'll have it for breakfast."

Silence—actual silence—for a moment. Then Azuba asked, in a half-smothered but much humbler voice, "Oh, Labe! WON'T you let me out?"

"Sure thing—if you've thought up that supper for me and Cap'n Dan'l."

"But I did so want—oh, if I could only tell you! It was SO necessary for me to go to that meetin'. You've spiled everything, and just as 'twas goin' so nice. What Gertie'll say I don't know."

Daniel developed a new interest. "Gertie?" he repeated. "Hush, Labe! wait a minute. What's Gertie got to do with it?"

"Nothin', nothin'. Oh, Labe, PLEASE."

"Well, I tell you, Zuby: it's close to nine now, and that's too late for you to be cruisin' out to meetin's. Sorry you have to miss the speeches and things, but—Say, I tell you what I'll do. If it's a sermon you want I'll preach you one, myself. Ready to come out and be good? That's right. Now, I bet you she's thought up somethin' that'll make our mouths water, Cap'n."

The crestfallen housekeeper emerged, blinking, from her thinking place. She removed her coat and, without even a glance at her employer, proceeded to adjust the dampers of the stove. Captain Dan rose from his chair. "I'm afraid I can't stop to have supper with you, Labe," he said. "I've got an—an errand to do outside, myself. I'll eat at a restaurant or somewhere. You'll stay here to-night, of course. I'll see you in the mornin'. Good-night! Good-night, Zuby!"

Azuba did not reply. Laban shouted protests. What was the sense of going just when supper was being made ready at last? Daniel, however, did not stay to listen. He had been too tender-hearted to remain in the kitchen and gloat, or appear to gloat, over a "free woman's" humiliation. Nevertheless, he astonished the waiter at the restaurant where he ate dinner by bursting into laughter at intervals, and with no obvious cause.

His dinner eaten, Captain Dan walked slowly home. Unlocking the front door with his latchkey he tiptoed through the hall and listened at the head of the back stairs. There was a steady murmur of voices in the kitchen. He heard a bass grumble from Mr. Ginn and Azuba's shrill reply. Then the pair burst into a laugh.

Evidently some sort of understanding on a peaceful basis had been reached. Still chuckling, the captain went up to his bedroom, removed his outer garments and his shoes, put on his bathrobe and slippers, and settled himself, with the evening paper, to await his wife's return. He resolved to be awake when she did return; he had news for her. Filled with this resolution, he read for three-quarters of an hour steadily, then at intervals between naps, and at last dropped into a sound sleep, the paper in his lap.

Gertrude and Serena came home at a surprisingly early hour. Not that the committee meeting was over; it was not. In fact, the elaborate dinner spread before her supporters by the grateful Mrs. Black had scarcely reached its last course when Gertrude suddenly rose from the table and hastened to her mother's side. She had been watching the latter with increasing anxiety all the evening.

"What is it, Mother?" she asked. "What is it?"

Serena, sitting with her elbow on the table, her hand to her forehead, and her untasted ice before her, looked up in a bewildered way. "What—why, what do you mean, Gertie?" she stammered.

"What is the matter, Mother?" repeated Gertrude. "Don't you feel well?"

Still Mrs. Dott did not seem to understand. She tried to smile, but the vague uncertainty of the smile caused even Annette, who had been deep in discussion of a plan for securing the vote of a still doubtful member, to cease speaking and regard her guest with surprise.

"What is it, Mother?" urged Gertrude. "Are you ill?"

Serena gazed at her for a moment, rose, stood looking about in the same hesitating, uncertain manner, and then, throwing her arms about her daughter's neck, burst into hysterical sobs. The alarmed guests clustered about them, asking questions, exclaiming, and offering suggestions.

"What IS it?" demanded Annette.

Serena, still clinging to Gertrude, continued to sob. "I—I don't know," she moaned. "I'm—I'm tired, I guess. I'm—I'm worn out. I—oh, Gertie, take me home. Take me home—please."

"Yes, yes, Mother, dear. We will go home at once."

She led her into the next room. Annette, hastening with a glass of wine and the smelling salts, caught the young lady's arm.

"She isn't going to be ill, seriously sick, is she?" she demanded.

Gertrude shook her head. "I don't know," she answered. "I certainly hope not. Will you call a carriage, Mrs. Black?"

"Yes, yes, I'll call one right away. Oh, I hope she isn't going to be sick. It would be dreadful—just now. The election is only two weeks off, and without her I—we should be almost certain to lose. Oh, Serena, DEAR! you WON'T be sick, will you? for my sake!"

It did not seem to occur to the agitated Annette that her friend might not care to be ill, for her own sake. But it was evident that Gertrude was thinking just that. "She is tired out," she said. "She has worn herself out working for her—for her friends, Mrs. Black. Will you call the carriage?"

"Yes, yes. They are calling it now. I'm so sorry the chauffeur—or—or Phelps—is out. If he—if they were not you could use our car. But, oh, Serena—"

Serena looked up. She was calmer now, she had heard, and loyally she answered.

"Don't worry, Annette," she said. "I am not going to be sick. I won't. You can depend on me. Oh, Gertie, I'm SO tired! My poor head!"

The carriage came and she and Gertrude were driven home. Annette did not offer to accompany them. It was such an important meeting and there were so many things to talk about, she explained. She would call the very next day.

Serena seemed better on the way home. When they reached the house she announced bravely that she was all right again; all she needed was a night's rest, that was all. Gertrude insisted on accompanying her to her room. They found Daniel asleep in the chair, and to him his daughter explained the situation.

"You get right into bed, Serena," he ordered. "Gertie, you call the doctor."

But his wife would not hear of the doctor. "Nonsense!" she declared. "I don't need any doctor. I want to go to bed. I'm tired—tired. Go, Gertie, please go. Your father will be with me. I am all right now."

Gertrude went, but she whispered to the captain that she would wait in the library and, if they needed her, he was to be sure and call. In the library she took a book from the shelf and tried to read, but that was impossible. She could not read, she could only think, and thinking was most unpleasant. Her conscience was troubling her. She had meant well, her plan had seemed the only solution of the family problem, but perhaps she had made a mistake. She loved her mother devotedly. Oh, if anything serious should happen—if, because of her, her mother should be ill—if—if she should. She would never forgive herself, never. It had been all wrong from the beginning, and she had been wicked and foolish. And yet—and yet, she had meant to do right. But now, after that misunderstanding and consequent sacrifice, if her mother should—She broke down and was very, very miserable.

Someone was at the front door, fumbling with a latchkey. Gertrude hurriedly sprang from her chair, wiped her eyes with her handkerchief and was on her way to the hall when the door opened. The hall was dark and for a moment she could not see who it was that had entered. She, however, was in the full glow from the electrolier in the library and Mr. Hungerford saw her.

"Ah, Gertrude," he said cheerfully. "Is that you? Don't go."

He was at the doorway before she could reach it. He had been dining out with some masculine friends and was in evening dress.

"Don't go," he repeated. "What's the hurry? Wait a minute and I'll join you."

He removed his overcoat and silk hat and tossed them carelessly upon the hall table. Then he entered the library. "What!" he exclaimed. "Alone? Where is old—er—where's your father?"

Gertrude replied that her father had retired. She was about to do so, she added. Cousin Percy, however, appeared decidedly conversational. "Well," he observed, "this is an unexpected pleasure. Didn't expect to find anyone up at this hour."

Gertrude curtly remarked that it was not late. "I didn't mean up, I meant in. Did I say 'up'? Most extraordinary. I thought you and Mrs. Dott were playing the political game this evening. Expected to find you out and old—the respected captain, I mean—in the arms of—what's his name?—Morpheus. That's all right, though; that's all right. So much the better. We can talk—you and I."

"I don't feel like talking. You must excuse me."

"What? Don't feel like talking? Why not? It isn't late; you said so yourself."

"I know but—really, you must excuse me."

She was moving toward the door, but again he stepped in her way. "Now, Gertie," he said. Then he broke into a laugh. "Called you Gertie, didn't I?" he said. "It slipped out before I thought. But you don't mind, do you? It's a pretty name. Just a little bit less formal than Gertrude, eh? Don't you think so—Gertie?"

Gertrude hesitated. She was humiliated and angry, but she did not wish a scene. Her parents might hear and her mother must on no account be disturbed.

"Perhaps it is," she answered.

"Then you don't mind?"

"No. Now, Percy, you must excuse me. Goodnight!"

"Wait! Wait! Gertie, I have something to say to you. Been wanting to say it for a long time, but haven't had the opportunity. You have kept out of my way. Perhaps you guessed I wanted to say it. Was that it?"

Gertrude did not answer. She moved toward the door. Mr. Hungerford laughingly blocked the passage. "No, no!" he cried. "Mustn't run away. I am going to say it, and you must hear me."

"Mr. Hungerford, will you stand aside? I can not talk with you to-night, or listen. I am going to my room."

The tone in which this was uttered should have been a warning, but Cousin Percy was in no condition to recognize warnings, or to heed them if he had. His smile grew more tender and his tone more intimate.

"Not yet," he smiled; "not just yet. I can't permit it. Gertie, I—"

"If you don't stand aside I shall call my father."

"What? Call the old gentleman? No, you don't mean it. You wouldn't be so unreasonable. Come, come! we're friends at least. We understand each other, don't we?"

"I understand YOU, thoroughly."

"Of course you do," with a triumphant leer. "And you know what I am going to say. Ah ha! I was sure you did. Gertie, my dearest girl, I—What! Going? Not until you pay toll. I'm keeper of the gate and you must pay before you pass, you know. If you won't listen you must pay. Ha! ha!"

He held out his hands. Gertrude shrank back. She was not afraid of him, but she did fear a scene. She moved away, to the other side of the library table.

Cousin Percy interpreted her retreat as a sign of surrender. He followed her, laughing. "Come!" he insisted. "I knew you didn't mean it. Come, my dear! Just one. I—"

He tripped over the captain's favorite footstool and fell to his knees. With a sudden movement Gertrude jerked the cord of the electrolier on the table. The lights went out. She dodged around the table, through the doorway, into the hall, and up the stairs.

Mr. Hungerford, pawing in the darkness at the offending footstool, swore. Then he laughed. "Good!" he exclaimed. "Very good, but not good enough. You can't escape that way. I shall find you. Where are you hiding? Ah, there you are!"

He had scrambled to his feet and hurried to the doorway. There were the sounds of footsteps and the rustle of skirts at the other end of the hall. "There you are!" he cried. "I've caught you. Now you must pay—twice."

He put his arm about a feminine waist and imprinted a kiss upon a feminine cheek. Then his own cheek received a slap which made his head ring, and the hall echoed with a shrill scream.

"Labe!" shrieked Azuba. "Help! Come quick!"

Mr. Ginn came up the back stairs three steps at a time. "What's the matter, Zuby?" he demanded.

"A man! He—he—"

"Where is he? What's he doin'?"

"He—there he is. Hear him? There!"

Mr. Hungerford, paralyzed with astonishment and dizzy from the slap, had moved, injudiciously. Laban heard him.

"Hey?" he bellowed. "Ah! I've got him. Stand still, dum you! I've got him, Zuby. Who is he? What did he do?"

"I—I don't know who he is," panted the frightened housekeeper. "He—he kissed me."

"KISSED you! Why—"

"It's a mistake!" cried Cousin Percy, frantically struggling in the grasp of his captor. "I—Stop! Stop! Help! Help!"

The hall became a pandemonium of thumps, struggles, cries for help, and pleas for mercy. From above Captain Dan shouted and Serena screamed. Then the chandelier blazed. Gertrude had pressed the button at the top of the stairs.

"Let him be!" ordered the young lady, rushing to the rescue. "Azuba, stop him!"

"Labe! stop! stop!" pleaded the housekeeper. "You—My soul! it's Mr. Hungerford."

It was what there was left of Mr. Hungerford. Mr. Ginn extended the disheveled, whimpering remnant at arm's length and regarded it. "Humph!" he grunted. "You know him, do you?"

"Know him! Of course I do. But—but I must say—"

Captain Dan came tearing down the stairs, his bathrobe fluttering and a slipper missing. In one hand he held a pair of scissors, the only offensive weapon which he had found available at the moment.

"What in blazes?" he demanded. "Burglars, is it?"

Gertrude answered. "No, Daddy," she said gravely. "It's no one but Cousin Percy. And—and Mr. Ginn. Why, Mr. Ginn, is—is it you?"

Laban nodded. "It's me, all right," he observed grimly. "Who the devil is this?"

Daniel turned to the captive. "Why—why, Percy!" he gasped. "What—what's happened to you? Let go of him, Labe Ginn! Percy Hungerford, what—what's all this?"

Mr. Hungerford, suddenly freed from the grasp upon his torn shirt collar, staggered against the wall. "It's—it's a mistake," he panted. "I—I—this—this blackguard assaulted me. I—I—"

"Assaulted you! I should say he had. Labe Ginn, what did you assault him for?"

Mr. Ginn glared at his victim. "Blackguard, am I?" he growled. "Humph! Well, if he starts to callin' me names, I'll—"

"Belay! What have you been doin' to him? Look at him! What do you mean by assaultin' him that way?"

"What do I mean? When a man comes home from sea and finds another man kissin' his wife, what would he be likely to mean?"

Daniel could not answer. Gertrude choked and turned away. "Kissin'!" repeated Captain Dan. "Kissin' ZUBA! I—I—am I crazy, or are you, or—or is he?"

Apparently he judged the last surmise to be the most likely. Cousin Percy, frantic with rage and humiliation, tried to protest. "It's a lie!" he cried.

The captain turned to his housekeeper. "Zuba," he demanded, "what sort of lunatic business is this? Do you know?"

Azuba straightened. "I don't know much," she announced sharply. "All I know is that I come upstairs in the dark and he grabbed me and—and said somethin' about my payin' him—and then he—he—done the other thing. That's all I know, and it's enough."

"But—but what's it mean? Can't anybody tell me, for the Lord sakes?"

Gertrude stepped forward. "I think I understand," she said. "Our cousin made a mistake, that's all. If—if you will all go away, he and I will have an interview. I think I can settle it better than anyone else. Go, please. I'm sure Mother needs you."

The mention of his wife caused her father to forget everything else, even his overwhelming curiosity. "My soul!" he cried. "She heard this; and—and I left her all alone."

He bolted up the stairs. Gertrude's next remark was addressed to the housekeeper. "Azuba," she said, "would you and your husband mind leaving us? Perhaps you'd better not go to bed. I—I may need Mr. Ginn later on; perhaps I may. But if you and he were to go down to the kitchen and wait just a few moments I should be so much obliged."

Azuba hesitated. "Leave you?" she repeated. "With—with him?"

"Yes. I have something to say to him."

She and Azuba exchanged looks. The latter nodded. "All right," she said decisively; "course we'll go. Come, Labe."

But Laban seemed loath to move. "I ain't got through with him yet," he observed.

"You come with me. Have you forgot all I told you so soon?"

"Hey? No; no, I ain't forgot. Is this part of it?"

"Part of it's part of it; the rest ain't. You come, 'fore you do any more spilin'. Come, now."

Mr. Ginn went. At the head of the back stairs he paused. "You'll sing out if you need me?" he asked. "You'll only have to sing once."

He tramped heavily down. Gertrude walked over to the victim of the "mistake" and its consequences. "I think," she said coldly, "that you had better go."

"Go?" Mr. Hungerford looked at her. "Go?" he repeated.

"Yes. I give you this opportunity. There will not be another. Go to your room, change your clothes, pack your trunk, and go—now, to-night."

"What do you mean? That I am to go—and not come back?"

"Yes."

"But, Gertrude—Gertie—"

"Don't call me that. Don't DARE to speak to me in that tone. Go—now."

"But, Ger—Miss Dott, I—I—don't you see it was all a mistake? I—"

"Stop! I am trying very hard to keep my temper. We have had scenes enough to-night. My mother is ill and she must not be disturbed again. If you do not go to your room and pack and leave at once, I shall call Mr. Ginn and have you put out, just as you are. I am giving you that opportunity. You had better avail yourself of it. I mean what I say."

She looked as if she did. Cousin Percy evidently thought so. His humbleness disappeared.

"So?" he snarled angrily. "So that's it, eh? What do you think I am?"

Gertrude's eyes flashed. When she spoke it was with deliberate distinctness. "Do you wish to know what I think you are?" she asked. "What I thought at the very beginning you were, and what I have been taking pains to make sure of ever since I came to this house? Very well, I'll tell you."

She told him, slowly, calmly, and with biting exactness. His face was flushed when she began; when she finished it was white.

"That is what you are," she said. "I do not merely think so. I have studied you carefully; I have stooped to associate with you in order to study you; I have studied you through your friends; I KNOW what you are."

His anger and mortification were choking him. "You—you—" he snarled. "You have been using me as a good thing. As a—as a—"

"As you have used my father and mother and their simple-minded goodness and generosity. Yes, I have."

"You have been making a fool of me! And Holway—confound him—"

"Mr. Holway was useful. And he, too, understands, now."

"By—by gad—I—I won't go. I'll—"

Gertrude walked to the rear of the hall. "Mr. Ginn!" she called, "will you come, please?"

Laban came. He looked happy and expectant. "Here I be," he observed eagerly.

"Mr. Ginn," said Gertrude, "this—gentleman—is going to his room for a few minutes. He is preparing to leave us. If he doesn't come down and leave this house in a reasonable time will you kindly assist him?"

Laban grinned. "He'll go."

"Thank you. Good-night!"

She ascended the stairs. The first mate looked at his watch. "Fifteen minutes is enough to pack any trunk," he observed. "I'll give you that much. Now, then, tumble up. Lively!"

At the door of her parents' room Gertrude rapped softly. Captain Dan opened it and showed a pallid, agitated face. "She's mighty sick, Gertie," he declared. "I wish you'd telephone for the doctor."

CHAPTER XIV

The doctor came, stayed for some time and, after administering a sleeping draught and ordering absolute quiet for his patient, departed, saying that he would come again in the morning. He did so and, before leaving, took Captain Dan and Gertrude into his confidence.

"It is a complete collapse," he said gravely. "Mrs. Dott is worn out, physically and mentally. She must be kept quiet, she must not worry about anything, she must remain in bed, and she must see no one. If she does this, if she rests—really rests—we may fight off nervous prostration. If she does not—anything may happen. With your permission I shall send a nurse."

The permission was given, of course, and the nurse came. She was a quiet, pleasant, capable person, and Daniel and Gertrude liked her. She took charge of the sick room. Azuba—the common sense, adequate, domestic Azuba of old—was in charge of the kitchen. Her husband remained, at Daniel's earnest request, but he spent his time below stairs.

"Sartin sure I won't be in the way, Cap'n, be you?" he asked earnestly. "I can go somewheres else just as well as not, to some boardin' house or somewheres."

"Not a mite of it, Labe," replied Daniel earnestly. "There's plenty of room and you can stay here along with your wife just as well as not. I'd like to have you. Maybe—" with a suggestive wink, "maybe you can kind of—well, kind of keep things runnin' smooth—in the galley. You know what I mean."

Laban grinned. "Cal'late you won't have no more trouble that way, Cap'n," he observed. "Zuby and I understand each other better'n we did. I THOUGHT she was mighty—"

"Mighty what?"

"Oh, nothin'. It's all right, Cap'n Dott. Don't you worry about Zuby and me. We'll boss this end of the craft; you 'tend to the rest of it. Say, that Hungerford swab ain't come back, has he?"

"No. No, he hasn't. He's gone for good, it looks like. Sent for his trunk and gone."

Laban seemed disappointed. "Well, all right," he said. "If he should come, just send for me. I'd just as soon talk to him as not—rather, if anything."

The captain shook his head in a puzzled way. "That business of—of him and Zuba was the strangest thing," he declared. "I can't make head nor tail of it, and Gertie won't talk about it at all. He said 'twas a mistake, and of course it must have been. Either that or he'd gone crazy. No sane man would—"

"What's that?" It was Mr. Ginn's turn to question, and Daniel's to look foolish.

"Why—why, go away and leave us without sayin' good-by," explained the Captain. "Er—well, so long, Laban. Make yourself at home. I've got to see how Serena is."

He hurried up the back stairs. Mr. Ginn, who seemed a trifle suspicious, called after him, but the call was unheeded. At the door of his wife's room—his room no longer—Captain Dan rapped softly. The nurse opened the door.

"How is she?" he whispered.

"She is asleep now," whispered the nurse in reply. "You must not come in."

"I wasn't goin' to. But—but—has she been askin' for me?"

"Yes. I told her you were out. If she wakes and asks for you I will call. She is easier when you are with her—or near by."

This was true. The one person Serena wished to see most of all was her husband. She asked for Gertrude, of course, but it was Daniel for whom she asked continually. If he were near her she seemed almost happy and contented.

"You are a good man, Daniel," she whispered. "A dear, good, unselfish man."

"No, no, I ain't any such thing," protested the captain hastily.

"But you are. And—and WHAT should I do without you now?"

"Sh-sh! I'm not much help. Land knows I wish I was more."

"You ARE the help; all the help I have. Gertie—Daniel, you will keep an eye on Gertie, won't you. You won't let her do anything foolish."

"Gertie? She won't do foolish things. She ain't that kind."

"I know, but she has changed so. It worries me. Percy—"

"Now don't you worry about Percy. He isn't here now."

"Not here? Where is he?"

"I don't know. He's gone away—for a spell, anyhow. Maybe that vacation he used to talk about is over."

Serena was too weak to ask further questions, even concerning so surprising a matter as Cousin Percy's sudden departure. But she did make one further plea.

"Daniel," she begged, "if Annette calls about the Chapter you tell her—"

"I've told her. She understands. She says it's all right."

"Does she? I'm so glad. Oh, Daniel, you'll have to take charge of everything now. I can't, and Gertrude—you must do it, yourself, Daniel. You WILL, won't you, Daniel?"

"Sure I will. I'm skipper now, Serena. You ought to see how the hands jump when I give an order."

It was true, too; the hands did "jump" at the captain's orders. He was skipper, for the time being. His wife's illness, Mr. Hungerford's absence, Gertrude's meekness all combined to strengthen Daniel's resolution, and he was, for the first time in years, the actual head of the household.

His statement concerning Mrs. Black was not the literal truth. Annette had called, that was true; she had called the very next morning after her chief aide was stricken. But she had not declared that everything was "all right"; far from it. "But can't I see her, Captain Dott?" she begged. "I MUST see her for just a minute."

"Sorry, ma'am, but you can't do it. Doctor's orders. She mustn't be disturbed."

"But I've got to see her."

"I know, but I'm afraid you can't. You can talk to me, if that will do any good."

"It won't. Where is Gertrude? Let me talk to her."

Daniel climbed the stairs to his daughter's room. He found her sitting at her desk; she had been writing "regrets" in answer to various invitations. She turned a careworn face in his direction. "What is it, Daddy?" she asked. "Mother is not worse, is she?"

"No, no; she's better, if anything. But that—er—Annette Black has come and, long as she can't see Serena, she wants to talk to you."

"About her precious politics, I suppose."

"That's what she wants."

"I can't see her. I don't want to see her. I don't want to hear the word politics. I—"

"That's enough, that's enough. I'll 'tend to HER. You stay right here." He descended to the drawing-room, where Annette was fidgeting on the edge of a chair, and announced calmly that Gertrude was not at home.

The caller's agitation got the better of her temper. "Nonsense!" she snapped. "How do you know she isn't?"

"Because she said so. Lovely mornin' for a walk, isn't it?"

Mrs. Black rose and stalked to the threshold. But there she turned once more. "If your wife knew," she cried hysterically, "how I, her best friend, was treated in her house, she—she—"

Daniel stepped forward. "I beg your pardon, Mrs. Black," he said. "Maybe I have been pretty plain spoken. But, you see, we're all upset here. I'm upset, and Gertie's as much so as the rest. She can't talk to you, or anybody else, now. I'm willin' to try, but you say my talkin' won't do any good."

"Of course it won't. I'm sorry Serena is not well, but this is IMPORTANT."

"I know, but so's her health, 'cordin' to my thinkin'."

"If I might see her just a moment. It is so provoking. Doesn't my—her election mean ANYTHING to you? Don't you care about the cause?"

The captain shook his head. "All I'm carin' for is my wife, just now," he said. "She's all I can think about. If some of us had thought more about her, maybe—" He stopped, cleared his throat, and added: "I know you'll understand and forgive us, when you think it over. I'll tell her you called. Good-mornin'."

If he supposed this was the end, he was mistaken. Annette was not so easily whipped or discouraged. She called again that afternoon, and again the next day. Each morning for a week she came, and, between times, other adherents of the Black-Dott party called. They all asked concerning the invalid, but their interest plainly centered upon her part in the campaign. Would she be well enough to take part in the election, that was the question. They sent flowers and notes. The flowers reached the lady for whom they were intended; the notes did not. And, after the first week, the calls became fewer. Annette and her followers had, apparently, given up hope of aid and advice from their candidate for vice-president. At any rate they ceased to trouble the captain and his daughter.

"It's all the better, Daddy, dear," said Gertrude. "Mother will have a chance to rest and improve now."

And Serena did improve, slowly at first, then with gratifying rapidity. She began to sit up for a portion of each day and to sleep through the greater part of each night. At the end of the tenth day the doctor announced that the nurse's services were no longer necessary.

"She will be all right now," he said, referring to his patient. "But she must continue to have absolute rest and she must not be worried or permitted to worry. If you and she could go somewhere, Captain Dott, to some quiet place in the country, and stay there for six months, I think it would help her more than anything. Can you do it?"

"I can do it, Doctor," replied Daniel eagerly. "I'll go anywhere, if it will help her."

"Good! Then I will advise it and you and Miss Dott must back my advice. Will you?"

"I will, and so'll Gertie, I'm sure. You speak to her, Doctor. We'll do the backin' up."

So the doctor made the suggestion. Serena received it quietly, but, when her husband came to do his share of the "backing up," she shook her head.

"I'd like to, Daniel," she said. "I'd like to, but I can't."

"You can't? Course you can! Now let's think where we'll go. Niagara Falls, hey? You always wanted to go to the Falls."

"No, Daniel."

"No? Well, then, how about Washin'ton? We'll see the President, and the monument, and the Smithsonian Museum, and Congress—we'll see ALL the curiosities and relics. We'll go to—"

"Don't, Daniel. It makes me tired out just to hear about them. I couldn't stand all that."

"Course you couldn't! The doctor said you needed rest and quiet, and Washin'ton is about as quiet as the Ostable Cattle Show. Well, what do you say to the White Mountains?"

"In winter? No, Daniel, if I went anywhere I should like to go to—to—"

"Where, Serena? Just name it and I'll buy the tickets."

"Daniel, I'd rather go to Trumet than anywhere else."

Captain Dan could scarcely believe it. "WHAT!" he cried. "You want to go to Trumet, Serena?"

"Yes. I've been wanting to go for some time. I never told you; I wouldn't even admit it to myself; but I've thought about it a great deal. I longed to be somewhere where there was nothing going on and where you and I could be together as we used to be. And, oh, Daniel—"

"Yes, Serena? Yes?"

"Oh, Daniel, since I've been really sick, since I've been getting better and could think at all, I've been thinking more and more about our old house at Trumet, and how nice and comfortable we were there, and what pleasant evenings you and

I used to have together. It was home, Daniel, really and truly home, and this place never has been, has it?"

"You bet it hasn't! Lordy, but I'm glad to hear you talk this way, Serena! I haven't thought anything else since we first landed, but I never imagined you did."

"I didn't, at first. It has been only lately since I began to feel so tired and my head troubled me so. Daniel, I'm not sure that our coming here wasn't a mistake."

The captain was perfectly sure.

"That's all right, Serena," he cried. "If it was a mistake it's one that can be straightened out in two shakes of slack jib sheet. You stay here and rest easy. I'll be back in a few minutes."

"Where are you going?"

"I'm going to make arrangements for our trip to Trumet. 'Twon't take me long."

"Daniel, stop! I didn't say I was going. I said I should like to go."

"That's the same thing. Now, Serena, I know what's frettin' you. You're thinkin' what'll become of this house and all the fine things in it. They'll be all right. We could rent this house in no time, I know it. I ain't sure but what we could sell it if we wanted to. That real estate fellow, the one Barney—B. Phelps, I mean—introduced me to down street one time, met me t'other day and told me if I ever thought of sellin' this place to let him know. Course I didn't pay much attention then; I judged you wouldn't think of sellin', but—"

"Stop! stop, Daniel! You are so excited it makes me nervous again to hear you. I wasn't thinking of the house at all. The way I feel now I had as soon sell it as not. But that isn't it. I can't leave Scarford."

Daniel's enthusiasm faded. There was determination in his wife's tone. "Oh!" he observed wistfully, "you can't? You're sure you can't, Serena? You know what the doctor said. Why can't you go?"

"Because I can't. It is impossible. I couldn't leave the Chapter. I am a candidate for vice-president. My friends are depending upon me. I couldn't desert them. I told you that before. Would they desert me?"

"I suppose likely they wouldn't," reluctantly.

"You know they wouldn't. No personal considerations, no selfish reasons, NOTHING could make them do it. But I've said this all before, Daniel. You must see why I have to stay. I'd like to go, I'd love to, but I can't."

Captain Dan sighed. "I presume likely you're right, Serena," he admitted. "It would seem like a mean trick, the way you put it.

But after the election? You said, when we was talkin' before, that after you was elected maybe you would go with Gertie and me somewhere. And we'll go to Trumet, that's where we'll go."

"All right, Daniel, dear, we'll see. And don't worry about me. I am almost well again and I am going to be completely well. Now won't you ask Gertie to come in and talk with me? I am beginning to think about the election. Gertrude must go. We need her vote and her influence. Send her to me, Daniel, please."

So the captain, his hopes somewhat dashed, but finding comfort in his wife's new longing to visit the one spot on earth which spelled home to him, left the room to carry Serena's message to their daughter.

He was busy at the desk in the library when, several hours later, Gertrude entered. She was wearing her hat and coat and, coming into the library, stood beside him. He looked up. His expression surprised and alarmed her.

"Why, what's the matter, Daddy?" she asked anxiously. "You look as if something dreadful had happened. What is it?"

Her father put down his pen. A sheet of paper, covered with figures, was on the desk before him; so, also, was the family checkbook which had been, until the illness of Mrs. Dott, in that lady's sole charge.

"Matter?" he repeated. "Do I look as if somethin' was the matter? Where have you been?"

"I have been out. Mother was so anxious about the election that I promised her I would see Mrs. Black and some of the others this very day. I have been calling on them."

"Have, hey? Well, what's the prospect? The cause of right and Black, and justice and Dott is goin' to prevail, I presume likely, isn't it?"

"I don't know. I couldn't find out anything. Mrs. Black was not in, at least that is what the maid said; but I am almost sure she was in. I think I saw her peeping between the curtains as I went down the steps."

"That so? Perhaps she was dosin' you with the same medicine I handed her when she called that first day after Serena was taken down."

"I thought of that. But I called on three other leaders of Mother's party—"

"Yours and your mother's, you mean?"

"Yes, of course. I called on three of our leaders. Two of them were in and I talked with them. I could learn nothing from either about the election. They would not discuss it, except to say that everything would be all right. They behaved so oddly and were so embarrassed. It was perfectly obvious that they wanted to get rid of me. I can't understand it."

"There's lots of things we can't understand in this world. Don't fret your mother about it."

"I shan't, of course. But what is troubling you, Daddy? Something, I know."

"Look that way, do I? See here, Gertie, I'm stumped. I've been goin' over back bills and the bankbook and the checkbook and—and—well, I'm on my beam ends, that's where I am."

"Why? Don't the books balance?"

"They balance all right. That's what's kicked me over. If they're true we've spent close to five thousand dollars since we made this town."

"Indeed! Well?"

"WELL! Five thousand dollars! I'm sayin' five THOUSAND; do you understand?"

"I understand. I'm not surprised. Living as we do, and moving in the—in the best society as we have, the expense is large, naturally. You must expect that."

"Expect! Gertie Baker Dott, STOP talkin' that way! Our income, not countin' what the store at Trumet is fetchin' in, ain't over six thousand at the outside. Six thousand a YEAR, that is. And we've got rid of five thousand in a few months! We've got a thousand or so to live the rest of this year on. One thousand—"

"Hush, Daddy! We shall have to use a part of the principal, I presume."

"Part of the prin—Oh, my soul and body! Use part of it this year, and some more next year, and some more the next, and—and—Do you know where we'll be ten year from now? In the poorhouse, that's where."

"Oh, I hope not as bad as that. And, besides, think what a beautiful time we shall have during those ten years. Just as beautiful as we have had so far; better, no doubt, for we have really only begun."

"Ger-tie DOTT!"

"Just think of it, Daddy. We have only begun."

"I—I won't think of it! I'll stop it, that's what I'll do!"

Gertrude smilingly shook her head. "Oh, no, you won't, Daddy," she said. "You never stop anything."

She turned to go. Captain Dan sat, speechless in his chair, staring at the bills, the figures, the checkbook, and the prospect of the poorhouse. Then he felt her hand upon his shoulder. "Never mind, Daddy, dear," she said softly. "I think—I am beginning to hope that YOUR worries are almost over."

She kissed him and hurried out before he could collect his senses sufficiently to ask what she meant. He did ask her at their next meeting, but she only smiled and would not tell him.

The next morning Serena's first remark was concerning the election, which was to take place that evening. All that day she spoke of little else, and when the evening came she insisted upon Gertrude's leaving for the hall immediately after dinner.

It was after ten when the young lady appeared. She was very grave when her father met her in the hall. "How is Mother?" she asked. "Asleep, I hope."

Daniel nodded. "Yes," he said, "she's asleep, for a wonder. She vowed and declared she was goin' to stay awake until you came, but I read out loud to her and she dropped off while I was doin' it."

"Then don't wake her, for the world. Tell her I have returned, that I am tired and have gone to bed, and will give her the news in the morning."

"That won't do. She'll want to know to-night. What is the news? Can't you leave some message? She won't rest if you don't."

Gertrude pondered. "Tell her," she began slowly, "tell her Mrs. Black is elected. Perhaps she will take—other things for granted."

But when morning, very early morning, came, Captain Dan summoned his daughter from her room.

"She's wide awake, Gertie," he said, "and she wants to know it all. You'd better come and tell her."

But Gertrude had been thinking. "I think you had better tell her first, Daddy," she said. "I think it may be wiser for you to tell her. Things were said and done at that election which she must not know. I will tell you the result and how it came about and you can tell her. Perhaps that will be sufficient. Listen, Daddy."

Daniel listened. "My soul and body!" he exclaimed, when the tale was ended. "My Godfreys! and those were the folks she figgered were her friends!"

"Yes."

"And Annette Black—"

"She was the moving spirit in the whole of it, I'm certain."

"My Godfreys! And she—and she—well, I guess maybe Serena'll be willin' to go back to Trumet NOW. She wanted to go before; 'twas only loyalty to that gang that kept her from goin'. She said she'd give anything to go back to the old house and be comfortable same as we used to be; she said—"

"Daddy!" Gertrude seized his arm. "Did she—did Mother really say that?" she demanded eagerly.

"Sure, she said it!"

"And she meant it?"

"She acted as if she did. Course we both realized 'twould be hard for you, Gertie, but—"

"Go! Go and tell her about the election." She fairly pushed him from her. "Don't wait," she urged, "go."

Daniel was on his way when she called him back.

"I almost forgot, Daddy, dear," she said repentantly. "I was so gl—I mean—well, never mind. What I want to say is that if you think the news will be too great a shock, if you think she is not strong enough to hear it now—"

Her father interrupted. "She's stronger than I've seen her for a fortnight," he declared. "And one thing's sure, she won't rest till she does hear it. I shall tell her, and get it over."

"Then be as gentle as you can, won't you?"

"I'll try. But, Gertie, what did you mean by sayin' you was so—so glad? I don't see as there's much to be glad about."

"Don't you? Well, perhaps. . . . Run along, Daddy, run along."

She closed the door of her room. Daniel, much perplexed, departed on his unpleasant errand.

His wife was eagerly awaiting him. "Where's Gertie?" she demanded. "Isn't she coming?"

"She'll come by and by, Serena. She isn't quite dressed yet."

"What difference does that make? Didn't you tell her I was dying to hear about the election? She must know I am."

"She does; she knows that, Serena. But she thought—she thought I'd better tell you first, myself."

Serena leaned forward to look at him. His expression alarmed her.

"Why don't you tell, then?" she asked. "Is it—oh, Daniel, it isn't bad news, is it?"

"It ain't very good, Serena."

"You don't mean—why, you said that Annette was elected; you said so last night."

"Yes—yes, she was elected, Serena; but—"

"But—but I wasn't. Is that what you mean, Daniel?"

"Well now, Serena—"

"I wasn't. Yes, it is true, I can see it in your face. Oh—oh, Daniel!"

Captain Dan put his arm about her. "There! there! Serena," he said chokingly, "don't cry, don't. Don't feel too bad about it. Politics is politics, inside Chapters and out, I guess. I'm as much disappointed as you are, for your sake, but—but don't care too much, will you? Don't make yourself sick again. Don't cry no more than you can help."

Serena raised her head from his shoulder. "I'm not crying," she said. "Really I'm not, Daniel. It is a relief to me, in a way."

"A RELIEF?"

"Yes. If it had happened a month ago I should have felt it terribly. I was crazy for office then. But lately I have dreaded it so. If I were vice-president I should have so much care, so much responsibility. Now, I shan't. The honor would have been great, I appreciate that. But, for the rest of it, I don't really care."

"Don't CARE!"

"No, I don't. And now," bravely, "tell me all about it. I don't quite see how Annette could win if I did not; but Miss Canby is popular, she has a great many friends. I hope," wistfully, "I hope I got a good vote. Did I, Daniel?"

Daniel's indignation burst forth. "You didn't get any votes, Serena," he cried angrily.

"What? No votes? Why—"

"Not a blessed one. They put up a low-down political trick on you, Serena. They left you out to save themselves. They took advantage of your bein' sick to—to—Here, I'll tell you just what they did."

What they had done was this: Mrs. Lake and Mrs. Black, heads of the opposing factions, each realizing how close the vote was likely to be, had, with their lieutenants—Mrs. Dott excepted—gotten together five days before the election and arranged a compromise, a trade. By this arrangement, Annette was to receive the Lake party's support for president; Miss Canby was to be given the Black support for vice-president; and the united support of both factions was to be behind Mrs. Lake in her struggle for office in the National body. Serena, not being on hand to protect her own interest, had been sacrificed, her name had not even been brought before the members to be voted upon.

Captain Dan told of this precious scheme, just as it had been told him by his daughter. At first his wife interrupted with exclamations and questions; then she listened in silence.

"That's what they did," cried the captain angrily. "Chucked you into the scrap heap to save themselves. And you sick abed! These were the FRIENDS you thought you had. And Annette Black was the worst of all. 'Twas her idea in the first place. Why, Serena—"

But Serena could hear no more. She threw her arms about her husband's neck and the tears, which she had so bravely repressed at the tidings of her own disappointment, burst forth.

"Oh—oh, Daniel," she sobbed, "take me away from here. I hate this place; I hate Scarford and all the dreadful people in it! Take me to Trumet, Daniel. Take me home!"

Half an hour later Captain Dan shouted his daughter's name over the balusters. "Gertie!" he called; "Gertie! come up here, will you?"

Gertrude came. She had feared to find her mother prostrate, suffering from a new attack of "nerves." She was prepared to obey her father's order to 'phone for the doctor.

But Serena did not, apparently, need a doctor. She was not prostrate, and, although she was nervous, it was rather the nervousness of expectancy, coupled with determination.

"Gertie," said the captain, "I've got some news for you. Your mother and I have made up our minds to go back to Trumet, and we want you to go along with us."

The young lady did not answer at once. She looked first at Serena and then at Daniel. The troubled expression left her face and was succeeded by another, an odd one. When she spoke it was in a tone of great surprise.

"To Trumet?" she repeated. "Not to live there?"

Captain Dan hesitated, but his wife did not. "Yes," she said decidedly, "to live. For the present, anyhow. At least we shan't live here any longer."

"Not live here? Why, what do you mean?"

Her father answered. "She means what she says, I presume likely," he observed impatiently. "Think she's talkin' for the fun of it? This ain't April Fool Day."

"But she can't mean it. She can't! Give up the Chapter, and all our friends—"

"Friends! They're a healthy lot of friends, they are!"

"Hush, Daddy; I'm not talking to you. Do you realize what you are saying, Mother? Give up the Chapter, and all your ambitions there? Give up Mrs. Black and Mrs. Lake and Miss Canby—"

"And that twist and squirm, antique Greece disgrace of a Dusante woman—don't forget her. Gertie, you stop now. Your ma knows—"

"Daddy, be still. Mother, are you willing to give them up? And all our society! You say yourself that there is no society in Trumet. Give up our bridge lessons, and our dancing, and our teas, and—"

"For the land sakes! What is this; a catalogue you're givin' us? Stop it! Serena, you tell her to stop."

But Gertrude would not stop. "Think what it would mean," she protested. "Think of your social position, Mother, the position we have worked so hard to attain."

Serena shook her head. "I don't care," she said firmly. "Our social position was good enough in Trumet."

"WHAT! Why, Mother! how often I have heard you say—"

"Never mind what I said. I have said a lot of foolish things, and done a lot, too. But I'm through. I'm sick and disgusted with it all. I'm going to be simple and comfortable and happy—yes, happy.

Oh, Gertie, DON'T talk to me about society! There isn't a real, sincere person in it, not in the set we have been in. I hate Scarford and I hate society."

"Mother! how can you! And opportunity and advancement—"

"I hate them, too."

Gertrude gasped. "Why, Mother!" she exclaimed. "And it was you who first showed me the way. Think what leaving here would mean to me. Think of Mr. Holway. Is there a young man like him in Trumet? Think of Cousin Percy!"

That was quite enough. Serena rose, her eyes flashing. "Stop!" she cried. "Gertrude Dott, your father and I are going back to Trumet and you are going with us."

"Oh, no, I'm not. Why, Cousin Percy—"

"Don't you dare mention his name to me."

"Why not? He is very gentlemanly and very aristocratic. You told me that when I first came, Mother. And I'm sure he moves in the highest circles; he says he does, himself."

"He is a good-for-nothing loafer. He has sponged upon your father—"

"You have often spoken of him as an honor to the family."

"A good-for-nothing, dissipated, fast—"

"Oh, a little dissipation is expected in society, isn't it?"

"I should think you would be ashamed!"

"Why? I haven't done a thing that you haven't done, Mother. That is, nothing which your friends don't do every day. They are ever so much more advanced than I am. I have only begun. No, indeed, I am not going back to plain, common, every-day old Trumet. I shall stay here and progress. Why, Mrs. Black says that, if I play my cards well, I may catch a millionaire, perhaps a foreign nobleman. How would you like to be mother-in-law to a—well, to a count, for instance?"

Mrs. Dott did not answer this question. Instead she turned to her husband. "Daniel," she cried, "are you going to stand this? Are you that girl's father, or aren't you? Are you going to make her mind, or not?"

Daniel would have spoken, but his daughter got ahead of him. "Oh, Father doesn't count," she observed lightly. "No one minds what he says. He didn't want to move to Scarford at all."

Serena stamped her foot. "Daniel Dott," she cried, "do you hear that? I call upon you, as the head of this family, to tell that girl what she's got to do, and make her do it."

Captain Dan stepped forward. Gertrude merely laughed. That laugh settled the question. "Gertie," ordered the captain, his voice, the old quarter-deck voice which had been law aboard the *Bluebird*, "you march your boots to your room and pack up. We're goin' to Trumet and you're goin' along with us. March! or, by the everlastin', I'll carry you there and lock you in! You speak another word and I'll do it, anyway. Serena, I'll 'tend to her. You're tired out; lie down and rest."

"But, Daniel—"

"Lie down and rest. I'm runnin' this craft. Well," wheeling upon his daughter, "are you goin'? Or shall I carry you?"

Gertrude looked at him and then at her mother. Her lips twitched. "I'll go, Daddy," she said meekly, and went.

When Captain Dan descended to the lower floor he found Mr. Ginn in the library.

"Hello!" hailed the latter, "you look kind of set-up and sassy, seems to me. YOU ain't had nothin' to drink, have you?"

"Drink? What do you mean by that? Has anybody around here had anything to drink?"

"I don't know. Some of 'em act as if they had. When I came into the kitchen a spell ago I found my wife and Gertie dancin' like a couple of loons."

"Dancin'?"

"Yes, sir, holdin' hands and hoppin' around like sand fleas in a clam bake. I asked 'em what set 'em goin' and they wouldn't tell me. I couldn't think of anything but liquor that would start Zuby Jane dancin'. I don't know's that would but 'twas the only likely guess I could make."

CHAPTER XV

Captain Dan was seated in his old chair, at his old desk, behind the counter of the Metropolitan Store. Over the counter, beyond the showcases and the tables with their piles of oilskins, mittens, sou'westers, and sweaters, through the panes of the big front windows, he could see the road, the main street of Trumet. Beyond the road, between the shops and houses on the opposite side, he saw the bare brown hills, the pond where the city people found waterlilies in the summer the sand dunes, the beach, the closed and shuttered hotel and cottages, and, beyond these, the cold gray and white of the wintry sea rolling beneath a gloomy sky. To the average person the view would have been desolation itself. To Captain Dan it was a section of Paradise. It was the picture which had been in his mind for months. And here it was in reality, unchanged, unspoiled, a part of home, his home. And he, at last, was at home again.

They had been in Trumet a week, the captain and Serena and Gertrude. Azuba had been there two days longer, having been sent on ahead of the family to open the house and get it ready. Laban remained behind as caretaker of the Scarford mansion.

Laban's remaining as caretaker was his own suggestion. "Me and the old gal have talked it over," he explained, "and it seems like the best thing to do. You've got to have somebody here, Cap'n Dott, you've got to pay somebody, and it might as well be me. I'm out of a job just now, anyway. As for me and my wife bein' separated—well, we're different from most married folks that way; it seems the natural thing for us to BE separated. I don't know as we'd get along so well together if we wasn't. There's nothin' like separation to keep husband and wife happy along with one another. I've been with Zuby for most three weeks steady now; that's the longest stretch we've had in a good many years. We ain't quarreled once, neither."

He seemed to consider the fact remarkable. Captain Dott grinned. "I suppose that shuttin' her up in the dish closet wasn't what you'd call a quarrel, hey?" he observed.

Mr. Ginn was momentarily embarrassed. "Oh, that!" he exclaimed. "Humph! I forgot that, for the minute. But that wasn't a quarrel, rightly speakin'. 'Twas just a little difference of opinion on account of my not understandin' her reason for bein' so sot on havin' her own way. Soon's I understood 'twas all right."

So, after consultation with Azuba, the arrangement was perfected. Laban was to receive ten dollars a week, from which sum he was to provide his own meals. He was to sleep in the house, but the meals were to be obtained elsewhere. Mrs. Dott would not consider his cooking in her kitchen.

Serena bore the fatigue of the journey well and the sight of her old home, with the table set for supper, plants in the dining-room windows, and all the little familiar touches which Azuba's thoughtfulness had supplied, served to bring her the contentment and happiness she had been longing for. Each day she gained in health and strength, and the rest and freedom from care, together with the early hours—they retired at nine-thirty each night—were doing wonders for her. Her husband was delighted at the improvement. He was delighted with everything, the familiar scenes, the smell of the salt marshes, and of the sea, the clear, cold air, the meeting with friends and acquaintances, the freedom from society all these things delighted his soul. And now, on the Saturday morning at the end of his first week at home, as he sat in his arm chair behind the counter of the Metropolitan Store, looking at the view through the windows and at the store itself, he was a happy man. There was one flaw in his happiness, but that he had forgotten for the moment.

He glanced about him and said aloud: "Well, if I didn't know 'twas the same place, I wouldn't have known it. I never saw such a change in my life."

Nathaniel Bangs, standing by the front window, turned. "I don't see much difference," he said. "The old town looks about the same to me."

The captain smilingly shook his head. "'Tain't the town," he observed. "It's this store. Nate, you're a wonder, that's what you are, a wonder."

For, if the view had not changed, if it was the same upon which Daniel Dott had looked for many winters, through the windows of that very store, the store itself had changed materially. Mr. Bangs had wrought the change and it was distinctly a change for the better. The stock, and there was a surprising deal of it, was new and attractively displayed. The contents of the showcases were varied and up-to-date. Neatly lettered placards calling attention to special bargains hung in places where they were most likely to be seen. There was a spruce, swept, and garnished look to the establishment; as Azuba said when she first saw it after her return, it looked as if it had had a shave and a hair cut. In other words, the Metropolitan Store appeared wide awake and prosperous, as if it was making money—which it was.

"You're a wonder, Nate," repeated Daniel. "I don't know how to get even with you, but I've got an idea. I've talked it over with Serena already and she's for it. I want to ask Gertie's opinion and if she says yes, and she will, I'm almost sartin, I'll tell you what it is."

"All right, Cap'n. Don't you worry yourself trying to 'get even,' as you call it, with me. I've enjoyed being in charge here. I always said there was money in a store in Trumet, if it was run as it should be. One year more and I can show you a few things, I'll bet."

"You've shown 'em already. Land of love! I should say you had."

"Give me time and I'll show you more. We have only begun. . . . Why, what's the matter? What made you look that way?"

"Oh, nothin', nothin'. Only your sayin' we'd only begun reminded me of—of other things. I don't suppose I'll ever hear 'only begun' without shiverin'. Humph! there's some kind of beginnin's I hope I'll never hear of again. Gertie been in this mornin', has she? She isn't in the house."

"No, I saw her go down street a little while ago. Gone for her morning walk, perhaps. How is Mrs. Dott to-day?"

"Tip top. I ain't seen her so satisfied with life for two months or more. She's gettin' better every minute."

"That's good. Contented to be back in Trumet, is she?"

"Seems to be. I am; you can bet high on that."

"And—er—Gertie, is she contented, too?"

This question touched directly the one uncertainty, the one uncomfortable doubt in the captain's mind. "What makes you ask that?" he demanded.

"Oh, nothing much. She seems changed, that's all. She used to be so full of spirits, and so bright and lively. Now she is quiet and doesn't talk much. Looks thinner, too, and as if something was troubling her. Perhaps it is my imagination. When's John Doane coming down? 'Most time for him to be spending a Sunday with you, ain't it? Engaged folks don't usually stay apart more than a week, especially when the one is as near the other as Boston is to Trumet."

Daniel knocked the ashes from his pipe into the wastebasket. "Oh, oh, John'll be along pretty soon, I shouldn't wonder," he said hastily. "He—he's pretty busy these days, I suppose."

"Nice thing his bein' taken into the firm, after Mr. Griffin died, wasn't it. Well, he's a pretty smart fellow, John is, and he deserves to get ahead. Did he tell you the particulars about it?"

"No. No, not all of 'em. Is that a customer in the other room?"

Mr. Bangs hurried away to attend to the customer. The captain seized the opportunity to make a timely exit. He went into the house, remained a while with his wife, and then returned.

Nathaniel had gone on an order-taking trip and Sam Bartlett, the boy, was in charge. Just as Daniel entered the store from the side door Gertrude came in at the front.

"Hello, Daddy," she said. "All alone?"

"Not quite, but I'd just as soon be. Sam, go into the other room; I'll hail you if I need you. Gertie, come here. I want to have a talk with you."

Gertrude came. She took her old position, perching upon the arm of her father's chair, with her own arm about his neck. "Gertie," began the captain, "what would you think of my makin' Nate Bangs a partner in this concern?"

Gertrude uttered an exclamation of delight. "Splendid!" she cried. "I thought of it, but I said nothing because I wanted you to say it first. It will be just the right thing."

"Ye-es, so it seemed to me. All that's good here in this store is due to Nathaniel. He's made a real, live business out of a remains that was about ready for the undertaker. I ought to give him the whole craft, but—but I hate to."

"You could. You could sell out to him and still have sufficient income to live upon in comfort here in Trumet. You might sell out, retire, and be a gentleman of leisure, one of the town's rich men."

Daniel grunted in disgust. "Don't talk that way," he repeated. "I've had enough gentleman of leisure foolishness to last me through. What do you think I am; a second-hand copy of Cousin Percy, without the gilt edges?"

Gertrude smiled. "I guess not," she declared. "You are not in the habit of 'dining out'—in Trumet, at any rate. Have you told Mother?"

"Yes, I told her. I don't think she was much surprised. She'd guessed as much before, so I gathered from what she said."

"No doubt; the explanation was obvious enough. Well, Daddy, I did not expect you would be contented to retire and do nothing. That is not your conception of happiness. But, if you do take Mr. Bangs into partnership, let him manage the entire business. You can be in the store as much as you wish, and be interested in it, so long as you don't interfere. And you and Mother can be together and take little trips together once in a while. You mustn't stay in Trumet ALL the time; if you do you will grow discontented again."

"No, no, I shan't. Serena may, perhaps, but I shan't."

"Yes, you will. You both have seen a little of outside life now, and it isn't all bad, though you may think so just at this time. You mustn't settle down and grow narrow like some of the people here in Trumet—Abigail Mayo, for instance."

"Humph! I'd have to swallow a self-windin' talkin' machine before I could get to be like Abigail Mayo. But you may be right, Gertie; perhaps you are. See here, though, how about you, yourself? You've seen a heap more of what you call outside life than your ma and I have. How are YOU goin' to keep contented here in Trumet?"

"Oh, I shall be contented. Don't worry about me."

"But I do worry, and your mother is beginnin' to worry, too. See here, Gertie, you ain't—you ain't feelin' bad about—about leavin' that Cousin Percy, are you?"

The young lady's cheeks reddened, but with indignation, not embarrassment. "DADDY!" she protested sharply. "Daddy, how can you! Cousin Percy!"

"Well, you know—"

"I hate him. I've told you so. Or I should, if he was worth hating; as it is I despise him thoroughly."

"That's good! But, you see, Gertie—well, when your mother and I first told you we'd made up our minds to come back here, you—you stood up for him, and said he was aristocratic and—and I don't know what all. That's what you said; and 'twas after the Zuba business, too."

Gertrude regarded him wonderingly. "Said!" she repeated. "I said and did all sorts of things. Daddy—Daddy, DEAR, is it possible you don't understand yet that it was all make-believe?"

"All make-believe? What; your likin' Cousin Percy?"

"Yes, that and Mr. Holway and everything else—the whole of it. It was all a sham; don't you see? When I came back from college and found out exactly how things were going, I realized at once that something must be done. You were miserable and neglected, and Mother was under the influence of Mrs. Black and that empty-headed, ridiculous Chapter and would-be society crowd of hers. I tried at first to reason with her, but that was useless. So I thought and thought until I had a plan. I believed if I could show her, by my own example, how silly and ridiculous the kind of people she associated with were, if I pretended to be as bad as the worst of them, she would begin by seeing how ridiculous I was, and be frightened into realizing her own position. At any rate, she would be forced into giving it all up to save me. Of course I didn't expect her to be taken ill. When THAT happened I was SO conscience-stricken. But it has turned out so well, that even that is—"

"Gertie! Gertie Dott! stop where you are. Do you mean to tell me that all your—your advancin' and dancin' and bridgin' and tea-in' and Chapterin' was just—"

"Just make-believe, that's all. I hated it as much as you did; as much as Mother does now."

"My SOUL! but—but it can't be! Cousin Percy—"

"Oh, do forget Cousin Percy! I was sure he was exactly what he was and that he was using you and Mother as conveniences for providing him with a home and luxuries which he was too worthless to work for. I was sure of it, morally sure, but I made up my mind to find out. I pretended to like him—"

"Hold on! for mercy sakes, hold on! YOU pretended, but—but HE didn't. If ever a feller was gone on a young woman he was, towards the last of it. Why, he—"

"Hush! hush! Don't speak of it. It makes me disgusted with myself even to think of him. It serves him right. And I think that it was with my—with your money, Daddy, much more than your daughter, he was infatuated. I had the satisfaction of telling him my opinion of him and his conduct before he left."

"Ho! you did, hey? I wish I might have heard it. But, Gertie," his incredulity not entirely crushed, "it wasn't ALL make-believe; all of it couldn't have been. Even Zuba, she got the advancin' craziness. She joined a—a 'Band,' or somethin'."

"No, she didn't. She pretended to, but she didn't. There wasn't any such 'Band.' She was helping me to cure Mother, that's all. It was all part of the plan. Her husband understands now, although," with a laugh, "he didn't when he first came."

Daniel drew his hand across his forehead. "Well!" he exclaimed. "WELL! and I—and I—"

"I treated you dreadfully, didn't I? Scolded you, and told you to go away, and—and everything. I COULDN'T tell you the truth, because you cannot keep a secret, but I was sorry, so sorry for you, even when you were most provoking. You WOULD interfere, you know. Two or three times you almost spoiled it all."

"Did I? I shouldn't wonder. And—and to think I never suspicioned a bit of it!"

"I don't see why you didn't. It was so plain. I'm sure Mother suspects—now."

"Probably she does. If I wasn't what I've called myself so much lately, an old fool, I'd have suspected, too. I AM an old fool."

"No, you're not. You are YOU, and that is why I love you—why, everyone who knows you loves you. And you are going to be happy now, aren't you?"

"I—I don't know. I ought to be, I suppose. I guess I shall be—if I ever get over thinkin' what a foolhead I was. So Zuba was part of it all, hey? And John, too? He was in it, I presume likely."

Gertrude's expression changed; so did her tone. "We won't talk about John, Daddy," she said. "Please don't."

"Why not? I want to talk about him. In a way—yes, sir! in a way I ain't sure that—that I didn't have a hand in spoilin' that, too. Considerin' what you've just told me, I wouldn't wonder if I did."

His daughter had risen to go. Now she turned back. "What do you mean?" she asked. "What do you mean? Spoiling—what?"

"Why—why, you and John, you know. Whatever happened between you and him happened that night when he come to Scarford. And he wouldn't have come—not then—if I hadn't written for him."

Gertrude was speechless. Her father went on. "Long's we're confessin'," he said, "we might as well make a clean job of it. I wrote him, all on my own hook. You see, Gertie, 'twas on your account mainly. Instead of straightenin' out your ma's course you were followin' in her wake, runnin' ahead of her, if anything. It looked as if you'd have her hull down and out of the race, if you kept on. I couldn't hold you back, and, bein' desperate, as I say, I wrote John to come and see if he could. And I told him to come quick. . . . Hey? What did you say?"

The young lady had said nothing; she had been listening, however, and now she seemed to have found an answer to a puzzle.

"So that was why he came?" she said, in a low tone, as if thinking aloud. "But—but without a word to me."

"Oh, I 'specially wrote him not to tell you he was comin'. I didn't want you to know. I wanted to have a talk with him first and tell him just how matters stood. After you'd gone to Chapter meetin' that night—I always thought 'twas queer, your bein' so determined to go, but I see why now; 'twas part of your plan, wasn't it?"

"Yes, yes, of course. Go on."

"Well, I judge John thought 'twas funny, too—but never mind. After you'd gone, he and I had our talk. I told him everything. He was kind of troubled; but he stood up for you through thick and thin. He only laughed when I told him—told him some things, those that worried me most."

Gertrude noticed his hesitation. "What were those things?" she asked.

"Oh, nothin'. They seem so foolish now; but at that time—"

"Daddy, did you tell him of my—my supposed friendship for Mr. Hungerford?"

Daniel reluctantly nodded. "Yes," he admitted. "I told him some. Perhaps I exaggerated a little. But he was so stubborn in not believin', that. . . . Hey? By Godfreys!" as the thought struck him for the first time, "THAT wasn't what ailed John, was it? He wasn't JEALOUS of that consarned Percy?"

Gertrude did not answer. "It couldn't be," continued Daniel. "He's got more sense than that. Besides, you told him, when you and he were alone together, why you was actin' so, didn't you? Or did he know it beforehand?"

Again there was no answer. When the young lady spoke it was to ask another question.

"Daddy," she said, not looking at him, but folding and unfolding a bit of paper on the counter, "are you SURE you mailed that letter I gave you the morning after—after he went away?"

"What? That letter to John that you gave me to mail? I'm sure as I can be of anything. I put it right in amongst the bills and checks I had ready, and when the postman came I gave 'em all to him with my own hands. Yes, it was mailed all right."

"And no letters came afterwards, which I didn't receive? You didn't put one in your pocket and forget it?"

"No. I'm sure of that. Why, your mother's cleaned out all my pockets a dozen times since. No, I didn't forget any letter for you, Gertie. What made you think I might have?"

"Oh, nothing; nothing, Daddy. Then, throwing down the bit of paper and moving toward the door, "I must go in and see Mother. I have scarcely seen her all the morning."

"But hold on, Gertie! I haven't found out what—Stop! Gertie, look at me! Why don't you look at me?"

She would not look and she would not stop. The door closed behind her. Captain Dan threw himself back in the chair. When Mr. Bangs, returning from his trip after orders, entered the store he found his employer just where he had left him. Now, however, the expression of high, good humor was no longer upon the captain's face.

"Well, Cap'n," hailed Nathaniel cheerfully. "Still on deck, I see. What are you doing; exercising your mind?"

"Humph! What little mind I'VE got has been exercised too blessed much. It needs rest more'n anything, but it don't seem likely to get a great deal. Nate, this world reminds me of a worn-out schooner, it's as full of troubles as that is full of leaks; and you no sooner get one patched up than another breaks out in a new place. Ah hum! . . . What you got there? The mail, is it? Anything for me?"

There was one letter bearing the captain's name. Nathaniel handed it to the owner of that name and the latter inspected the envelope and the postmark.

"From Labe Ginn," he observed. "Nobody else in Scarford that I know would spell Daniel with two 'l's and no 'i.' What's troublin' Laban? Somethin' about the house, I presume likely."

He leisurely tore open the envelope. The letter was a lengthy one, scrawled upon a half dozen sheets of cheap note paper.

"From Laban, is it?" asked Mr. Bangs casually.

"Yup, it's from Labe."

"There was another from him, then. At any rate there was one addressed in the same hen-tracks to Azuba. I met her as I was coming out of the post-office and gave it to her; she was on her way to the grocery store, she said."

Daniel nodded, but made no comment. Occasionally he chuckled. Laban began by saying that he expected his term as caretaker of the Scarford property to be of short duration. The new tenant would move in within a fortnight, he was almost sure. Mr. Ginn, personally, would be glad of it, for it was "lonesomer than a meeting-house on a week day."

"I spend the heft of my daytimes out in the Back yard," he wrote. "I don't offen meet anybody I know, but tother day I met barney Black. He asked about you and your fokes and I told him. He was prety down on his Luck I thort and acted Blue. His wife is hed neck and heles in Chapter goins on. I see her name in the Newspaper about evry day.

"He said give you his Regards and tell you you was a dam lukky Man."

Captain Dan's chuckle developed into a hearty laugh. He sympathized with and understood the feelings of B. Phelps.

"He has sold his summer Plase at Trumet," the letter went on. "Mrs. Black don't want to come thare no more. He has sold the Plase to some fokes name of Fenholtz. I know thats the rite name becos I made him spel it for me. Do you know them?"

Daniel uttered an exclamation of delight and struck his thigh a resounding slap.

"What's up?" asked Nathaniel. "Got some good news?"

"You bet! Mighty good! Some people I knew and liked in Scarford have bought the Black cottage here in Trumet."

"What I realy wrote you for," continued Mr. Ginn, at the top of page four, "was to tell you that I had a feller come to see me Yesterday. It was that forriner Hapgood who used to work for you. He told me a lot of things but manely all he wanted to talk about was that Swab of a Coussin of yours, that Hungerford. He sed Hungerford was a mene sneak and had treted him bad. He told me a Lot about how Hungerford worked you fokes for sukkers and how he helped. Seems him and Hungerford was old shipmates and chums and had worked your ant Laviny the same way. Hapgood says if you knew what he knows you'd be intterested. He says Hungerford pade him to get a hold of Tellygrams and letters that he thort you had better not see. He had one Coppy of a tellygram that he says come to him over the Tellyfone 3 days after John Doane left your house. It is from John to Gertie, but she never got it becos Hapgood never told her. I send it in this letter."

Captain Dan, who had read the latter part of this long paragraph with increasing excitement, now stopped his reading and began a hurried search for the "Coppy." He found it, on a separate sheet.

And this was what the captain read:

"MISS GERTRUDE DOTT,
"No. — Blank Avenue,
"Scarford, Mass.

"Why haven't you written? Did you receive my letters? The firm are sending me on urgent business to San Francisco. I leave to-night. If you write me there I shall know all is well and you have not changed. If not I shall know the other thing. I shall hope for a letter. San Francisco address is—"

Then followed the address and the signature, "John Doane."

The "Coppy" dropped in Daniel's lap. He closed his eyes. Nate Bangs, glancing at him, judged that he was falling asleep, but Mr. Bangs's usually acute judgment was, in this instance, entirely wrong. So far from sleeping, the captain was just beginning to wake up.

"Why haven't you written?" That meant that John had never received the letter which Gertrude wrote, the letter which she had given him to post. Why had it not been received? It had been posted. He gave it to the carrier with his own hands.

Before the captain's closed eyes that scene in the library passed in review. He was at his desk, Gertrude entered and handed him the letter. He commented upon its address and placed it with the others, the envelopes containing bills and checks, upon the table.

Then the postman came and—No—wait. The postman had not come immediately. Serena had called and he, Daniel, had gone up to her room in answer to the call. But he had come down when the postman rang and... Wait again! There had been someone in the library when he was called away. He dimly remembered. ... What? ... Why, yes! Cousin Percy had come in and—Daniel leaped to his feet. His chair slid back on its castors and struck the safe behind him. Mr. Bangs looked up.

"Why, what's the matter?" he cried, in alarm. "Is—Where are you going?"

Captain Dan did not answer. He was running, actually running, toward the door. Bareheaded he dashed across the yard. His foot was on the threshold of the back porch of the house, when he stopped short. For a moment he stood still; then he turned and ran back to the store again.

Nathaniel, who had followed him to the side entrance of The Metropolitan, met him there. "For mercy sakes, Cap'n Dott!" he began. "What IS it?"

Daniel did not answer. He pushed past his perturbed manager and, rushing to the closet in which the telephone instrument hung, closed the door behind him. He jerked the receiver from the hook, placed it at his ear, and shouted into the transmitter.

"Hello! Hello there, Central!" he bellowed. "I want a long distance call. I want to talk to Saunders, Griffin and Company, Pearl Street, Boston. ... Hey? ... Yes, I want to talk to Mr. Doane. ... NO, not Cone! Doane—Doane—Mr. John Doane. ...Hey? ... You'll call me? ... All right, then; be as quick as you can, that's all."

He hung up the receiver and, flinging the door open, dashed out into the store again, and began pacing up and down.

Nathaniel ventured one more question. "Of course it ain't any of my business, Cap'n Dott," he stammered, "but—"

Daniel waved his hand. "Sshh! shh!" he commanded. "I'll tell you by and by. But now I want to think. To think, by time!"

Ten minutes later the telephone bell rang. "Hello! Here is your Boston call," announced Central.

"All right! all right! Is this Saunders, Griffin and Company? ... Hey? ... Is Mr. Doane there? ... What? I want to know! Is that you, John? ... This is Dott, speakin'. ... Yes, Dan Dott. ... No, no, of Trumet, not Scarford. ... Yes. ... YES. ... Here! you let me do the talkin'; you listen."

Captain Dan ate scarcely any luncheon that day. He seemed to have lost his appetite. This was a good deal of a loss and his wife commented upon it.

"What does ail you, Daniel?" she asked anxiously. "Why don't you eat?"

"Hey? Oh, I don't know, Serena. Don't feel hungry, somehow."

"Well, it's the first time you haven't been hungry since you came back to Trumet. I was beginning to think Azuba and I couldn't get enough for you TO eat. And now, all at once, you're not hungry. What does ail you?"

"Ail me? Nothin' ails me."

"Don't you feel well?"

"Never felt better in my life. Don't believe I ever felt quite so good."

"You act awfully queer."

"Do I? Don't you worry about me, Serena. My appetite'll be back all right by dinner time. You want to lay in an extra stock for dinner. I'll probably eat you out of house and home then. Better figure on as much as if you was goin' to have company. Ain't that so, Zuba?"

He winked at the housekeeper. His wife noticed the wink. "What is it?" she demanded. "Are you and Azuba planning some sort of surprise?"

"Surprise! What sort of surprise would Zuba and I plan? She's had one surprise in the last six weeks and that ought to be enough. Laban's droppin' in unexpected was surprise enough to keep you satisfied, wasn't it, Zuba? I never saw anybody more surprised than you was that night in the kitchen. Ho! ho!"

Azuba smiled grimly. "A few more surprises like that," she observed, "and I'll be surprised to death. Don't talk to ME about surprises."

"I wasn't talkin' about 'em, 'twas Serena that started it."

Mrs. Dott was still suspicious. She turned to her daughter. "Gertie," she asked, "do YOU know what your father is acting so ridiculous about? Is there a secret between you three?"

Gertrude had been very quiet and grave during the meal. "No," she said. "There is no secret that I know of. Father is happy because we are back here in his beloved Trumet, I suppose."

"Well, his happiness hasn't interfered with his appetite before. There's something else; I'm sure of it. Why, Gertie! aren't you going to eat, either? You're not through luncheon!"

The young lady had risen from the table.

"You've eaten scarcely anything, Gertie," protested her mother. "I never saw such people. Are YOU so happy that you can't eat."

Gertrude did not look happy. Instead she hastily declared that she was not hungry, and left the room.

Serena stared after her. "Was she crying, Daniel?" she asked. "She looked as if she was just going to. Ever since she came in from her walk she has been so downcast and sad. She won't talk and she hasn't smiled once. Daniel, has she said anything to you?"

The captain shook his head. "She and I had a little talk out in the store," he admitted. "I shouldn't wonder if she was thinkin' about—about—"

"About John, do you mean?"

"Maybe so."

"Did she talk with you about HIM? She won't let me mention his name. Daniel, I feel SO bad about that. I'm afraid I was to blame, somehow. If we hadn't gone to Scarford—if . . . Daniel, I'm going to her."

She rose. Her husband laid a hand on her arm. "Sit down, Serena," he urged. "Sit down."

"But, Daniel, let me go. I must go to her. Perhaps I can comfort her, though how, I don't know. John Doane!" with a burst of indignation. "If I ever meet that young man I'll give him my opinion of his—"

"Sshh! shh! Serena! You sit down and finish your luncheon. Don't you worry about Gertie. And you needn't worry about her appetite or mine. I tell you what I'll do: If she and I don't have appetite enough for dinner to-night—or breakfast to-morrow mornin', anyhow—I'll swallow that platter whole. There's a fair wind and clear weather comin' for the Dott frigate, or I'm no sailor. You just trust me and wait. Yes, and let Gertie alone."

He positively refused to explain what he meant by this optimistic prophecy, or to permit his wife to go to their daughter. Gertrude went out soon afterward—for another walk, she said—and Serena retired to her room for the afternoon nap which the doctor had prescribed as part of her rest cure.

Captain Dan and Azuba had a short conference in the kitchen. "Understand, do you, Zuba?" queried the captain. "A late dinner and plenty of it."

"I understand. Land sakes! I ain't altogether a numskull or a young-one, even if I do have to be shut up in the closet to make me behave."

"Ho! ho! I expect you could have knocked my head off for bein' in the way just at that time."

"Humph!" with a one-sided smile, "I could have knocked my own off for not listenin' afore I come downstairs. If I'd heard Laban's voice I bet you I wouldn't have come. All I needed was a chance to be alone with him and explain what Gertie and I were up to."

"Well, I'm glad you didn't have the chance. I wouldn't have missed that show for somethin'. How you did holler!"

He roared with laughter. Azuba watched him with growing impatience. "Got through actin' like a Bedlamite?" she inquired tartly, when he stopped for breath. "If you have you can clear out and let me get to my dish-washin'."

"I'm through. Oh, by the way, what did Labe say in your letter? I've told you what he wrote me, but I forgot that he wrote you, too."

Mrs. Ginn looked troubled. "I don't know what to do with that man," she declared. "I expect any minute to get word that he's been put in the lock-up. Do you know what he's done to that Hungerford critter?"

"DONE to him! What do you mean? He hasn't seen him, has he?"

"No, he ain't seen him, thank goodness, but Labe is so wrought up over what that Hapgood thief told him, about your precious cousin stealin' your telegrams and so on, that he and Hapgood have gone in cahoots to play a trick on Mr. Percy. Labe says Hapgood told him that Percy was keepin' company now with another woman there in Scarford, a young woman with money, of course—he wouldn't chase any other kind. Well, Hapgood knows a lot about Hungerford and his goin's on in the past, and he's got a lot of the Percy man's old letters from other girls. Anyhow, Labe and Hapgood have sent those letters to the present young woman's pa."

Daniel whistled. "Whew!" he exclaimed. "That's interestin'."

"Ain't it, now! Laban says the old commodore is a holy terror and sets more store by his daughter than he does by his hopes of salvation, enough sight. Well, anyhow, the letters are gone and Labe says he's willin' to bet that Cousin Percy'll be GOIN' when papa gets after him."

Captain Dan whistled again. "Well, Zuba," he observed, "we can't help it, as I see. What's done's done and chickens do come home to roost, don't they?"

"Humph! I wish my husband would come home and roost where I can keep my eye on him. He says he's gettin' sick of bein' a land lubber. He'll be aboard some ship and off again afore long, that's some comfort. The only time I know that man is safe is when he's a thousand miles from dry land."

CHAPTER XVI

Serena and Daniel were together in the parlor. It was past dinner time, but Azuba, for some reason or other, had not gotten dinner ready. This was unusual for, if there was one thing upon which the housekeeper prided herself, it was in being "prompt at meal times."

She was setting the table now, however, and they could hear her rattling the knives and forks and singing, actually singing.

"Azuba is in good spirits, isn't she," observed Serena. "I haven't heard her sing before for a long time. I suppose, like the rest of us, she has been too troubled to sing."

Captain Dan listened to the singing, "There's some comfort to be got out of trouble, then."

"Why don't you light the lamp, or let me light it? It's getting so dark I can hardly see you."

"Never mind; let's sit in the dark a spell. Gertie comin' down pretty soon, is she?"

"Yes. She's changing her dress, because you asked her to. Why did you ask her? Why should she dress up just for you and me?"

"Oh, just a notion of mine. I like that red dress of hers, anyway; the one with the fringe trimmin's along the upper riggin'."

"That dress isn't red, it's pink."

"I thought 'twas about the color of my nose, and if that's pink then I'm losin' my complexion."

"Daniel!" with a laugh, "how you do talk and act to-day! At luncheon you were as queer as could be and now you're worse. What IS going to happen? Something, I know. You wouldn't tell me this noon; will you tell me now?"

"Pretty soon, Serena; pretty soon. Now let's talk about somethin' interestin'; about ourselves, for instance. How do you like bein' back here in Trumet? The old town doesn't seem stupid; hey?"

"No, indeed! Don't speak that way, Daniel."

"Well, I just mentioned it, that's all. Soon as you do get tired and want to see somethin' new, we'll take that cruise to Washin'ton or the Falls or somewheres. Never mind the price. Way I feel now I'd go to the moon if 'twould please you."

Serena laughed again. "I shan't say it for a long while," she declared. "I am having such a good time. The house seems so snug and homey. And all our old friends and neighbors have been so kind. They seemed so glad to see us when we came, as if they were real friends, not the make-believe sort."

"Not the Annette kind, you mean. That particular breed of cats is scarce on the Cape—at least I hope it is."

"So do I. I never want to see her again. I am so glad they have sold their cottage here, and that the Fenholtzes have bought it. You always liked the Fenholtzes, Daniel. I did, too, or I should if Annette hadn't told me—"

"I know, I know. Some day that woman will tell the truth by accident and the Ladies of Honor crowd'll be mournin' a leadin' light that went out sudden. But never mind her. The folks here HAVE been nice to us, haven't they?"

"Indeed they have! And so thoughtful! Why, Sophronia Smalley even came to ask me if I wouldn't consider taking my old place as president of Trumet Chapter. She is president now, but she declared she would resign in a minute in my favor."

For an instant Captain Dan's exuberant spirits were dashed. "She did!" he cried. "Well, if that woman ain't. . . . Humph! Are you thinkin' of lettin' her resign, Serena?"

"No."

"I—I wouldn't stand in your way if you did, you know. Trumet ain't Scarford, and if you want to—"

"I don't, I don't. I may attend a meeting once in a while, later on, but I never shall hold office again. I have had all the 'advancement' I want."

"Advancin' backwards, some folks would call what you're doin' now, Serena, I cal'late. There! I've said 'cal'late' again. I haven't said it before for a long time. This Cape sand has got into my grammar, I guess. I must be careful."

"You needn't be. Say 'cal'late' if you want to, I am not going to fret you about your grammar any more, Daniel. I'd rather have you, just as you are, than any other man in the world, grammar or no grammar."

"Whew! Hold on, old lady! If you talk that way I'll get so puffed up I'll bust into smoke when you touch me, like a dry toadstool. I—Hello! what was that? The train whistle, was it?"

"Yes. Here is the night train in; it is almost mail time, and no dinner yet. What IS the matter with Azuba? I'll speak to her."

She was rising to go to the dining-room, but her husband detained her. "No, you wait; no, you mustn't," he said, hastily. "Speakin' of dinners, this talk of ours is like that everlastin' long meal that you and I went to at Barney Black's house just after we landed in Scarford. You remember it took half an hour to get to anything solid in that dinner, don't you? Yes, well, I'm just gettin' to the meat of my talk. And I want Gertie to come in on that course. She is on her way downstairs now; I hear her. Hi! Gertie! come in here, won't you!"

Gertrude entered the room. "Where are you, Daddy?" she asked.

"Here I am, over here by the window."

"But why haven't you lighted the lamp? Why are you sitting here in the dark?"

Serena answered. "Goodness knows," she replied. "Your father would insist on it."

"You see, Gertie," he explained, "'twas on account of my bashfulness. Your mother, she wanted to sit along with me and hold hands, so—. Oh, all right; all right. You can show a glim now, Serena, if you want to. I'll cover up my blushes."

The maligned Mrs. Dott announced that she had a good mind to box his ears. "That's what I should do to a child," she added, "and nobody could act more childish than you have this afternoon."

"Second childhood and dodderin' old age are creepin' over me fast. There!" as the lamp blazed and the parlor was illuminated, "now you can see for yourself. Do I dodder much?"

Even Gertrude was obliged to laugh. "Daddy!" she cried; "you silly thing! I believe you ARE getting childish."

"Am I? All right, I'm willing to be, at the price. My! Gertie, you look awfully pretty. Don't she look 'specially pretty to you to-night, Serena?"

Serena smiled. "That gown was always becoming," she said.

"I know it was; that's why I wanted her to put it on. And she's fixed her hair the way I like, too. My! my! if some folks I know could see you now, Gertie, they'd. . . . Ahem! Well, never mind. She looks as if she was expectin' company and had rigged up for it, doesn't she, Serena?"

Gertrude paid little attention to this rather strained attempt at a joke. She merely smiled and turned away. But her mother appeared to suspect a hidden meaning in the words. She leaned forward and gazed at her husband.

"Daniel," she cried, sharply and with increasing excitement; "Daniel Dott, what are you—"

The captain waved her to silence. She would have spoken in spite of it, but his second wave and shake of the head were so emphatic that she hesitated. Before the moment of hesitation was at an end Captain Dan himself began to speak. He spoke in a new tone now and more and more rapidly.

"Serena, don't interrupt me," he ordered. "Gertie, listen. I'm goin' to tell you both a story. Once there was a couple of married folks that had a daughter. . . . This couple, as I say, had a daughter. This daughter was engaged to be married. The old folks moved away from the place they had always lived and went somewhere else. There they both commenced to make fools of themselves. The place was all right enough, maybe, but they didn't belong in it. The daughter, she came there and she saw how things were goin' and, says she: 'I'll fix 'em. I'll cure 'em and save 'em, too, by showin' 'em an example, my example. I'll—'"

Gertrude broke in. "Daddy," she cried, with a warning glance at her mother, "be careful. Don't be silly. What is the use—"

"Hush! Never mind what she did. All is, she showed 'em and she cured 'em and she saved 'em. But meanwhile her meddlesome old father had got worried, not understandin' what was goin' on, and he put his oar in. He wrote for the young chap she was engaged to to come down and help cure HER. The father meant all right. He—"

Again the young lady interrupted. "Mother," she said, "this is nonsense, the way father is telling it. I meant to tell you, myself, by and by. I'm sure you have guessed it, anyway, but—"

"There's one part she hasn't guessed," shouted Captain Dan; "or that you haven't guessed either, Gertie, God bless you. I guessed it myself, this very day, and I guessed it because I had a letter from Labe Ginn up at Scarford that put me on the right track. Gertie, that letter you wrote to John WASN'T mailed; the postman DIDN'T get it; John himself never got it."

"Daddy! Daddy, what—"

"Wait! wait! How do I know? you were goin' to say. I know because I know who did get it. Cousin Percy Hungerford—confound his miserable, worthless hulk! HE got it; he stole it from my table, where it laid along with my other letters, when I was out of the room. And—wait! that isn't all. John DID write you, Gertie. He wrote you two or three times and he telegraphed you once. And you didn't get either letters or telegram because that Hapgood butler—Oh, if I had only known this when I chased him out of the back yard! He'd have gone over the fence instead of through the gate—he was helpin' our dear cousin and gettin' paid for it, and HE stole 'em. There! that's the truth and. . . . My soul! I believe I've scared the girl to death."

But Gertrude, although white and shaken, was far from being "scared to death." She was very much alive.

"Are you sure, Daddy?" she cried. "How do you know?"

"I know because Labe wrote that Hapgood told him. And I know that's what happened to your letter because John didn't get it."

"How do you know he didn't get it? How do you know John didn't get my letter, Father?"

"I know because. . . . Is that a wagon stoppin' at our gate, Serena?"

"Never mind if it is. Answer Gertie's question. HOW do you know?"

Steps sounded on the front porch. Captain Dan strode to the hall and stood with one hand on the knob of the front door.

"I know," he declared triumphantly, "because I telephoned John this very day and he told me so. And now, by the everlastin', he'll tell you so himself!"

He flung the door wide. "Come in, John!" roared Captain Dan. "There she is, in there, waitin' for you."

And Mr. Doane came, you may be sure. Serena and Daniel waited in the dining-room. The captain's triumphant exuberance continued to bubble over. He chuckled and laughed and crowed vaingloriously over his success in keeping the secret ever since noon.

"I was bound I wouldn't tell, Serena," he declared. "I told John over the 'phone; I said: 'I won't tell a soul you're comin', John. We'll give 'em one surprise, won't we.' And, ho! ho! he didn't believe I could keep it to myself; he said he didn't. But I did, I did—though I felt all afternoon as if I had a bombshell under my jacket."

Serena laughed; she was as pleased as he. "You certainly exploded it like a bombshell," she declared. "I didn't know at first but that you really had gone crazy. And poor Gertie! you didn't prepare her at all. You blurted it out all at once. I wonder she didn't faint."

"She isn't the faintin' kind. Serena, we never can be grateful enough to Gertie for what she's done for us. And she sacrificed her own happiness—or thought she did—for you and me and didn't whimper or complain once."

"I know, Daniel, I know. And pretty soon now we must give her up to someone else."

"So we will. But I'd rather give her to John than any other man on earth. The thought that it was all off between them and that she was grievin' over it was about the hardest thing of all."

"So it was. Well, now we can be completely happy, every one of us."

Azuba flounced in from the kitchen. "Ain't they come out of that parlor YET?" she demanded. "I can't keep roast chicken waitin' forever, even for engaged folks."

But the "engaged folks" themselves appeared at that moment. As one of those who, according to Mrs. Dott, were to be completely happy, Mr. Doane looked his part. Gertrude, too, although her eyes were wet, was smiling.

John and the Dotts shook hands. Daniel turned to his daughter. "Well, Gertie," he asked, "are you ready to forgive me for what happened on account of my sendin' that summons to John—that one up in Scarford, I mean?"

"I think so, Daddy."

"I thought maybe you would be, considerin'," with a wink at Mr. Doane, "the answer you got to my telephone to-day. But, see here, young lady, I want to ask you somethin' and I expect a straight answer. Can I keep a secret, or can't I?"

"You can, Daddy, dear. You kept this one almost seven hours."

"'Twas a strain, but I kept it."

"You managed it all beautifully, Daniel," declared Serena. "I am proud of you."

"We're all proud of you, Captain Dan," said John.

The captain smiled happily. "Much obliged," he said, "but I ain't the one you ought to be proud of. When it comes to real managin' I ain't knee-high to the ship's cat alongside of Gertie there. No sir-ee! if you've got any time to spare bein' proud of folks, don't be proud of Cap'n Dan, but of Cap'n Dan's daughter. Sit down, all hands. Here comes dinner—at last."

THE END